CRAFTS AND THE VISUAL ARTS

© **Editions Didier Millet, 2007**
Published by Archipelago Press *an imprint of* Editions Didier Millet Pte Ltd
121, Telok Ayer Street, #03-01, Singapore 068590
Tel: 65-6324 9260 Fax: 65-6324 9261 E-mail: edm@edmbooks.com.sg

First published 2007

Editions Didier Millet, Kuala Lumpur Office:
25, Jalan Pudu Lama, 50200 Kuala Lumpur, Malaysia
Tel: 03-2031 3805 Fax: 03-2031 6298 E-mail: edmbooks@edmbooks.com.my
Websites: www.edmbooks.com • www.encyclopedia.com.my

Colour separation by United Graphic Pte Ltd
Printed by Star Standard Industries (Pte) Ltd
ISBN 978-981-3018-57-0

CONTRIBUTORS

Abdul Halim Nasir
Malay woodcraft expert and writer

Assoc. Prof. Dr Anuar Talib
Universiti Teknologi MARA

Henry Bong
Pucuk Rebung Royal Gallery-Museum

Laura Fan
Curator and writer

YM Raja Datin Paduka Fuziah bte Raja Tun Uda
Crafts consultant/Sari Ayu Consult Sdn Bhd

Prof. Dr Ghulam-Sarwar Yousof
Universiti Malaya

Assoc. Prof. Ham Rabeah Kamarun
Universiti Teknologi MARA

Kamil Yunus
Freeform Design

Khoo Joo Ee
Crafts historian and writer

Barbara Leigh
University of Technology, Sydney

Li-En Chong
Art historian

Vasanthi Marimuthu
Formerly of Specialist Teachers' Training Institute

Dr Mohd Kassim Hj Ali
Culture and heritage consultant

Assoc. Prof. Dr Muliyadi Mahamood
Universiti Teknologi MARA

Heidi Munan
Researcher and writer on the material culture of Borneo

Redza Piyadasa
Artist and art historian

Patricia Regis
Sabah Ministry of Tourism, Culture and Environment

Prof Dr Haji Rudin Salinger
Consultant

Dr Siti Zainon Ismail
Artist, poet and Malay art, culture and heritage consultant

Syed Ahmad Jamal
Artist and former Director of the National Art Gallery Malaysia

Yeoh Jin Leng
Artist and art educationist

Assoc. Prof. Dr Zakaria Ali
School of Fine Arts, Universiti Sains Malaysia, Penang

THE ENCYCLOPEDIA OF
MALAYSIA

Volume 14

CRAFTS AND THE VISUAL ARTS

Volume Editor

Datuk Syed Ahmad Jamal

Artist and former Director of the National Art Gallery Malaysia

ARCHIPELAGO PRESS

Contents

Although the use of a copper stylus to draw designs with wax on *batik* (*batik canting*) was a technique introduced from Indonesia, a Malaysian innovation in the 1970s led to new ways of applying colour and different types of fabric being used.

PREVIOUS PAGE: The damascened blade (length 32 cm) of this *keris sepukal* has verses from the Qur'an etched into it. The hilt is carved from wood.

HALF TITLE PAGE: A variety of Malaysian handicrafts.

Iban *spirit* carvings such as this *Hudok Kelunan* are used for protection and to drive away evil spirits which could bring sickness to the longhouse.

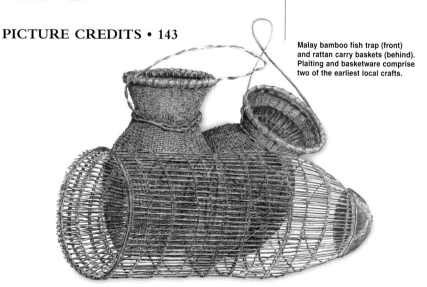

Malay bamboo fish trap (front) and rattan carry baskets (behind). Plaiting and basketware comprise two of the earliest local crafts.

Introduction

This volume surveys the rich and varied craft traditions of Malaysia and the development of Malaysian modern art into a medium which expresses its own unique subject matter, viewpoints and realities. As a discussion of these subjects inevitably touches on the country's history, culture and multi-ethnic population, other volumes in this series, such as Early History, Performing Arts *and* Peoples and Traditions, *also have relevance. The extensive nature of the subject being dealt with in this volume means that not everything can be covered. However, readers of this book should gain a holistic understanding and appreciation of Malaysia's crafts and visual arts and its vibrant cultural heritage.*

Malay pottery is not made using a potter's wheel or spinner, nor are glazes used. Its colour results solely from the firing process and the properties of the clay used.

Colourful Sarawak Iban warrior shield which portrays courage and bravery.

The beginning and influences

Objects crafted for the needs of early societies—such as pottery, woven fibres and stone tools—can be traced to the habitat in which these people lived. Among the significant early examples of artistic creation in Malaysia are the roughly hewn stones and rocks known as menhirs or megaliths and cave paintings, which have basic generic similarities to those of other early societies in other parts of the world. Some of these simple objects later developed aesthetically to exhibit higher levels of artistic attainment, for example, with the addition of engraving and carving. The abundance of wood in the region inspired artistic creativity with this material from very early times.

The movement of migratory peoples from parts of the Asian mainland and nearby islands has helped to inspire the creative process, and the development of trade with India, China and parts of West Asia from the early centuries CE enhanced the materials, techniques and design elements. This is especially so in relation to weaving, which became one of the main creative accomplishments, as evident in fine examples of woven cotton and silk textiles. Another craft which exhibits indigenous innovation is the making of objects using bamboo, rattan and palm leaves, initially for daily needs, but later reaching a high level of craftsmanship, artistry and sophistication in technique and design.

The arrival of Islam in the Malay Peninsula in the 14th century CE led to a shift in design emphasis from that of the earlier Hindu and Buddhist forms and motifs towards stylization and abstraction. Other influences include immigration as well as colonization by the Portuguese, Dutch and British. Cross-migration and trans-pollination between the Malay Peninsula and its neighbours, particularly Indonesia, the Philippines and Thailand, had a strong effect on local techniques and designs, such as batik from Indonesia, metalware from Thailand and textiles from the Philippines, while Wayang Kulit (shadow puppet play) was strongly influenced by Thailand and Indonesia.

TOP: The weaving of *songket* on the frame loom is a skilful traditional Malay craft that has been handed down from generation to generation.

ABOVE: Iban woman in Sarawak crafting a beaded shoulder yoke using a hat as a base.

Chinese and Indian migrants to the Malay Peninsula and Sarawak and Sabah in the 19th century brought their own culture and traditions with them which have added to the diverse range of crafts and visual arts that can be found here. In the case of the Peranakan or Straits Chinese, intermarriage with locals from the 1400s resulted in the unique and distinct products of a sub-culture.

One manifestation of the Malaysian cultural melting pot and local ingenuity is the fusion of elements from Malay, Chinese and Islamic traditions seen in the Melaka Terengkera Mosque with its *nusantara* (regional) roof, Chinese-style minaret and Islamic decorative motifs and Malay woodcarving in the pierced panels interpenetrating its spaces.

Modern art

What started from relatively humble beginnings in the form of renditions of the lush local landscape introduced by the British in the 19th century continued into the pre-World War II period with the establishment of the Nanyang Academy of Fine Arts in the 1930s and the introduction of Post-Impressionist and modernist forays into painting.

Malaysian modern art had a resurgence in the years following Merdeka (Independence). The spirit of the newly independent nation seemed to inject interest in the visual arts, together with support given by the first Prime Minister. Official and political support for the arts had its beginnings in the early 1950s with the establishment of the Malayan Arts Council in 1952, and culminated in the establishment of the National Art Gallery in 1958, just one year after independence was declared.

The Ministry of Education has played an important role in the advancement of art, beginning with the establishment of the Specialist Teachers' Training Institute in 1960 and then other teacher training colleges. The main force in art activity began with art teachers in the Ministry of Education, who were later sent for further art education overseas and thus were introduced to international art movements such as Impressionism, Post-Impressionism, Cubism, Fauvism, Surrealism, Expressionism, Constructivism, abstract art and further evolutions in Modernism and Post-modernism. The establishment of government-sponsored and private art establishments followed, resulting in locally trained artists and designers.

All of these factors had a significant impact on the evolution of art in the country, resulting in a burgeoning of modern Malaysian art which began to receive local support. The local art infrastructure has gone from strength to strength, especially since the late 1980s. The question of identity raised by the National Cultural Congress in 1971 gave rise to inquiries into the uniqueness of Malay art (as postulated by the *Rupa dan Jiwa* (Form and Soul) exhibition), indigenous (*pribumi*) regional identity, the 'Malaysian-ness' of Malaysian art and other probings into the inner dimensions of art, against the background of a developing nation with a multi-ethnic pluralistic society. The response from the general public, with positive interest in Malaysian art by collectors and corporate bodies, has resulted in a vibrant local art scene.

'Tepak Sirih' gift presented by the people of Malaysia to the United Nations in 2003. The cross-cultural piece, which comprises a composite of traditional craft elements including a *sirih* centrepiece and antique Malaysian weapons, was designed by Henry Bong and produced by the Pucuk Rebung Royal Gallery-Museum. The concept was conceived by Foreign Minister Datuk Seri Syed Hamid Albar.

ABOVE: This watercolour by Nik Zainal Abidin entitled *Wayang Kulit* depicts figures from the Wayang Kulit puppet shadow play for which Kelantan is well known. The characters are from the Hindu epic *Ramayana*.

LEFT: Steel sculpture, *Gotong Royong* (1959) by Anthony Lau (ht 118 cm).

Woman walking past an Islamic mosaic which was part of an exhibition during the launching of National Craft Day in 2003. Since the 14th century CE, Islamic motifs and design principles have become a component of Malay crafts and visual arts.

7

1. Festival village houseboat at Taman Negara (National Park) decorated in traditional style with an atap roof and woven panels, nets, a bamboo fishing trap, textiles and a carved and painted ornamental head at the front.

2. This *pua sungkit* ceremonial head and shoulder cloth (c. 1900) from Sarawak was used by a shaman. The crocodile motifs represent the spirit of the land.

3. Ivory and silver *sirih* set (container to hold the ingredients for betel chew). The meticulously shaped silver patterns feature flowing leaves and tendrils with the addition of a seal (perhaps royal) at the front of the container.

4. The Iban use baskets for some of their rituals. The baskets pictured are embellished with beads, shells and other decorative elements.

5. Malay woodcarver painstakingly creating a cut-out panel with floral and vine designs, according to age-old traditions.

6. The art of making colourful decorative kites is an important Malaysian craft, particularly in Kelantan where kite-flying remains a popular pastime.

7. Nonya beadwork doily of spring flowers and leaves from Penang, c. 1920s.

A LIVING VISUAL TRADITION

Malaysia is characterized by its great cultural and ethnic diversity, its population comprising Malays, Chinese, Indians, Orang Asli, the numerous indigenous peoples of Sabah and Sarawak and others. The Malay Peninsula's location adjacent to the Melaka Strait—one of the world's most important maritime trading routes—and the resulting heterogeneous population, have led to indigenous crafts and art being subjected to the influence of other cultures. Sarawak and Sabah, being somewhat removed from the international thoroughfare of the Melaka Strait, developed markedly different arts and crafts.

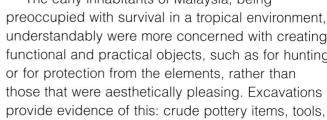

Early examples of locally produced unglazed earthenware from Neolithic times (c. 2800–500 BCE).

The early inhabitants of Malaysia, being preoccupied with survival in a tropical environment, understandably were more concerned with creating functional and practical objects, such as for hunting or for protection from the elements, rather than those that were aesthetically pleasing. Excavations provide evidence of this: crude pottery items, tools, megaliths and grave decorations have been found as well as simple cave paintings that were used to record daily life and events. These primitive craft and art forms gradually developed, over thousands of years, until artisans mastered the production of more sophisticated vessels, weapons, stone and wood craft, cloth, and personal adornments.

As the aesthetic value of objects became more important, specialists in the various art forms developed their skills with the intention of making objects as visually beautiful as possible, taking design beyond an object's utilitarian role. A balance between the elements of form, space and the inherent natural qualities of the materials was required. The resulting creations reflected the skill of the artist or artisan at producing works that did not allow one element to overpower the others.

Foreign influences affected the development of Malaysia's visual art tradition. Hindu and Buddhist influences from Indonesia and India played a large role in artistic development, particularly in weaving, metalwork and woodcarving. The conversion of the Malays to Islam led to the embrace of decoration based on the use of vegetal forms without figures. This is apparent in Malay pottery, textiles, metalware, woodcarving and stone carving. Chinese and Indians, and to a lesser extent Europeans, brought with them their own visual art traditions, some of which were integrated and assimilated into local crafts.

Malaysian artisans continue to produce crafts and visual art based on a well-tried formula: an inherited framework determined by tradition. However, new ideas and expressions are constantly being developed—with the only real limit being the imagination of the artist/craftsman.

Sundatang two-string long-necked strumming lute from Sabah.

Influences on arts and crafts:
A historical perspective

Malaysia's artistic evolution has to a large extent been driven by influences from afar. From the 5th century CE, the Buddhist and Hindu religions prevailed, but to a large extent had been displaced by Islam by the 15th century CE. Settlers from Europe, China and India provided further inputs; each precipitated a change in art forms, many of which have survived—and are still being practised—to this day.

Haematite cave paintings found in Gua Tambun, Perak in 1959 feature animals, human figures and abstract designs. It is thought that these may date from the Neolithic period.

Standing bronze Buddha found in Kedah, believed to date from the 5th to 9th centuries CE.

Early manifestations of art

The earliest examples of indigenous art that have been found in Malaysia date from the Mesolithic (c. 40,000–2500 BCE) and Neolithic (c. 2800–500 BCE) eras. These comprise cave paintings and unglazed pottery found in the Niah Caves, Sarawak and at Gua Cha in Kelantan. Undated cave paintings have also been discovered in Perak.

Motifs on a number of bronze Dongson artefacts such as drums and elephant bells, dating from the Metal Age (c. 500 BCE–500 CE), found at various sites throughout Peninsular Malaysia, indicate influences from North Vietnam. Many indigenous tribes in Sarawak and Central Borneo used similar motifs and patterns in their artwork.

Buddhist and Hindu influences

Buddhism in Malaysia dates from the 5th century CE, reaching its height of influence during the Srivijaya Empire (c. 680–1025 CE), which had its main centres of control in the Malay Peninsula in Perak and Kedah. The later conquering of Kedah by the Hindu Chola kingdom of South India (1025–1100 CE) also left a strong impression on Malay art. Both Buddhist and Hindu influences in the region are evidenced by stone inscriptions with Sanskrit Buddhist texts and Hindu-Buddhist sculptures made from terracotta, bronze and stone found in the Kinta Valley in Perak, the Bujang Valley in Kedah and Santubong in Sarawak dating from 400 CE. Indian and more specifically, Hindu influence is also seen in the many Sanskrit words incorporated into the Malay vocabulary and in elements of the local royal court ceremonies. Hindu epics such as the *Ramayana* and the *Mahabharata* were introduced and feature heavily in Malaysian performing arts. The ancient Buddhist kingdom of Langkasuka (c. 2nd–14 centuries CE) in the Patani area is recorded in Arabic, Chinese, Indian, Javanese and Malay writings. In particular, it influenced the cultural development of the regions of the east coast states of Kelantan and Terengganu in terms of woodcarving, metalwork, weaving, drama, music and dance traditions.

Melaka and Islam

Buddhist and Hindu influences waned with the arrival of Islam, which has no precise date. The earliest evidence of Islam in Malaysia is the Terengganu Stone inscription dated 1303. Melaka's strategic location enabled it to become a thriving entrepôt, trading in spices, forest products and textiles, especially those from India, and silk, iron and porcelain from China. Its establishment and the conversion of Parameswara, the ruler of Melaka, in the 1400s led to the spread of Islam throughout the country. Over the course of the next century, Islam began to have a tremendous influence on various Malay visual art forms, particularly stone- and wood-carving, metalwork, fabric and pottery.

The Malay rulers employed highly skilled craftsmen within their palaces to manufacture their jewellery, decorative items, weapons and textiles. This patronage of master craftsmen contributed to the development of the Malay craft tradition.

Kedah tombstone with Islamic motifs and forms.

Megaliths

One very early art form is the megalith, several examples of which still exist. Some of the most important examples of these were found at Keramat Sungai Udang near Pengkalan Kempas in Negeri Sembilan, close to the grave of one Sheikh Ahmad Mallari, who died in 1467 CE. Among other things, they provide evidence of the early adoption of Islam by the people residing in that area.

The megaliths comprise three carved, flat-faced, upright stones, surrounded by several smaller stones. The tallest of the three, some 2.5 metres in height, is commonly known as 'the Sword' due to its shape, and is decorated with carvings which conform to the basic form of the stone. The stone is an ancient sculptured work of high artistic quality, with a fine balance between form, line and space. The area in the middle of the stone has circular shapes, spirals and forms that resemble human figures. In the section below there is a dragon-like shape with two ears. A curved line in relief in the middle crosses the sculpture just above the circle, joining the two sides. The word Allah, in perpendicular Kufic script, is carved in bas-relief in the space above.

From left, the Rudder, the Spoon and the Sword, now situated at the historical complex in Pengkalan Kempas.

'The Rudder,' some 1.9 metres tall, has low relief carving portraying a scene of plants growing on a hill slope. There are also carvings of a horse, a barking deer and a tiger. These shapes are arranged on a flat background, as in a painting. This is one of the earliest works of art found in Malaysia to present the idea of a landscape.

'The Spoon,' some 2 metres in height, is placed between the other two stones. It is devoid of any carving, but remains important because it forms part of a trio.

Art forms and decoration were, and still are, based almost entirely on vegetal forms, resulting in an almost total absence of figurative forms except in puppetry (see 'Puppetry') and highly stylized or abstract forms in weapon handles (see 'Metalworking and weapons') and woodcarving. The use of Arabic calligraphy, the supreme form of Islamic visual art, is mainly restricted to religious uses such as tombstones and as decorative features on mosques and pulpits (see 'Islamic design principles and motifs'). Such calligraphy is almost wholly in Arabic, presenting verses from the holy Qur'an. Holy verses were also etched on kris blades and waist buckles. Another non-religious use of calligraphy was on gold coins issued during the 15th and 17th centuries, as well as on the Malay rulers' seals and royal regalia (see 'Gold jewellery and regalia').

Peranakan

Chinese immigrants settled in the region from the 14th century in Melaka and also Penang, Terengganu and Kelantan. Although they considered themselves Chinese, some adopted local customs and married locally. Their descendants are known as 'Peranakan' ('local-born' Chinese) or Straits Chinese. Their custom of specially ordering items from Malay, Chinese and Indian craftsmen for their homes has resulted in a number of hybrid crafts being created. The legacy that resulted from this assimilation of cultures may be seen in beautifully crafted wood carvings, beadwork, embroidery, jewellery, metalware, and porcelain preserved in museums, and in modern versions manufactured today.

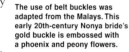

The use of belt buckles was adapted from the Malays. This early 20th-century Nonya bride's gold buckle is embossed with a phoenix and peony flowers.

Other influences

The conquest of Melaka by the Portuguese in 1511 brought Christianity to the Peninsula, but overall Portuguese influence was largely confined to the Eurasian community of the Portuguese settlement in Melaka. However, the style of decoration using colourful ceramic tiles to decorate the walls and floors of Chinese shophouses in Melaka, as well as the staircases of many Malay houses in the state, possibly originated from Portugal or some other part of Europe. The Dutch and then the British also influenced local arts and crafts with the introduction of different materials such as gold, crystals, English porcelain and English cotton, which sometimes replaced already existing local materials. European watercolour painting traditions influenced the art scene in Malaysia from the 1930s (see 'The beginning of landscape painting'). Cross-migration with neighbouring countries had its own impact, for example, migration from the Philippines led to a diversity of colourful textiles in Sabah (see 'Textiles of Sabah').

The arrival of Indian and Chinese people, some traders, some workers for the tin-mining and rubber

Harmonious blend of cultures

The diverse range of visual art in Malaysia today encompasses the culmination of years of intermingling of cultures, an effort to retain age-old traditions and a national identity. Examples of this can be seen in Malaysian style batik (an influence from Java) which is more highly coloured than Javanese batik. Boat-making traditions resemble those in Indonesia and elsewhere but have been modified to suit local requirements and preferences in decoration. Some of the *mimbar* (pulpits) in the mosques of Melaka are carved with designs which show distinct Chinese visual art features, lacquered and embellished with a profusion of gold, a practice which is not found in other states (see 'Islamic design principles and motifs'). In parts of Sabah, the style of decoration of buildings, including mosques, displays a fusion of local and Islamic traditions

This Melaka house has the intricate woodcarving usual for traditional Malay houses. However, the use of coloured tiles (often of European origin) on the staircase, akin to the decoration of Melaka Chinese shophouses, is characteristic of this region.

industries, particularly in the 19th century, also resulted in an influx of craft and art forms from their respective countries which has influenced Malay art.

A fine example of the intermingling of local, Islamic and Chinese art forms can be found in Melaka mosques, some dating to the 18th century. These structures, built of brick and stone with wooden fittings and tiled roofs, have pagoda-like minarets and Chinese-like decorative extensions on the roofs.

Some indigenous groups have not been affected by outside influences, their art still reflecting the local environment. Examples are woodcarvings of human and animal figures and masks in Sarawak and the animistic spirit figures created by the Mah Meri and Jah Hut tribes in Peninsular Malaysia.

Looking forward

Modernization of craft production techniques has enabled mass production in various fields and is the impetus needed to cater for export and local tourism needs. In order to protect and promote Malaysian handicrafts and traditions, one initiative by the Government was the establishment of the Malaysian Handicraft Development Corporation (Kraftangan Malaysia), whose centres provide for the purchase of local handicrafts, heritage craft exhibitions, and the viewing of handicraft demonstrations and participation in interactive craft activities. Various training programmes also enable young people to become skilled and keep old traditions alive. However, the challenge for today's craftspeople is to produce items of purpose, quality and beauty while adapting to the ever-changing society of a country caught up in the tide of development.

Karyaneka handicraft shop at the Kraftangan Malaysia complex in Kuala Lumpur.

Traditional crafts: Forms and functions

The forms in traditional Malaysian design grew from the purpose or function of the utensil, and from the characteristics of the material used. However, aesthetic consideration is evident in most cases, making the resulting object satisfying to the senses. Styles of form and ornamentation have evolved to suit the requirements and personal tastes of the users.

The Orang Ulu 'Tree of Life' mural painting at the Sarawak Museum shows many forms of life including tigers, peacocks, snakes and man.

ABOVE: Labu air (water gourds) from Kampung Kuala Sayong.

BELOW: This pandan prayer mat from Kampung Rusila (Kuala Terengganu) has a number of different motifs and colours incorporated in it to produce a striking visual effect (Muzium Negara Collection).

Pottery forms

The evolution of pottery in Peninsular Malaysia is of interest. One reason, paradoxically, is its lack of technical sophistication. Because of this, contemporary Malay pottery has retained some of its original elements including its flowing form and quality of clay used. Decoration is restricted to impressed and engraved motifs, with ribs added.

All Malay pottery products are unglazed, with the focus on retaining the natural quality of the clay used. Malay pottery, mostly water containers and cooking pots, has a few basic forms (see 'Pottery forms and motifs') that differ from Indian (simple and unadorned) and Chinese (glazed) pottery and the two types of pottery manufactured in Sarawak (hand-moulded and glazed Chinese pottery).

Fibres

Easy access to and availability of pandanus, bamboo and rattan, which grow abundantly in the jungle and along riverbanks, have made them the material of choice for numerous functional and domestic objects, such as fish traps, baskets, trays and food containers. Of these, even everyday objects such as portable fish traps exhibit an elegance of form and proportion. Another art is plaiting. Leaves and reeds, trimmed into thin strips and dyed, are plaited into articles such as mats, baskets, pouches and food covers, incorporating a wide array of geometrical patterns arranged with complementing and contrasting colours. Plaited bamboo was also used as a housing material—an excellent example of this is the patterned bamboo walls of the Istana Kenangan in Kuala Kangsar, Perak.

Woodcarving

With the abundance of wood available in Malaysia, it is natural that creativity is emphasized in objects made from this material. Many of the favourite motifs and designs are floral and geometrical, while a number of them suggest inspiration sourced from the animal kingdom. Examples can be found in wall panels—in both relief and pierced work, partitions, boxes, on boats, sculptures, musical instruments and carved kris handles. Some carvings take on the form of *awan larat* (floating clouds) inspired by the form of clouds in a clear, tropical sky.

Two Orang Asli groups, the Jah Hut and the Mah Meri, are known for their wood sculptures and masks based on animistic beliefs (see 'Wood and other carvings'). Originally carved only for spiritual purposes, interest in them is so great that they are now manufactured for others.

The indigenous groups of Sabah and Sarawak produce objects for domestic use and others for ritual purposes and decoration. Items made from wood have particular significance, as trees are believed to be the origin of all life. The carved decoration of longhouses, burial poles, sword sheaths, shields, masks and sculptures possibly began as symbols from nature or the imagination to ward off evil. Designs do not seem to have changed a great deal over time despite outside influences.

ABOVE: The sea Bajau people of Semporna, Sabah, carve with intricate details these miniature *lepa-lepa* replicas of the houseboats on which they live.

BELOW: The old Perak royal palace, Istana Kenangan in Kuala Kangsar, built in 1926, is unique. Totally built from timber with no nails. Its walls are made of plaited bamboo strips (called *kelarai*) which form lattice-like diamond patterns in white, yellow and black, the colours of the state.

Textiles

Bark cloth and woven cotton were the earliest materials to be used as textiles. But as more varied and 'superior' imported materials became available through trade with India. China and Europe, there was a gradual shift to their use (see 'Development of local textiles'). The availability of luxury items such as silk and metal thread enabled weavers to make prestigious materials for the ruling class. Influenced by Indian weaving and design methods, weavers all over Malaysia adopted the use of the backstrap loom. Later, the frame loom was introduced from Europe, which allowed for more freedom of movement and enabled weavers to produce wider pieces of cloth than those made on the backstrap loom. The indigenous groups of Borneo still use the backstrap loom and the use of natural dyes is a feature of the muted, natural colours of indigenous textiles, particularly the Iban *pua kumbu* of Sarawak (see 'Cultural significance of textiles: Sabah and Sarawak'). Besides the basic function of using textiles to cover the body, textiles are also often used as art.

Metal weapons

A wide range of tools and cutting implements with elegantly shaped blades developed in all areas of Malaysia as needed for domestic, farming and ceremonial purposes. The Kenyah and Kayan of Sarawak were particularly well known as metalsmiths. Generally, decoration is found on the wood or bone hilts and knife sheaths rather than the blades themselves.

Among the glories of Malay visual art are weapons (blades). In this case, the kris reigns supreme. Ordinary kris are workmanlike weapons, but ceremonial kris are far more elaborate and ornamental. In contrast to other blades, such as the Japanese sword, the blade of the kris has organic characteristics. The blade, which is not poured into a mould, is made out of iron strips beaten while the metal is hot. The double-sided blade is broad at its base, tapering in various arrangements of odd-numbered curves—5, 7, 9, 11, 13, 15, 17, and so on. Kris blades with large numbered curves are rare, while the *keris sepukal* has no curves at all. The curvy shape of the kris blade reflects the flow of the river and waves at sea. Various metals, hard and soft, are applied in layers, and finished with the application of acid to provide the desired finish (see 'Metalworking and weapons').

Utilitarian metalwork

Products made from brass, such as cooking pots and kettles, evolved as items for use by the common folk. Over time, many items related to religious ceremonies were also made from brass. The states of Terengganu and Kelantan are well known for brassware production (see 'Brassware'). Terengganu craftsmen took the craft to Brunei, which led to the craft being imported to other areas of Borneo. Brassware from Terengganu and Kelantan differs greatly from those made in neighbouring countries in that there is little decoration, with an emphasis on the shape and function of the object rather than ornamentation.

Regalia and jewellery

A tradition of wearing elaborate regalia and personal adornment was inculcated by the Malay rulers and also adapted by the Peranakan in their elaborate wedding trousseaux. Gold was the metal of choice, but silverware was also used liberally (see 'Silverware' and 'Gold jewellery and regalia').

Due to the influence of Islam, vegetal and geometric motifs were often used as decoration. Repoussé and filigree techniques were enhanced in Malay gold and silver jewellery, such as waist buckles and breast ornaments as well as kris sheaths, tobacco boxes and *sirih* (betel) sets. Many of the traditional forms of jewellery are now only worn on ceremonial occasions and modern forms more suited for everyday wear have evolved.

Modern silver and jewel-encrusted handbags made by Kelantanese silversmiths using traditional patterns.

In Sarawak, the Maloh were renowned for their silversmithing and also brasswork. Jewellery and ornamentation were made from materials readily available such as wood, shells, ivory, beads, and silver and brass combined with rattan rings. Heavy brass earrings that stretched the earlobes—a symbol of beauty and status—were a common ornament. These are generally not worn by the younger generation. The Kayan and Kenyah people also have a long metalworking tradition.

In Sabah, Rungus women wore coiled brass wire rings on their legs, arms and necks; however, in modern times they are rarely worn as a whole set (see 'Jewellery and ornaments of Sabah and Sarawak'). Bead jewellery, on the other hand, remains popular among many of the indigenous groups of Sabah and Sarawak.

ABOVE: **A Terengganu brass kettle with engravings and long spout.**

LEFT: ***Pua kumbu* textile from Sarawak (Sarawak Museum Collection).**

FAR LEFT: **The artistry of the Malays is shown in the fluid curved form of the kris.**

BELOW: **Sarawak Kelabit metalsmiths still use simple implements to make tools and weapons.**

Islamic design principles and motifs

Islamic art forms were traditionally used on a wide variety of items both functional and decorative, and the range of their application has increased over the years. Early local examples of Islamic art were heavily influenced by that of the Middle East as a result of Arab trade with the Malay Peninsula. However, local artisans soon began to draw inspiration from the local environment and culture, creating a distinct Malay style of Islamic art.

Two *sura* from the splendidly illuminated *Al-Qur'an Mushaf Malaysia*, a national project first published in 2000. Sura an-Nas, one of the most often recited sura (left). The al-Fatihah, the opening sura of the Qur'an (right).

Principles of Islamic art

Islam forbids excess and promotes moderation and humility. These principles are applied equally to art forms—a balance between beauty, virtue, peace and harmony is thus sought. The use of human and animal forms, unless stylized or abstract, is also forbidden, as this may lead to idolatry. Floral and geometric designs, the cosmos, patterns, motifs, arabesques and calligraphy are therefore favoured. Originally, decoration and splendour was not the main objective, but artists and architects have added their own creativity and interpretations to works that glorify Allah. Symbols are used to balance the negative and positive, to evoke tranquillity, and to give praise to Allah.

Space and arrangement are particularly important to Islamic design as Islam requires man to use space (that is, the world and the universe created by Allah) wisely. The elements within an artwork should be balanced and contain a harmonious arrangement of space and colour.

The mimbar

The quintessential Malay design is the *mimbar* (pulpit). Examples of designs in traditional Malay woodcarving found in Melaka, Negeri Sembilan, Perak, Penang and Kedah suggest a uniformity of style whose religious underpinnings are detected in the fine and rigorous workmanship.

The type of design is determined by the location on any given surface on the *mimbar*. The most common is the square border with plain mouldings that tone down the continuous interlacing of scrolls of stalks and leaves. Rectangles and right-angled triangles (**1**) are employed as well, designed to impose order upon the wild surging of undulating foliage that threatens to overwhelm the neighbouring spaces. Such is the ornamental design on the *mimbar* of the Masjid Aceh in Penang built in 1808—inspired by *bunga Cina* (Chinese flowers) (**2**), buds, and scroll motifs, in a restrained composition, painted in gold on a pink background.

The *mimbar* of Masjid Permatang Pasir, Bukit Mertajam, Penang is composed of square and rectangular borders. It was built, according to the inscription on the arch of the gateway (**3**), in 1267 Hijrah or 1847 CE. The jasmine flower design is expressive with sprays and tendrils spreading out in exuberant profusion painted in deep blue, interlacing the knots of faith (**4**); two out of the four panels depict a flowerpot, metaphors of the appointed moments of birth and death (**5**).

Circles in the form of rosettes, or cinquefoils, or quatrefoils are often placed on the arch or the sides of the *mimbar* to denote the emanation of light (*nur*) upon the holy sanctuary. A rosette of a pineapple fruit is placed at the intersection of the arch and pillar of the gate of the *mimbar* of Masjid Permatang Pasir in Penang, while another situated in the bracket is made of continuous interlacing bands. A simplified four-petal quatrefoil is on a cluster of jasmine leaves that animate the main rafter of the *mimbar*. At Masjid Telok Buntar in Perak the rosettes are a unifying device in the band of scrolls on the pillars and on the side panels, painted in gold in contrast to the black background (**6**).

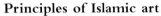

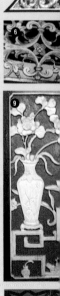

LEFT: Chinese styling, Malay classical forms and Islamic influences are evident in this elaborately carved wooden *mimbar* in the Terengkera mosque in Melaka, which features heavy gold lacquer work.

Motifs

Traditional Malay Muslim designs are found on houses and palaces (see 'Techniques, forms and motifs of Malay woodcarving' and 'Traditional wooden architecture'), carved on pulpits (*mimbar*) in mosques (see also 'Influences on arts and crafts: A historical perspective'), woven into mats (see 'The artistic tradition'), engraved on kris and other weapon handles (see 'Metalworking and weapons') or adorning pottery (see 'Pottery forms and motifs' and 'Malay pottery'), batik cloth and other textiles (see 'Cultural significance of textiles: Malay' and 'Malay woven cloth'). They are largely floral and geometrical, or a combination of the two. A set of motifs is employed that is susceptible to repetition, elaboration and distortion, stylized in curvilinear scrolls and convolutions.

Repeated patterns are a strong element in Islamic art; the repetition signifies continuity—no beginning and no end. Floral designs may be interwoven in continuous coiling spirals of leaves; they are smooth and uncluttered, emitting a classicism imitated by contemporary designers.

ABOVE: Royal *tekat* early 20th century pillow end from Kuala Kangsar with Jawi script Islamic verses in gold thread (Henry Bong Permanent Collection).

BELOW: Gilt embellished wooden chest carved with verses from the Qur'an (19th century CE). Such chests were used by wealthy Malays to keep clothes and valuables (Islamic Arts Museum Malaysia Collection).

Calligraphy

Calligraphy is a key feature of Islamic art. The names of Allah and the Prophets and excerpts from the Holy Qur'an are frequently used as decoration on coins (see 'Silverware' and 'Gold jewellery and regalia'), ceramic ware, metalware, carpets, textiles (see 'Cultural significance of textiles: Malay'), tombstones, books, woodcarvings (see 'Techniques, forms and motifs of Malay woodcarving') and as architectural features, particularly in palaces and mosques (see 'Techniques, forms and motifs of Malay woodcarving' and 'Traditional wooden architecture'). It is also used extensively in modern Malaysian art (see 'Contemporary Islamic art').

Silver betelnut *sirih* set dating from the late 19th to early 20th century CE. The set would have been commissioned by a Malay patron of distinction. Its repoussé decoration with floral and foliate motifs is in accordance with Islamic design requirements (Islamic Arts Museum Malaysia Collection).

19th century Malay jewellery: a set of three *kerongsang* brooches with a star motif (Henry Bong Permanent Collection).

Examples of mimbar motifs and forms

1. Scroll motifs, Masjid Aceh, Penang, 1808. 2. *Bunga Cina* (Chinese flowers), Masjid Aceh, Penang, 1808. 3, 4 & 5. Jasmine spray and tendrils, potted scrolls, inscription (all Masjid Permatang Pasir, Penang, 1847). 6. Rosettes, Masjid Telok Buntar, Perak. 7. Top details and dome, Masjid Pengkalan Rama, Melaka, 1728. 8. Cherry blossoms, Masjid Kampung Hulu, Melaka, 1728. 9. Still life, Masjid Terengkera, Melaka, 1728. 10. *Bunga ketumbi*, Masjid Kampung Hulu, Melaka, 1728. 11. Lotus, Masjid Terengkera, Melaka, 1728. 12. 12-pointed stars, Masjid Ubudiah, Kuala Kangsar, Perak, 1913. 13. Hadith Ibnu Abbas, Masjid Ubudiah, Kuala Kangsar, Perak, 1913.

Chinese influence is best seen in the design, the composition and the choice of subject matter on the *mimbar* at the three Melaka mosques, Masjid Terengkera, Masjid Pengkalan Rama (**7**), and Masjid Kampung Hulu, all completed around 1728. Under the Dutch, Melaka attracted wealthy Chinese Muslim traders who were probably of the Hanafiah persuasion. They most likely financed the construction of these mosques with their elaborate *mimbar*, whose designs bear witness to a feeling of 'Chineseness', maintained over the years by having pink reapplied to the background. Even a winter vignette of cherry blossom (**8**) is included on the gateway at Masjid Kampung Hulu; at Masjid Terengkera, a perfect still life is featured, showing a vase and a small bowl of fruits, both of which sit on a table of right-angled fret design (**9**).

In all three *mimbar*, the ends (*pemeles*) of the ridges (*tulang perabung*) swirl dramatically skywards, resembling the eave corners found on the roofs of Chinese temples. At Masjid Kampung Hulu (**10**) and at Masjid Pengkalan Rama, the motif is either the *bunga ketumbi* or the mangosteen corolla, while it is the lotus at Masjid Terengkera. (**11**). Such ostentatious display of the designer's skills and, by extension, of the patron's wealth runs counter to the deep austerity of Shafie school that permeates Malay Islam. Perhaps this explains why *mimbar* in the 19th and the 20th centuries were rigorously simplified, largely unadorned and minimally decorated.

Twentieth-century *mimbar* adopted the fret design, as can be seen in the *mimbar* of the Masjid Ubudiah, Kuala Kangsar, Perak, built in 1913. Hardwood *belian* seems ideal to carve the geometric patterns of the twelve-pointed stars (**12**). And on the archway of the *mimbar*, the beautiful *naskh* inscription quotes from the Hadith (**13**) attributed to Ibnu Abbas concerning the silence that must be maintained while the imam delivers his sermon to ensure bountiful grace.

1. A Murut *bobohizan* (female shaman) in the Sook district, south of Kota Kinabalu, sips *tapai*—a traditional rice wine—from a stoneware jar during a religious ceremony.

2. Brown and olive-green stoneware jars manufactured between the 10–12th centuries, such as these pictured in an Iban longhouse, are considered precious heirlooms (*pusaka*). More common jars would be used for storing food items and rice wine (*tuak*).

3. Lotud potter in Kg Tutu, Tuaran, Sabah making a *taranang* (water jar) in 1983. Pottery ceased to be made in this area a few years later with the passing of this potter.

4. Made from the mid-19th century to the early 20th century the decorative enamelled porcelain now known as Nonya

porcelain was imported from China to Malaysia. This Nonya porcelain joss-stick holder features flora and fauna motifs in striking colour combinations.

5. Applying the finishing touches of vertical raised relief ribs to a *labu panai* vessel from Tarit, Perak. This form resembles the *asam gelugur*, an acidic fruit.

6. A potter throws a pot on his wheel at a pottery in Kuala Selangor, one of many such family-run potteries that manufacture clay pots used in Indian weddings and religious ceremonies, as well as others for daily activities.

7. This modern version of a *buyung*, a wide-bellied pot used for carrying water, features an elegant, leafy motif around its unglazed body.

POTTERY AND EARTHENWARE

Shards of pottery excavated from caves in Kedah, Kelantan, Pahang, Perak, Perlis and Sarawak suggest that pottery-making was widespread as early as the Neolithic period (3000–2000 BCE). Early methods of pottery-making were the same as those used throughout the world; only the forms, motifs and firing methods differed. One of the oldest craft forms of human civilization, it is believed that pottery was discovered by 'accident' when early humans began coating the insides of woven baskets with clay before drying them in the sun to make waterproof containers. With the discovery of fire, it was found that by placing these containers over intense heat, the outer layer of fibre or other organic matter would burn away. All that remained was the hardened clay. Pottery went on to be used not just for storing, carrying and cooking, but also for religious rituals and ceremonies.

Ceramic items found in the Niah Caves, including a double-funnelled funerary jar, suggest that pottery was made in Malaysia during Neolithic times.

Potters from the Malay and other indigenous communities did not traditionally use a potter's wheel. Instead, they placed a lump of clay on square pieces of wood or metal plates lined with banana leaves to prevent sticking. This improvised base allowed them to rotate their clay pieces while they hand-moulded them to the desired shapes, after which the surfaces were decorated by beating with carved wooden paddles. The potter's wheel was invented later, for moulding purposes, as were kilns—proper firing systems that allowed for better control of temperature.

In Sabah and Sarawak, indigenous communities used basically the same pottery-making techniques as were used in the Peninsula, although motifs and purposes differed. It is believed that Chinese traders introduced sturdy glazed clay jars to coastal communities in Sarawak in the early 16th century. These huge jars with intricate dragon motifs were exchanged in barter trade and soon found a strong following in the local community, being highly prized as heirlooms.

Under the British, Chinese and Indian immigrants who arrived to work in the tin mines and rubber plantations brought with them their knowledge of earthenware manufacture and design. The Chinese produced pottery with symbolic floral and fauna motifs, which can still be seen in modern examples of the craft. Almost all Chinese pottery is glazed either on the inside or the outside. The Indians, on the other hand, focused on making plain, unadorned water and cooking pots. Unlike the Malays, however, the Chinese and Indians used kilns to fire their pottery.

Through the years, technological improvements and a better understanding of the materials have both played an important role in the advancement of pottery, both in studio and industrial pottery. Many artisans working in the clay media in Malaysia today are pushing its boundaries and, through experimentation, are producing new ceramic forms and finding local and international markets for their products, though traditional forms remain popular.

Pottery forms and motifs

Created to serve a particular purpose, various pottery forms have evolved within the various ethnic groups of Malaysia. Decoration in motif form is often inspired by elements of nature. Religious influences, too, are evident in the pottery of some communities. Generally, the Malay and Chinese are largely influenced by plant and animal motifs. Indian pottery is better known for its plain forms and often unadorned cooking pots and water containers, and tribal communities for their clay containers and burial urns.

Functions and decorations

In the area of pottery, each community in Malaysia is seen to have its own identity in crafting items for their daily and ceremonial use. The need for containers for cooking, storing and carrying were age-old reasons for the fashioning of pottery items such as pots, cooking urns and water containers. As pottery was formed to be functional, the cooking pot, for example, had to be circular in shape and deep enough to contain food. However, it also had to be reasonably shallow to allow for easy cooking. Water containers, on the other hand, had to be slimmer and taller to prevent spillage.

It was not long then before potters wanted to adorn these forms. Local flora and fauna provided much inspiration for motifs, as did traditional beliefs about the supernatural world. Motifs included wave-like designs incised by carvings or stampings using pieces of wood. These indentions actually strengthened the pottery, giving it a certain hardness and making it less fragile.

Generally, the Malays and Chinese are largely influenced by plant and animal motifs. Indian potters are known for the form of their pots and water containers, while indigenous communities are known for their clay incense braziers and burial urns.

Ornamentation is applied with a variety of tools including sharp implements and wooden sticks with carved motifs that are stamped onto the vessel.

Some common pottery motifs and forms

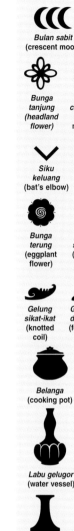

Bulan sabit (crescent moon)	Tulang ikan (fish bone)	Huruf 'V' (letter 'V')	Pucuk rebung (bamboo shoots)
Bunga tanjung (headland flower)	Bunga cakar ayam (chicken markings)	Bunga keduduk (rhododendron flower)	Bunga padi (rice flower)	Pucuk rebung (bamboo shoots)	Susur kelapa (coconut palm frond)
Siku keluang (bat's elbow)	Huruf 'F' (letter 'F')	Huruf 'X' (letter 'X')	Bunga cengkih (clove flower)	Bunga lawang (anise flower)	Bunga pecah empat (four petalled flower)
Bunga terung (eggplant flower)	Buah semunjing (kemuning fruit)	Gelung bekaul (entwined pattern)	Gelung kelindu (a type of fern)	Kelangai tabak (pattern used on base of brass tray)	Gelung ulu jempul (parang handle)
Gelung sikat-ikat (knotted coil)	Gelung demam (fevered coil)	Gelung bunga tapang bubut (Ketapang tree pattern)	Juring (sharp edge)	Janggut udang (prawn's whiskers)	Dilah kebumbu (decorative torch)
Belanga (cooking pot)	Periuk (cooking pot)	Buyung (jar)	Bekas perasap (incense burner)
Labu gelugor (water vessel)	aLabu tela (water vessel)	Labu gombol (water vessel)	Labu belalai gajah (water vessel)
Pasu tinggi (tall vase)	Pasu tinggi (tall vase)	Pasu bertangkai (urn with handles)	Pasu tinggi (tall vase)

Source: Kraftangan Malaysia 2004

Sabah pottery

Although much of the traditional earthenware pottery production in Sabah has become obsolete, on the east coast the Bajau of Semporna at Tampi Tampi still make on demand, and for a limited market, *lapohan* pottery stoves and selected traditional earthenware receptacles, such as incense burners (*tugtugan*), water jars (*bingki*) and cooking pots. These were usually plain earthenware, sometimes with decorative markings of no particular design, made with the edges of thin strips of bamboo or pieces of wood repeatedly stamped or scratched on the surface to create a pattern around the receptacle.

Incense burner (*tugtugan*).

On the west coast, the Dusun of Kg Malangkap, Kota Belud made small, usually plain, cooking pots with lids called *kuron* from clay. Production was small-scale and limited. The pots were used to cook herbs or medicine. The Lotud produced earthenware for the kitchen such as cooking pots and water jars (see 'Pottery and earthenware'), also using the paddle and anvil technique, but production stopped with the death of the last potter at Kg Tutu, Tuaran in the 1980s.

The seafaring Bajau Laut people of Sabah still use this simple pottery stove called *lapohan*. It is portable and suitable for use on the houseboats in which they live and travel.

Sarawak pottery

There are two main types of pottery in Sarawak. One type is Chinese glazed pottery produced in dragon kilns and the other is the hand-moulded, simple low-fired pottery of the Iban, Lun Bawang and Kelabit groups. Iban pottery resembles Neolithic pottery excavated at the Niah Caves in Sarawak where Stone Age weapons and utensils made of stones, bones, shells and clay have been found. The people of that period conducted primary burial by leaving the body in open spaces or in caves for a certain period of time, and a secondary burial in earthen jars. Included with the bodies were colourful pottery items. Decoration of Iban pots is done simply by using a wooden paddle carved with lines that the potter uses to shape the pot.

This Neolithic three-coloured clay burial urn with angular patterns and short incisions was found in the Niah Caves, Sarawak.

It is believed that the Chinese introduced their sturdier clay jars to the coastal community of Sarawak when plying the trade routes in the early 16th century. These huge jars with intricate dragon motifs were exchanged in barter trade and soon found a strong following among the indigenous community. However, they soon introduced elements of their own rich cultures and beliefs in the spirit world into the decorative motifs of their pottery. It was soon common to find flora and fauna motifs taken from the longhouse paintings and tribal musical instruments like the *sapeh*, a guitar-like stringed instrument. It is these designs that make Sarawak pottery so distinctive today.

A clay seat with a leather upper and bottom features motifs taken from nature.

Malay pottery

There are four main types of Malay pottery—mainly water and cooking containers—the *labu* (gourd-shaped water container); *belanga* (cooking pot); *buyung* (wide-mouthed water jar); and the *terenang* (angular shaped water container). The many types of water containers are categorized according to their forms, motifs and shape of the spout. The clay *labu* uses the gourd shape—a symbol of the continuity of life for the Malay community. Due to the porous properties of the clay used, the water kept in these *labu* stays cool.

Another popular drinking container associated with Malay potters is the *kendi*. A vessel with two openings—a mouth and a spout—the *kendi* has no handle and usually has a neck,

Unglazed earthenware cooking pots *belanga* (left) and *periuk* (above) with handles, covers and slight impressions as decoration.

characteristics that distinguish it from the other water containers. A *kendi* is commonly used for serving water, for administering medicine, and in rituals such as for pouring libations or holy water. These vessels have been prized for their form as much as for their use, and have been known to be included as grave offerings in burials.

The round shape base of the *belanga* provides for even distribution of heat and is favoured for cooking curries. A smaller form also used for cooking is known as *periuk*. *Belanga* and *periuk* are mostly made in Kampung Mambong, Kuala Krai, Kelantan and Kuala Tembeling, Pahang.

The *kendi* water vessel has no handle. It is grasped by the neck and tilted towards the mouth, allowing water to pour into the mouth through the spout.

Motifs

Motifs in traditional Malay pottery draw inspiration from nature, especially from elements found in the rainforest. Some common motifs include bamboo shoots (*pucuk rebung*), rice flowers (*bunga padi*), clove flowers (*bunga cengkih*). Animal-inspired motifs include tiger prints, fish scales and deer hoofs. Most motifs are carved on the ends of sticks and pressed into the clay. Serrated bamboo strips are also used to produce continuous dotted patterns.

A form of *labu panai* with vertical ribs of clay and a floral relief motif.

LEFT: Malay cooking pots are simple in form and mostly unglazed. This example of *belanga* has a wide, thin brim and simple but elegant decoration on its lid and handles.

BELOW: The *bunga pecah empat* (four-petalled flower) motif can be seen on the lid handle of this *belanga* (cooking pot).

Chinese pottery

Traders from China are believed to have traded their pottery in Southeast Asia since the Sung Dynasty (960–1279 CE). There was a mass influx of Chinese brought in to mine tin in Malaya prior to World War II under British rule (1786–1941). Along with many other aspects of their rich culture, the Chinese brought along with them large storage jars decorated with motifs of flowers and dragons. Porcelain items were also used to hold offerings on ancestral altars. Auspicious floral and fauna and Chinese religious motifs were used to decorate Chinese pottery, particularly the colourful porcelain known as Nonyaware. Daoist and Buddhist motifs often ran along the bands at the edges of Nonya porcelain.

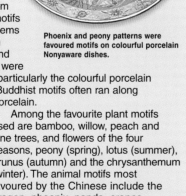

Phoenix and peony patterns were favoured motifs on colourful porcelain Nonyaware dishes.

Among the favourite plant motifs used are bamboo, willow, peach and pine trees, and flowers of the four seasons, peony (spring), lotus (summer), prunus (autumn) and the chrysanthemum (winter). The animal motifs most favoured by the Chinese include the dragon, phoenix, panda, cranes, magpies, ducks and fish, with each having its own symbolic meaning. The dragon is the symbol of wisdom, strength and pride of place. It is often placed besides its 'queen', the phoenix, which is symbolic of peace in self-sacrifice and rebirth. Besides fauna and flora motifs, the Chinese also emphasize the natural elements of the moon, clouds and waves in their background designs.

Examples of glazed ceramic Chinese flowerpots that have proved popular in the domestic and export markets.

Indian pottery

Contact between India and the Malay Peninsula has been recorded as early as the 3rd century CE. The oldest signs of Indian elements in Malay culture date from the 5th century. Indians were believed to have sailed to the port of the Bujang Valley, Kedah, where they first made clay figurines and related pottery items for use in temples to worship Hindu gods and Buddha.

Prior to World War II under British rule (1786–1941), more Indians were brought to Malaya to work in the plantations. This community took to producing their traditional earthenware, mainly cooking pots. These items were never glazed—the red brick colour on the outer surface was due to the oxidation of iron particles in the clay when fired.

Other earthenware items used include incense braziers for religious purposes and matrimonial ceremonies. During burials, shards of earthen pots are strewn over the grave. According to folklore, this is to ensure the happiness of the deceased's children and relatives. Unlike Malay and Chinese pottery, Indian pottery does not have much surface decoration. Cooking pots are left unadorned and unglazed. The emphasis is on the form, and one of the more popular forms is that of the shape of a woman (flowing curves): it symbolizes love, bounty, beauty and fertility.

Dated from the 10th–11th century, this terracotta Bodhhisattva votive tablet found in the Bujang Valley, Kedah, reflects similarities with Southern Indian images of the same period.

BELOW: Indian cooking pots are often unadorned and simple in form.

Malay pottery

Traditionally in Malay communities, pottery was typically a woman's work which she would do once her chores were over, or perhaps when harvesting was completed and the rice field was not yet ready for ploughing. Malay pottery—mainly round-bottomed, wide-mouthed cooking pots and tall, bulbous-bottomed water containers—was distinctive because of its geometric decoration applied with stamped marks or carved wooden paddles. No significant Malay pottery older than 250 years has been found; its fragility was probably due to the corrosive nature of the soil and the humid conditions of the Malay Peninsula.

Various forms of *labu* from the collection of the Perak Museum.
1. *Labu tela*
2. *Labu pucung*
3. *Labu gelugur halus*
4. *Labu bucung*
5. Slight differences in form and decoration allows for many variations of the *labu* (gourd-shaped water containers). Sometimes *labu* of special quality are embellished with silver mountings on the mouth rim and provided with silver stoppers.

Characteristics of Malay pottery

In the Malay Peninsula, a major characteristic of Malay pottery is that potters do not use the potter's wheel or spinner. Another characteristic is the non-use of dyes or colours to decorate the pottery. Instead, the colour of the item is a product of the firing methods used on the natural properties of the clay. Malay pottery is generally unglazed and decoration is by stamping a design in the wet clay or by applying low relief such as the band or raised ribs.

Traditionally, Malay pottery is usually fired in the open, but more recent methods have been introduced including firing in gas kilns, electric wheels and plaster-mould production techniques, thus allowing for mass production, precise quality control and a larger variety of forms of pottery to be produced.

Today, the craft of making traditional Malay pottery survives in a few places in Peninsular Malaysia, namely Sayong, Mambong, Tembeling and Pulau Tiga.

Building up a pot the traditional way from coils of clay spun on a hand-rotated board.

Sayong

Kampung Kuala Sayong, near the royal town of Kuala Kangsar in Perak, is a famous pottery-making village. The Sayong potters are predominately women. They use the greyish clay of the district to make a specialized water vessel called *labu air* (water gourd), named for the gourd upon which it is modelled. The *labu air* has a long, narrow neck, bulging gently in the middle and rising to a slightly everted mouth rim. The body of the vessel is rounded, sometimes oval, in shape, standing on an out-turned foot rim. In one type, *labu gelugur,* the body is decorated with vertical round ridges resembling the fruit of the *asam gelugur* (*garcinia atroviridis*), an acidic dried fruit.

Many water gourds made in Sayong have a distinctive black burnished surface. This finish is obtained by plunging the gourds into rice husks

Wooden paddles and thin bamboo pieces are common tools used to form clay pots.

after wood-firing. The husks ignite from the heat of the pots, causing an oxidation process that gives the pottery its sooty look.

The forms and motifs used in Sayong pottery emphasize natural elements. Hand moulded, the surface designs often draw inspiration from nature, for example, *bunga padi* (rice flower), *pucuk rebung* (bamboo shoots), *bunga cengkih* (clove flowers) and other natural geometric shapes.

Some contemporary forms of Malay pottery, produced using modern techniques, but still maintaining some original characteristics, such as simple relief decoration.

Making Sayong pots

The traditional pottery-making process in Malaysia requires clay to be gathered from riverbanks or anthills. The clay is kneaded, moulded by hand, smoothed with river pebbles, decorated with motifs, dried in the sun and then fired. The traditional way of making the *labu Sayong* is featured below, however, today it is more commonly manufactured using moulds and electric kilns as this allows for mass production and quality control.

1. The clay is prepared in a foot-pounder (*lesung kaki*) and sieved to remove stones. Kneading of the clay removes air bubbles. The clay is formed into a cylindrical shape.

2. The pots are built up by hand from coils of clay spun on a simple board which can be rotated by hand. The clay is pressed gently and raised to form the body, neck, head and mouth.

3. A wooden paddle (*penepek*) is used to shape the body and a thin piece of bamboo (*sudip*) to scrape off excess clay. River pebbles (*batu luru*) are used to smooth the surface of the pot.

4. The vessel is decorated with motifs using a piece of wood (*kayu matera*) with engraved motifs, and then left to dry in the air for several days.

5. The dried pots are placed inverted on a rack with a fire pit below. They are covered with banana and coconut leaves and slowly fired.

6. After about four to five hours the rack is removed and the fire stoked with bamboo splints. The pots are left to fire for a second time for about an hour.

7. After the second firing, the vessels are removed from the embers and buried in rice husks which combust, from the heat, giving the pots their black colour.

Source: Kraftangan Malaysia 2005

Mambong

Situated upriver of Sungai Galas in Kuala Krai, Kelantan, Kampung Mambong is known for its unglazed reddish or terracotta pottery, decorated with animal forms on the lid, making it unique compared with other pottery in the country.

Dug from riverbanks, the clay is originally yellowish-brown but turns reddish upon sunning or open firing. The clay's plasticity is very high, with an estimated 10 per cent shrinkage. It does not require mixing with other materials as is the practice elsewhere. Only a little sand is added for porosity. Clay from this area is very resilient in that it does not crack easily when dried under the sun. When fired, the body becomes even stronger. Elements of golden particles in the clay from this area lend Mambong pottery a distinctive burnished look.

The potters of Mambong are keen on fashioning instruments to leave motifs on the body of the pottery when pressed. They tend to utilize the abundant supply of rattan for these instruments. As such, Mambong pottery is often covered with decorated motifs. The most favoured motif is that of the crescent moon.

Tembeling

Pottery is a small cottage industry in Pasir Durian in Kuala Tembeling, Pahang. This village is particularly known for its earthen cooking pots, the *belanga* and *terenang*.

The *belanga* has a shape similar to that of a steel helmet with a wide, thin brim and simple decorations. A smaller version, also used for cooking, is called a *periuk*.

The *terenang* has an elegant shape with unique proportions. It is believed that the *terenang's* shape is based on the brassware containers once made in Kelantan and still made in Terengganu. The *terenang's* concave neck curves outwards, providing a contrast with the convex-shaped body and sharp-edged foot. Delicate flower motifs are arranged horizontally on the main body and vertically on the neck.

Terenang from Kuala Tembeling, Pahang, highly adorned with relief and stamping patterns, mostly of floral motifs. *Terenang* are mostly unglazed.

Pulau Tiga

Pulau Tiga in Perak is known for its high quality pots. Using white clay found two metres underground, the body is hand-moulded, decorated and fired before resin is applied to the foot. After firing, the pots take on a reddish tint and an attractive surface texture.

The form of *labu* here is similar to that of Sayong but the proportions of the various parts differ. According to legend, the origins of the Pulau Tiga *labu* were linked to the *padi* (rice) spirit, on account of the discovery of an earthen pot balanced on three clay rocks in the *padi* fields one day. This inspired potters to fashion the three-legged *nenek kemang* earthen container for water/storage.

Other popular forms include *geluk gelugur* and *geluk kepek*. The *geluk gelugur* has a rounded main body, a straight neck and a lipped rim and foot. The *geluk kepek*, on the other hand, is footless but also possesses elegant lines and a formal balance.

Applying a decorative pattern around the neck of a *labu* by the stamping technique using wooden tools.

Indian and Chinese pottery

In the late 19th and early 20th centuries, a number of Indian and Chinese pottery enterprises were established, catering to local market requirements for vessels used in marriage, birth and death rites, religious festivals, celebrations and daily use. Some potteries still use traditional methods in the making of these vessels, but plaster moulds are used to increase production and new mixtures of clay have been introduced for certain ranges of pottery. The number of Indian potters is decreasing, while Chinese enterprises often import goods from China to sell alongside locally manufactured goods.

RIGHT: Pots are neatly stacked to dry on top of a wood-fired kiln at Ramadas Chettiar's Indian pottery factory in Kuala Selangor, Selangor.

BELOW: Workers removing fired pots from the kiln and checking for any defects.

TOP: Clay pot used for storing dry goods and cooking.

MIDDLE: Decorated pot for the ponggal harvest festival.

ABOVE: Cooking pot.

Indian pottery areas and forms

The two notable Indian pottery centres are in Kampung Kedah in Parit Buntar and Batu Dua, Jalan Kelang, Kuala Selangor—coastal areas where a pulpy and brackish clay is found. Potteries in both places produce low-fired terracotta ware of South Indian origin in a formula handed down from Indian immigrants to their descendants.

A limited number of vessel forms are produced in the potteries. Wide-mouthed cooking pots in many sizes are common, as are oil and incense burners. The oil burner is a small dish pinched at the rim to keep the wick in place and is used for religious ceremonies. The incense burner, a perforated dish fixed to a foot and provided with a handle, is used on religious and ceremonial occasions. Some statuary is also produced for temple and religious purposes. Although there is competition from other types of cooking pots available, traditional cooking pots are still used, as food cooked in terracotta ware is tastier than that cooked in metal pots.

Methods of producing Indian pottery

Finding suitable clay is always the first task for a potter, the next being cleaning the clay of small stones and pebbles. Formerly the clay was kneaded by hand because there were no electric mixers to smooth the muddy clay. The mixing machine is a larger version of a kitchen mixer.

In the past, Indian potters used a wheel much like a wooden bullock cartwheel balanced by a metal pin in the centre. The potter's helper would spin the wheel using a pole inserted into a hole at the rim. The wheel's weight gave the momentum and the potter would throw a pot as the wheel was spun. This old tradition is no longer practised here but has been replaced by electric motors which drive the wheels. These wheels allow the potter to pull up or 'jigger' the pots from a hump of clay. This innovation to Indian pottery production was introduced in the 1980s when the potteries were visited by the then Head of the Art Department of the Specialist Teachers' Training Institute (see 'Art education'), Yeoh Jin Leng, and a visiting Scottish potter.

Small oil lamps are made by throwing a small amount of clay on the wheel and pinching the rim to hold a wick. The lamps are used at temple ceremonies and festivals.

Pots are thrown without a bottom and allowed to dry. Stacking them over the top of the brick kiln exposes them to the heat or they are left to dry out in the sun. At the leather-hard stage, the open-ended base of a part of the pot is closed by repeatedly beating the wall towards the centre into a rounded form using the paddle and anvil method. When the pots are thoroughly dried, they are fired. Traditionally this was done using an open-fire method. Pots were placed inverted over a pile of brushwood, coconut shells and husks. Thicker wood and branches and *lalang* grass, mixed with a thick slurry of mud, were plastered all round to form a conical mould. A fire was started at the bottom and the pots were fired hard in about an hour. Today, a wood-fire kiln is used. The pots are stacked one above the other inside the kiln, with the larger ones below. Lighting the kiln is often a woman's work—she starts the fire early in the evening, so that it is burning well by late evening and stokes it up again before going to bed so that there is a good heart to the fire that will take it through the night. By morning the clay vessels will all be fired and rendered non-porous. When the kiln is cool, the tan-coloured products that were formerly grey are ready to be removed, the colour having changed because of the heat. They are not glazed, although sometimes Hindu temples request that storage pots for use in wedding ceremonies be painted. Plaster moulds are used to increase production and new mixtures of clay have been introduced for certain ranges of pottery.

Most Indian pottery is usually reddish, never over-decorated and sometimes has simple stamped designs running over the shoulder of the pot. The reddish colour is the result of an iron red slip brushed over the pots before firing.

Chinese pottery

At the turn of the 20th century, rubber plantations in Peninsular Malaysia had a vast demand for small ceramic cups to hold latex running down the cuts of trees. Chinese immigrants, mostly Teochew from Swatow in the Guangdong province of China, came to Malaya and set up potteries in locations with rich clay deposits and usually near a river, as a large water supply was needed. Long dragon kilns (so named because their vast length is likened to a dragon on the side of a hill; flames from the side openings and furnace are also considered 'dragon-like') of Chinese potters, of 18 to more than 30 metres in length, are located along the west coast of Peninsular Malaysia, north of Ipoh, and in the Segambut area of Kuala Lumpur.

Chinese pottery salvaged from shipwrecks in the Melaka Strait, left to right: 540-year-old Celadon plate and 170-year-old Chinese urn.

Mass production ware such as vases and bowls for the tourist market is produced in many Chinese pottery factories like this one in Sarawak.

Elsewhere, dragon kilns can be found in Kedah and Johor and also on the outskirts of Sibu and Kuching in Sarawak (see 'Sarawak Pottery') and Kota Kinabalu in Sabah. The dragon kilns are roofed with corrugated iron stretching from the fire mouth to the chimney ends, with internal dimensions of up to two metres high and two metres wide. The kilns are usually built on gentle slopes.

Many of the potteries set up by Chinese immigrants have remained family businesses and descendants of the original potters in the Ipoh area have established their own potteries in other areas such as Sungai Siput, Batu Gajah, Gopeng and Beruas. Many of these potteries manufacture flowerpots and jars for both the domestic and export markets. Container loads of glazed stoneware pots and jars are exported to the United States, Australia, Europe and the United Kingdom. In the 21st century, many of these potteries have closed. Others have turned to importing wares, particularly from China.

Products, clays and glazes

Beside flowerpots and water jars, dragon kilns are also used to produce joss stick holders, latex cups, drainpipes and specially designed items. The large jars are partly thrown on the wheel and partly built up with thick coils of clay. They are then beaten with wood paddles and refined on the wheel.

The clay that is used for these wares is a composition of ball clay and sandy clay mixed and extruded through a pug mill. The use of glazes is a strong feature of Chinese pottery compared with Malay and Indian ware. A glaze makes an item stronger than an unglazed piece, renders it waterproof and is also used for decorative purposes. There are many different types of glazes and some potters in Malaysia use a recipe of marine clay or sea mud and lime. The sea mud comes from Port Klang, Selangor. Salt glazes are also used.

Tenmoku Pottery

Tenmoku Pottery was established in 1989. The founder named his enterprise Tenmoku Pottery after a Japanese glaze which originated from the Chinese words *tien mok* (heaven's eyes). In China, the original black glaze found in the red earth had spots on it after firing caused by the mineral content. Tenmoku pottery was originally distinguished by these spots, but in more recent years its hallmark is the use of fish, leaves and branches pressed into the hundreds of various products created. A computer is used to calculate the formula for each of the products. The company has expanded dramatically and Tenmoku Pottery is now operating its own retail chain and can be found in Malaysian department stores around the country with the company also exporting overseas.

Glazed plant pots such as these with a bamboo design are common items manufactured in Malaysian potteries.

A potter working a tall vase on his wheel. As the demand for traditional pottery decreases, items such as colourfully decorated vases have become a staple item manufactured by potters in Sarawak for sale to tourists.

Ritual jars such as these are used by the Lotud in Sabah to make and store *tapai*—a traditional rice wine.

Sarawak pottery

There are two distinctive types of pottery made in Sarawak. One is by the indigenous people, particularly the Iban, Lun Bawang, Kelabit, Melanau and Orang Ulu who hand-moulded and low-fired their pottery to be used as utensils as well as for ceremonial purposes. The other type is wheel-thrown Chinese pottery introduced by immigrant artisans, descendants of potters from Swatow (Shantou) in Guangdong province in China, a famous pottery production area. As cheap imports flood the market the manufacture of tourist ware becomes more obvious, with less emphasis on goods made and used for daily use.

Ceramic pieces from as early as 10th century CE have been found in the possession of the indigenous peoples of Borneo. The Melanau coastal people often possess very fine, old pieces of Chinese and Siamese ceramics, such as these pictured above, due to their participation in maritime trade from early times.

Indigenous pots with various relief patterns applied by the potter with carved wooden beaters when forming the pots using the paddle and anvil technique. The example directly above, an Iban pot with a rounded bottom, has a rattan stand that allows the pot to sit evenly when not in use.

A long pottery tradition

As early as 3000 BCE, Sarawak's tribal communities were making pots of all shapes and sizes for domestic uses such as cooking and storage. Native pottery was primarily manufactured by women in a tradition handed down from generation to generation. Similar methods (hand-moulding and low-firing) were used by most tribes to make traditional cooking pots (*periuk tanah*) and it was found that food cooked in these earthenware pots was much tastier than food cooked in metal pots. The pots were decorated by beating them with patterned wooden paddles. Jars were also produced for ritual use, particularly burials. Imported stoneware and earthenware were used particularly as prestige and storage vessels, and for other domestic purposes, but native potters continued to produce for home use until the turn of the 20th century.

Traditional Iban pottery and the wooden beaters used to imprint patterns on the pots.

Heirlooms

Trade relations in the region brought the indigenous people into contact with colourful and attractive objects, amongst them fine ceramic ware from China, Vietnam, Thailand, Japan and Europe. These objects were treasured by the indigenous people as heirlooms (*pusaka*) and passed from generation to generation, with one's status being measured by the number of ceramic items owned.

Early trade objects such as these ceramic heirloom jars, seen in an Iban longhouse in Sarawak, are not only highly valuable, but also useful, often being used for storage and in religious ceremonies and rituals.

Into the South Seas

In the 18th century, potteries were established in Sarawak by immigrant Chinese artisans. One pottery stood near Kuching's old port at Tanah Puteh (white earth), by a creek called Sungai Priok (pot river), when James Brooke, later Rajah of Sarawak, arrived in 1839.

The potters must have been a law-abiding class of men; they are seldom mentioned in official records. The *Sarawak Gazette* of June 1887 briefly announced that 'enterprising Chinamen' were building a pottery kiln in Sibu and had engaged an experienced potter from the Tanah Puteh kilns as their foreman of works. Whoever the financier was, the man at the wheel was almost without exception a Teochew, from Swatow. Potters who had served their apprenticeship there came 'into the South Seas' to seek employment.

Not many of them settled permanently as family traditions among Kuching and Sibu potters suggest that each workman saved up a good sum of money and retired to China. If he had been prosperous enough to buy his own factory in Sarawak, he would recruit staff from his own clan.

Early production at the Sarawak kilns centred on large vessels, treasured by Borneo natives who could usually tell a genuine old jar from a 'country-made' piece. The new, lower-status locally produced jars were used for storage, brewing and other household purposes.

The clay bed at Tanah Puteh has long been exhausted. Kuching potters now purchase their raw material from further upriver. Clay comes off the lorry in coarse lumps, so impurities have to be picked out and the whole mass vigorously kneaded. In the past, this was carried out by men treading the clay pile with their feet until the advent of the pug mill relieved them of this arduous task. All Sarawak pottery used to be wheel-thrown, but moulding is becoming increasingly common.

Modern pottery

These days, various utility products—once traditionally glazed honey-brown with burnt rice husks—are now slip-coated white with painted designs in pastel colours. Flower pots and stands, low garden stools and curry pots with this simple kind of decoration are offered for sale beside the old-fashioned brown ones. Colour and design have invaded the hitherto rather monochrome pottery stores. But the traditional pottery is not entirely gone, for new consumers are making their presence felt: tourists. They buy the colourful pottery because it is durable, reasonably priced and some of it small enough to stuff into a travelling bag at the last moment.

The switch from utility ware to tourist ware took a few years. It is now nearly complete; not every kiln still produces brown jars, or even a complete range of cooking and medicine vessels. Only flower pots remain in full production, both for the local market and increasingly for export. Tourist ware ranges from huge jars (over one metre high) to tiny jars of five or six centimetres. Each is decorated with at least two colours, though most sport a veritable rainbow of colours. The main shapes are jars, round containers with and without lids, ashtrays, plates and shallow bowls, drinking mugs, low stools, angular and irregularly shaped trays and shallow boxes for flower arrangements, and mould-cast money boxes ranging in shapes from frogs to Dutch shoes.

There is a local trend towards pottery to commemorate special occasions—a presentation piece may be embellished with a particular logo, even dainty little 'baskets' to present to wedding guests. Much of today's tourist ware is decorated

Assorted types of colourful pots and vases, many with native motifs, are manufactured for sale to tourists.

A modern potter: Gerald Goh

Gerald Goh, a descendant of a long line of potters, is one artist who, unlike many of his cousins, is staying in the family business. He is a young man of artistic talent and innovative spirit; ceramics courses overseas have opened his eyes to new techniques, new kilns, new glazes and new colours.

Gerald is excited about the ancient Borneo method of making pottery freehand by the stone-and-anvil technique. There is one very good reason for producing traditional artefacts by modern methods and selling them in the open market: it helps to keep the real, old, handmade pots in the country. The production and sale of good quality replicas is a step towards heritage conservation; in some countries, such replicas are sold in museum shops.

Gerald with a clay hornbill.

with friezes of Sarawak native designs, or what passes for such. Others are painted with picturesque renditions of Sarawak scenery or native lifestyle vignettes more or less accurately observed. Hedda Morrisson's classic Sarawak photos are a favourite treasure trove for ceramic painters in search of a motif. Kuching photographer Dennis Lau (see 'Photography'), too, enjoys the compliment of being immortalized on clay.

Besides painting decorations on unglazed clay, designs may also be cut out. The leather-hard artefact is covered with a wet slip of another colour, and the design is lifted out with a sharp little knife or lino-cutting tools. Eager to cash in on the new tourist ware trend, potteries are modernizing. The only person who laments the passing of the kick-wheel is the photographer who wants shots of a 'real traditional pottery.' The craftsman who had to sit at the wheel all day finds the pedal-controlled electrical rotor a blessing.

Is tourist ware artistic? Thousands of people each year vote with their money that it is—the proof of the pot is in the selling. There were eight potteries registered in Sarawak in 1986 (not including 42 brick works, which are listed under a different heading), nine in 2006, and the mainstay of this industry is tourist ware. To keep the potteries going in Sarawak, it is now up to the creative artists, by their individual efforts, to branch out into 'art pottery' as distinct from mass-produced products.

Pottery kilns

In an average-sized pottery employing about 20–25 hands, two kiln-loads a month are fired, more if necessary. Most Sarawak potteries use a wood-fired tunnel kiln known as a 'dragon kiln' which slopes gently upwards, encouraging natural updraft. An average kiln is between 18 to sometimes over 30 metres long; fully packed, it holds about 1000 items of all sizes. Access to the kiln is via two or more openings in its sides. It is fired from the lower end, where the furnace mouth is in a pit about a metre below ground level.

Firing takes 36–48 hours. After firing, the kiln has to be left to cool off; premature opening and draughts of cold air could seriously damage the contents, especially the delicate glazes. Although the prices of firewood vary, the cost is not the main reason why some potters prefer to install oil- or gas-fired kilns. The main advantage of such modern furnaces is that they permit exact temperature control.

Workers removing pots from a dragon kiln at the Ng Li Seng pottery in Sarawak.

Recent developments

Pottery has never been a major industry in Sarawak. In fact, after World War II, it languished considerably. Over time, the demand for locally produced utility ware dwindled with the appearance of aluminium and plastic. The earthenware dish for simmering curry has become an optional extra in most modern kitchens, while the unglazed spouted medicine pot and the one-footed shallow incense burner are only used by traditional healers nowadays. Insecticide aerosol sprays are so generally used that water-filled earthenware ant traps and perforated mosquito coil burners are less in demand. Piped water makes large water jars in kitchens obsolete. Well-stocked supermarkets mean fewer households keep large reserves of sugar, flour, rice and other staples, in big-bellied brown storage jars. Even the humpy brown coin box faces competition from plastic money boxes which are handed out free by local banks.

As the demand for traditional pottery decreases, items such as colourfully decorated vases have become a staple item manufactured by potters in Sarawak for sale to tourists.

1. Elaborately carved and decorated wedding bed reflecting the fusion of Chinese and local cultures characteristic of the Peranakan.

2. Orang Asli Jah Hut carver creating sculptures of spirit figures.

3. Kenyah woodcarving of a dragon-like dog creature with horns, long snout and large fangs from the Sarawak Museum collection.

4. These intricately carved east coast fisherman's rice and tackle boxes are practical yet ornate objects.

5. A spirit wood carving from the Monsopiad Cultural Village in Sabah.

6. Rural village (*kampung*) scene. The timeless Malay wooden house is still built in the traditional way and displays fine examples of Malay decorative woodcarving.

WOODCRAFT AND CARVING

Historically, much of Malaysia was covered with forests and wood was abundant. The first objects made of wood were utilitarian; designs and forms were simple, functional and unadorned. Simple wooden utensils used for carrying, storing and cooking were common. Later, as civilization developed, agricultural implements and tools, buildings and boats were made out of wood, as many still are today, and the wooden items used became more sophisticated. A proliferation of forms, and the designs and motifs carved, characterized the development of the wood tradition. Sometimes, design styles differed according to region, as in the case of boats and housing.

It is difficult to say exactly when decorative woodcarving in Malaysia began, but, in relation to the Malays, the history of woodcarving is closely intertwined with the progression of their culture over the centuries. Early forms and motifs were closely associated with the traditional way of life and sometimes took the form of symbols based on creatures perceived to have the power to ward off evil and malicious spirits. Pre-Islamic influences were commonly found in motifs of animals such as birds, tigers, snakes, dragons, monkeys, squirrels and others. The embrace of Islam by the Malays brought a new impetus to the art of woodcarving, in particular stylized or abstract designs and motifs based on the cosmos, plant life and calligraphy, in Arabic or Malay Jawi script, became the new stylistic focus. Few carvings more than 300 years old exist today, but many of them have been preserved in traditional Malay buildings. The best examples of exquisitely executed woodcarvings that are more than a century old are those displayed in the old palaces of the Malay rulers found in Kelantan at the Istana Balai Besar and Istana Jahar and in Negeri Sembilan at the Istana Ampang Tinggi. Particularly fine examples dating from the early to mid-18th century can also be seen in certain mosques, including in Kelantan, Melaka and Kuala Terengganu.

With the emergence of the Peranakan came unique woodcraft blending Chinese, Malay and European motifs and styles. In comparison, later 19th-century Chinese migrants preferred more traditionally Chinese designs. A great wood sculpture tradition exists among the indigenous peoples of Malaysia, including the Mah Meri and Jah Hut Orang Asli animist groups of Peninsular Malaysia. Coastal dwellers, the Mah Meri's carvings (often ritual masks) reflect spirits related to water, while the Jah Hut, who live in the jungles of Pahang, carve sculptures of forest spirits. Originally carving only for their own purposes, the work of both groups is now sought after by museums, galleries and private collectors. Besides utilitarian items, in Sarawak and Sabah a large number of decorative woodcarved items are seen, such as musical instruments, walking sticks and carvings on rafters, walls, doors and posts of longhouses. Carved ritual objects include masks, sculptures, burial poles and huts, sickness images and carved sword handles and sheaths. Ivory, bone and bamboo are also used as a carving medium, the latter for tobacco and other containers, smoking pipes and blowpipe dart holders.

Sarawak Melanau fish charm figurine carved from deer antler. This charm is tied to fishing nets to enhance the catch.

Techniques, forms and motifs of Malay woodcarving

The forms and motifs long seen in Malay woodcarving are influenced by nature—flora, the environment, natural elements and the cosmos—and the Islamic religion. While some of the early pre-Islamic themes and motifs are still evident today, they are now only manifested in stylized or abstract form. Many of the motifs used by the Malays have symbolic meaning and, traditionally, carving ornamental embellishments on houses and perahu *(boats) were not simply for aesthetic appeal, but also to protect homes and livelihoods from evil and the elements.*

Cut-out carved 19th-century wooden screen from Kelantan incorporating Qur'anic verses, floral and geometric motifs. The combination of different motifs is common in Malay woodcarving.

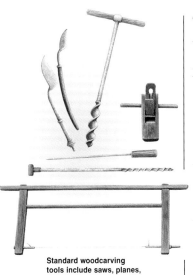

Standard woodcarving tools include saws, planes, borers, files, shavers and various types of knives among which is the *pisau wali* used for fine work.

Techniques employed

Malay woodcarving employs two main techniques—*ukiran timbul* bas-relief carving and *ukiran tebok*, a pierced and cut-out design technique. Bas-relief carvings are usually found on panels, walls, pillars and doors of traditional Malay houses and palaces, as well as furniture and objects such as *sirih* boxes. This technique allows for intricate carving of a multitude of designs, and commonly uses pieces of wood 2–3 centimetres thick. The cut-out technique is used for parts of a building where ventilation is required, such as windows, balustrades, verandahs, partitions or in fanlights above doors and windows. Such cut-out panels also serve the purpose of decoration. These carvings may sometimes be painted, very often in gold, to contrast with the dark background of the surrounding wood and thereby better display the carver's skill. Usually, selected motifs are outlined directly onto the wood without the benefit of draft drawings. However, only a skilled and experienced carver will attempt to carve without first drawing the design on the wood.

Motifs and Malay beliefs

The forms and motifs of Malay woodcarving have always been closely associated with the Malay way of life and are illustrative of their culture, values and beliefs. Many of the traditional motifs had symbolic meanings and formed part of an extensive repertoire of designs reflecting a heritage handed down from generations of woodcarvers.

Before the coming of Islam, the Malays were influenced by animism, Buddhism and Hinduism, reflected in depiction of many living creatures including birds, tigers, seahorses, dragons, monkeys, rhinoceros and snakes. These influences were gradually alienated as the Malays embraced Islam which did not encourage such images. When in use, forms taken from nature, such as animals and plants, became stylized or abstract, the most sophisticated depiction. Islamic principles also played a part in the structure of design compositions which should generally be symmetrical and thus harmonious, but not in total perfection—as only God can be thus—

Wooden window of the Terengkera Masjid in Melaka featuring floral and tendril patterns in the top panels and carved railings. No glass is used in the window, allowing ventilation in a tropical climate.

and the choice and deeper religious and cultural symbolism behind the motifs used. The use of Islamic calligraphy in the form of Qur'anic verses developed as a major design element, giving rise to variations of woodcarving which can be found in mosques, palaces, houses of the wealthy and other religious places. For example, *mimbar* (pulpits) are carved using a combination of calligraphic and geometric patterns (see 'Islamic design principles and motifs'). Other examples can also be seen in mausoleums and wooden tombstones at several old graves on the east coast of Peninsular Malaysia (see 'Carvings and sculptures: From cradle to grave').

The raw material

The type of wood chosen by a craftsman depends on the purpose of the carving—common examples include *kemuning* (Chinese myrtle) (**1**) and *sena* for sculptures, kris sheaths and hilts; *nangka* (jackfruit) (**2**) for musical instruments; and *jati* (teak), *cengal* (*Neobalanocarpus heimii*) (**3**) and *merbau* (*Intsia palembanica*) for buildings and boats.

Pattern and design elements

ABOVE: 'Ducks coming home' motif. Such carvings were normally found on furniture and in prominent places such as in the fanlight above a main door.

RIGHT: The fighting cock motif.

Choosing a pattern

As pattern and motifs play an important role in ensuring beauty and aesthetics in Malay woodcarvings, the selection of the right motifs is an integral part of the process and a carver will exercise care in choosing those that are appropriate for the position and place the carvings will occupy. A traditional Malay woodcarver will first select the form or pattern before choosing the motifs which are based on various influences or elements.

The three types of patterns can be described as the shadow pattern, the frame pattern or the complete pattern. Generally, shadow and frame patterns are more suited to freestanding motifs, such as flowers, fruits and those based on geometric shapes. In a frame pattern the motifs are linked by the border of the frame. Common motifs of this type include bamboo shoots normally seen on roof eaves or fascia boards. Other motifs traditionally used were the rhinoceros, seahorse, 'ducks returning home', 'fighting cockerels', waves and the sun.

A complete pattern has a fuller aesthetic value in the sense that it encompasses the motifs used in a wider natural context, for example, a complete network of flowers, trees, branches, twigs, fruits and leaves may be shown. Complete patterns normally appear gentle and swaying and are done in a continuous line. The commonly favoured Malay design motif, *awan larat*, is one example of this pattern style. Other examples include *daun sesayap* (wing-like leaf), *sulur kacang* (bean sprout), *saga kenering* (creeper with red and black-spotted beans) and *kerak nasi* (creeper with flowers like rice scrapings).

BELOW: This carving with the *sulur kacang* motif has a deeper symbolism. The design emanates from a hidden central seed (which represents God) and sprouts identical curling foliage branching out left and right (which shows God's creations in pairs).

LEFT: This illustrates the various components of a wall structure which has various patterns and designs, such as these sunray (**1**), sea-horse (**2**) and *kepala cicak* (lizard head) (**3**) motifs in the highest abstracted floral form.

Geometric patterns

Geometric designs may appear on their own or in combination with other patterns, such as flowers or foliage, and have been used even from pre-Islamic times. Common motifs include triangles, squares, octagons and hexagons, circles and the swastika.

Early 20th-century carved panel tile from Kelantan incorporating diamonds, squares and circles.

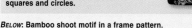

BELOW: Bamboo shoot motif in a frame pattern.

Living creatures

After the advent of Islam, decorative motifs in conflict with Islamic teachings, such as those based on animal or human forms, were generally avoided or appeared in stylized or abstract form. Traditional Malay motifs featured a number of living creatures, which often held symbolic significance. For example, the 'fighting cock' (*ayam berlaga*) motif of two cocks locked in combat portrayed two strong characters in a fierce struggle without recourse to a peaceful solution, each stubbornly trying to subdue the other. It also cautioned against gambling in the popular Malay sport of cock fighting. The 'ducks coming home' motif conveyed the message that Malays should obey their leaders and abide by the tenets of cooperation and unity. Another example is the rhinoceros, a big, quiet animal normally at peace with others, representing those who seek wealth without causing inconvenience to other people. Other common animals depicted included tigers, eagles, seahorses, snakes, dragons, monkeys, horses, cats and squirrels.

Kris hilt carved in the shape of a bird.

Cosmic elements

The cosmos has inspired Malay carvers to create designs featuring sun, moon and star motifs, sometimes seen adorning the gables of homes and roofs of mosques. Other natural elements are also depicted in traditional architecture. For example, a mountain is represented in the architectural style of *atap tumpang*, also known as *masjid bentuk meru* (mountain-shaped mosque), and mountain ranges have inspired the creation of scallop-like carvings known as *gunungan*, frequently featured on roof eaves. The arabesque *awan larat* (translated variously as floating clouds, parading clouds, meandering clouds or meandering pattern) is another commonly used Malay motif in many art forms.

Wooden panel with *awan larat* motif carved in bas-relief in a shadow pattern, originally from a house in Negeri Sembilan, c. 1869 CE.

LEFT: The roof gable wall and window header frames of this house in Bukit Gantang, Perak, use radiating sunray motifs and stars. Small stars are also punched through, creating patterned light effects.

Plants

Plants are widely featured in Malay woodcarvings because of their close association with daily life. Various parts of plants and trees, including leaves, roots, creepers, fruits, flowers and branches appear. Among other popular motifs are yam, ladies' fingers, bamboo shoots and hibiscus. Motifs commonly found decorating Malay houses include the *bunga tanjung* (*Mimusops elengi*) which indicates that visitors are always welcome to the house and *bunga mawar* (rose) for protection and to ward off bad charms and efforts to cause harm to the occupants or owner. The *bunga matahari* (sunflower) motif symbolizes a beautiful world as the sun brings brightness, turning night into day and *bunga melati* (jasmine) epitomizes Malay customs and courtesies.

A complete pattern of tendril and leaf motifs decorate this Terengganu panel.

Calligraphy

Calligraphy (*khat*) carvings of Arabic or Jawi script can be found in Islamic buildings and Malay palaces. Most calligraphic carvings found in religious buildings use verses from the Qur'an and *Hadith* (sayings of the Prophet), while those found in old palaces and wealthy homes normally feature the names of the owners. Since the 15th century, calligraphic carvings have also been used to decorate mausoleums and headstones. Calligraphic designs will often be emphasized and combined with floral, plant or cosmic elements.

Early 19th century Patani woodcarved panel with calligraphy from a royal ship (Muzium Seni Asia collection).

BELOW: Late 19th-century wooden wall from the palace of Sultan Muhammad IV, Kota Bharu, Kelantan. *INSET*: Detail of carved panel using combination of calligraphy and floral motifs.

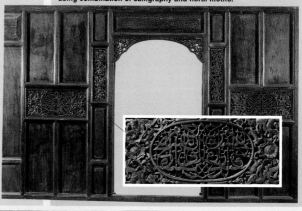

Traditional wooden architecture

Fine wooden architecture has been a feature of many types of buildings in Malaysia for many centuries—examples include traditional Malay houses, istana (palaces), mosques, mausoleums and the houses and graves of the indigenous peoples of Sabah and Sarawak. Decorative carving can be seen in wall panels, balustrades, pillars, roof eaves and gable ends and gateways.

Dato Dagang's long-roofed house in Sri Menanti, 1874. From afar, traditional Malay houses looked similar, but close-up, decoration and motifs and the number of columns (16 for nobles and 12 for everyone else) revealed the status of the owner.

The wooden staircase at the upper floor of what was the headquarters of Bank Bumiputra (now CIMB), Kuala Lumpur.

INSET: The arabesque motif of the staircase railing in detail.

The Malay house

Traditional Malay houses have evolved and adapted over generations but have always reflected the Malay way of life and cultural traditions. Early simple dwellings were built with timber and plant materials, such as bamboo and palm leaves, for the walls and roof. Later development included long roofs of different types with wooden shingles and then tiles, new techniques for securing pillars and roofs, timber rather than bamboo or thatched walls and floors, and colonial period pyramid-shaped roofs which also underwent modification. A characteristic that has remained is the elevation of the Malay house on stilts which served to protect its inhabitants from flooding and wild animals, provided natural air circulation and could be utilized for storage or as a working area. Another feature is that homes are transportable—although the preparation and cutting of the wood and beams may take up to 10 months, the prefabricated modular components of a Malay house can be assembled within eight to nine days and dismantled within three to four days.

Aside from being constructed from wood, part of the beauty of a Malay house is its carved decorative features. At the roof section, carvings are mounted on the facade which cover the space between the wall and the roof and also cover the roof eaves. These commonly depict bamboo shoots or wave motifs. In Perak houses, one may find 'hanging bees' (*lebah bergantung*) mounted at the intersection of the long and cross beams. According to an old belief, if the 'hanging bees' carvings break and drop to the ground, this foretells that a calamity will happen, in which case special measures must be taken. The gable (*tebar layar*) of a building is also often a carved plank.

Rumah Melayu—the traditional Malay house

Many Malays have, at one point in their lives, lived in a traditional Malay house. However, as the country has developed, more and more people live in modern concrete houses and apartments. Still, the typical Malay house continues to be built in the *kampung* (villages), and by those enamoured and appreciative of the skill and effort it takes to build one. Some builders today have incorporated aspects of the traditional house and its ornamentation into modern homes and even skyscrapers. There are two types of traditional Malay house: the long-roofed house (*rumah bumbung panjang*) and the house with a pyramidal roof (*rumah bumbung limas*). The long-roofed house has an older history than the pyramidal-roofed house which was introduced in the 19th century. In the *kampung*, building a long-roofed house was largely dependent on the skills and craftsmanship of Malay builders and on the immediate environment for the building materials. The pyramidal-roofed house, on the other hand, could be built by non-Malays as materials such as tiles for the roof, nails to secure the joints, and cement and bricks for the walls and stairs were increasingly used.

The Malay house typically consists of three sections, namely the roof, main body of the house and its pillars. The strength and durability of the house depends on the type of wood used for the pillars. These pillars are secured by crossbeams, to which walls and partitions are attached, serving to separate the different sections of the house. Traditionally, a special pillar (*tiang seri*) was installed ceremoniously to ensure the well-being of the occupants. Floors are usually simply wooden planks, although long ago, split bamboo arranged on top of the joists and secured with cane or creepers was also used. The walls may be embellished with bas-relief carvings or woven in attractive *kelarai* (interwoven bamboo patterns). Doors and partitions may have decorative fretwork panels and fanlights above. Windows open outwards and are often of floor-to-ceiling height, with part of the opening latticed with decorative balustrades. Wooden shingles edged with carved or scalloped roof eaves may be used for roof tiles.

Rumah Penghulu Abu Seman, a traditional Malay house, was originally located in a small village in Kedah. Purchased in 1996 by Badan Warisan, it was moved to Kuala Lumpur where it was restored to its former glory and opened for public viewing in November 1997.

TOP: The main house (*rumah ibu*) of Rumah Penghulu Abu Seman, where guests are entertained.

ABOVE: The carved arched partition leading to a bedroom has floral and geometric patterns.

LEFT: Carved railing on the verandah with an abstracted seahorse motif.

On the west coast (Perak, Penang, Kedah and Selangor), its apex possibly might sport a carved lizard head (*kepala cicak*), a guardian symbol.

In older Malay houses, walls were decorative as well as functional. In the past, the walls of the nobility were made from wood panelling while those of others were made and adorned with interwoven bamboo or bertam splits (*kelarai*). Eventually, walls made of panelled planks became a feature of the contemporary Malay house.

ABOVE: Hanging bees.

BELOW: *Kepala cicak* hanging at the apex of the *tebar layar* (gable).

Decorative carvings are also found on interior partitions, on panels above doors and windows, verandah railings and balustrades. Cut-out fretwork panels above windows allow cooling breezes to circulate, providing

ventilation. Malay houses typically have open verandahs. These are enclosed with low, carved railings called *pagar tinggalung*. The lower section of tall windows often display the same feature, mainly to prevent children from falling.

Mosques

In the Peninsula, early mosques were constructed from timber and shared common structural and design elements with Malay houses. Examples of wooden mosques still survive throughout the country, such as Masjid Kampung Laut in Kelantan. The decorative piece at the crown of the roof known as the *mahkota atap*, symbolizing a building as a mosque and enhancing its appearance, might also be made of wood, as at Masjid Lama Kampung Barok in Jasin, Melaka and at Masjid Lama Kampung Sungai Machang Ulu in Lenggeng, Negeri Sembilan. Intricate woodcarving embellishment of posts, the areas above doors, window screens and ventilation panels can also be found in traditional mosques. Designs range from direct calligraphy of Islamic revelations to symbolic carvings of abstracted floral motifs (see 'Techniques, forms and motifs of Malay woodcarving').

Palaces

It is in the palaces of the Malay rulers that some of the most extravagant and highly refined examples of woodcarving, some more than a century old, can be found decorating audience halls, walls, brackets, pillars, windows, doorposts and gateways. Traditional palaces contain abundant evidence of the early royal patronage of woodcraft and the immense creativity and skill of Malay craftsmen. Examples include the elaborate carved cut-out screens and panels, especially in the audience hall of Istana Balai Besar, Istana Seri Akar and Istana Jahar in Kelantan; the

intricate low relief carved pillars, borders, panels and doors of Istana Ampang Tinggi and Istana Sri Menanti in Negeri Sembilan; and the gilded cut-out work featuring Qur'anic script of Istana Tengku Nik and Istana Maziah in Terengganu.

Some magnificent palaces now only exist in classical Malay literature. One is the palace built for Sultan Mansur Shah (1456–1477 CE) in Melaka detailed in the *Sejarah Melayu* (Malay Annals) as having carved cupolas, gilded spires, trelliswork with pendants and pyramidal decoration. Aspects of the architecture of the palace built at Pulau Indera Sakti during the reign of Sultan Iskandar Dzulkarnain (1756–65 CE) of Perak have also been documented as including walls and windows with ivory balustrades adorned with gold, silver and precious metals, wall panels carved and encrusted with precious stones arranged in various patterns, and carved timber panels alternated with mirrors and glass.

Indigenous wooden architecture

Most Malaysian indigenous groups utilized wood to create their living accommodation, especially for the framework, pillars and stairs. In Sarawak and Sabah, this is represented by large traditional communal longhouses whose architecture varied by region and group. These residences would sometimes be embellished with woodcarved decoration. In the past, the walls and doors of longhouse individual *bilik* (rooms) of Kayan and Kenyah aristocrats of Sarawak were carved with designs that included human figures and powerful motifs as a symbol of their status, power and authority. Such decoration was forbidden to commoners who dared not risk supernatural punishment. The Iban also used doors in this way, sometimes with carved lintels. Modern Iban longhouses may have bas-relief carvings and cut-out panelling for decoration as well as ventilation.

The magnificent and imposing burial poles and woodcarved grave sites of Sarawak (see also 'Wood and other carvings') are noteworthy, the construction and decoration of these immense structures both time-consuming and surrounded by ritual.

ABOVE: This Kenyah door depicts the victory of the protective spirit over evil spirits.

ABOVE RIGHT: A typical Iban door carved in relief featuring crocodiles, pythons (both powerful figures) and frogs.

TOP: People gathered on the verandah (*ruai*) of an Iban wooden longhouse at Rh. Garu, Nanga Ngemah, Kanowit District, Sarawak (1951).

The old Istana Sri Menanti in Negeri Sembilan was built in 1902. At this time, palace architecture was similar to, but substantially more elaborate than, traditional Malay houses. Features include timber construction with massive beams, no nails and ornate woodcarved embellishment.

Peranakan and Chinese woodcarving

From the intermarriage between early Chinese merchants and traders and local women, evolved a unique people, the Peranakan. Female elements such as the phoenix and peonies were the symbols of choice in their decorative arts and culture, largely due to assimilation of the local Malay concept of matrilocal control. Colonial and European influences are also evident in their woodcraft. In comparison, later 19th-century Chinese migrants favoured more purely Sinic forms and motifs.

Late 19th century Peranakan home interior displaying typical woodwork. This image was developed from an original glass plate negative (Henry Bong Permanent Collection).

Trade links, Chinese settlement and evolution of the Peranakan

Excavations of maritime trade ceramics indicate that the Chinese were trading with the present-day Malay region and the Malay Archipelago as early as the 10th century CE. This is evidenced by the southern Song ceramics found in the Sarawak River delta, Limbang and the Kinabatangan areas of Sabah, in the Bornean states of Malaysia, as well as on Tioman Island and the waters off Pahang and Johor and in the Bujang Valley Archaeological Park in Kedah, in Peninsular Malaysia.

Chinese migrants of the mid-19th century preferred the traditional culture and customs, costumes and hairstyles of China as reflected in this 1880s picture well-to-do men.

The earliest settlement of the Chinese in the Peninsula would have been in Melaka, where the tombs on Bukit Cina can be traced back as far as the Ming Dynasty period (1368–1644 CE). These early merchants and traders intermarried with the locals, including the Malays, to evolve into the Peranakan group, also known as Baba (men) and Nonya (women) or the Straits Chinese. The Peranakan are essentially a long settled Chinese-based group with strong links to the Malay World and distinct from mainland Chinese in their locally integrated approach to language (they used Nonya patois, a Malay-based dialect, and many did not know how to speak, read or write Chinese), food (a fusion of Malay and southern Chinese flavours) and culture and dressing (sarong and *kebaya* for the ladies—see 'Straits Chinese embroidery and beadwork' and 'Chinese and Indian dress'). Another distinction is epitomized by the fact that while the early Peranakan remained Chinese in their worship and their distribution of property only to male offspring, their social structure was matrilocal, a practice most likely adapted from the Minangkabau Malays of the neighbouring Negeri Sembilan area. Their unique eclecticism and fusion resulted in the exotic and adventurous expressions of the Baba and Nonya as a well assimilated sub-group of overseas Chinese in both the Nanyang and Malay worlds.

ABOVE: Chinese craftsman in Penang carving a camphor teak wood chest in bas-relief. Intricate handcarved chests, altar cabinets, altar tablets and furniture are usually produced on a commission basis.

BELOW: A drawer being handcarved at Malacca Woodwork, a family-run business in Melaka specializing in the reproduction of antique and classic Chinese furniture from local hardwoods. Traditional woodworking techniques are still used.

In the 19th century CE, the British colonial practice of importing migrant 'coolie' labour for the tin mines and the rubber estates resulted in another wave of Chinese—*sinkeh* as they were known (meaning 'new guests' in the Hokkien dialect) or *Cina Gek*, as they were patronisingly referred to by the long settled and established Peranakan. Some of these later migrant arrivals established themselves to become towkays (bosses) in the tin mining, textile and herbal trades.

Woodcarving traditions in Malaysia

The wealthy Peranakan families of the Straits Settlements of the 19th century provide the best examples of existing Peranakan style in the woodworking tradition of this nation. The assimilation of Malay and British colonial elements in their carvings resulted in a distinct robust and hybridized vernacular style based on, and yet different from, the mainland Chinese style. On the other hand, another group

Auspicious guardian lion or *fu* dog, carved from *cengal* wood and gilded, of the type that would have graced the entrance (usually on a pillar) of an early 19th-century Chinese Straits Settlement building.

of patrons, the Chinese towkays emerging from the tin mining and trading enterprises of the later Chinese migrants, had a more purist Chinese approach to woodwork commissioned by them.

Serving both of these groups, as well as the wealthy Malays and colonial masters, were a group of skilled *tukang Shanghai*—generations of highly skilled immigrant Shanghainese cabinet makers and carvers, Malaysian descendants of whom still run thriving traditional Chinese furniture enterprises in Melaka today. As a result, while the carvers were Malaysian of Shanghainese descent, their two main categories of patrons would have exacted two distinct styles of execution in the resultant woodcraft.

Types of crafted wood and styles

With the exception of China-imported blackwood and namwood Chinese and made-to-Peranakan taste furniture, local woodcraft traditions produced all the necessities for local use in architecture and artefacts for both secular and religious use. Items produced ranged from lintels, windows and their surmounts, doors, gables, ventilation vents, balusters and stairways to lanterns, lamps, furniture and palanquins. Their applications included domestic secular use in various parts of the late 19th- to mid-20th-century shophouses, clanhouses and Kongsi, wealthy Malay and Indian residences and Malay royal palaces. Other works embellished Chinese temples and shrines, including some Melaka mosques, whose windows sport gilded Chinese surmounts (see 'Influences on arts and crafts: A historical perspective' and 'Islamic design principles and motifs').

RIGHT: Main door of a Peranakan link house, usually at the five-footway entrance. It features cut through wood on its panels with incised work on the bottom panels and gold leaf decoration on the carvings (Penang, c. 1880s).

BELOW: Opium day bed in the red and gold style made of *cengal* and *seraya* local indigenous woods from Penang (c. 1890s).

Woods used included both imported and local woods—the later Chinese towkay migrants preferring imported blackwood/rosewood of the purple sandalwood (*zitan*) and rosewood or various *huali* types of the subtropical Dalbergia species. Most of these have a distinct Chinese Ming or Qing domestic furniture look and feel. The Peranakan taste was for using the same types of wood sparingly as well as imported species of Chinese cedar, namwood (*Machilus namu*) and Burmese/Thai teakwood (*Tectona grandis*). Among the local rainforest hardwoods used were *cengal*, *balau*, *merbau* and *rengas* (of the Dipterocarpaceae and Leguminosae families). Some rare Chinese furniture was also made from local Bornean *belian* (ironwood species) timber.

Specifically, blackwood/rosewood woodwork tended to be very Ming Chinese and austere in style. Namwood furniture was often carved and richly gilded on a red lacquer base—hence the name red and gold—and was a distinctly Nonya favourite. After the war between the Kuomintang and the communists in the late 1920s, the production of red and gold was severely disrupted resulting in the local production of Anglo-Nonya pieces in Burmese/Thai teakwood commonly available then in the Straits Settlements and used as an imported status symbol raw material preferred over local wood. Over time, the British colonial influence of the Straits Settlement became evident and teakwood carvings and furniture incorporating the English Jacobean, Regency, Georgian, Queen Anne, and Chippendale styles with Chinese Peranakan ornamentation on a European body began to evolve. Some without animal motifs were also known as the Anglo-Malay style as seen in the Istana Besar Royal Sultan Abu Bakar Museum (Bukit Serene) collection.

Symbols and their cultural significance

The assimilation with local cultures and their matrilocal social structure influenced Peranakan taste in adornment and decorative styles as seen in their ceramics, beadwork and woodcarvings and manifested by a distinct preference for depiction of female icons. This is why they favoured the phoenix, peony and other flowers, symbols of the female and a yin element, which was otherwise unusual in the Chinese cultural milieu. The presence of a dragon was very rare and, even then, it was understated or highly stylized or secondary to the total composition or aesthetics of the work. When prominent, it usually indicated marriage to a newer pure Chinese immigrant (*sinkeh* or *Cina Gek*) whose tastes were more Sinic and conservatively Chinese with a resistance to the local influences.

Melaka lintel made from *cengal* wood with a traditional Malay style *awan larat* inspired foliage and a central flower (*bunga*).

One of a pair of rare tall stand wedding mirrors with a strong colonial influence, made from teakwood in the brown and gold style (Penang, c. 1910s).

Grand wedding tall sideboard, locally made from imported teakwood, for the main hall of a wealthy Nonya home with a strong neoclassic form and marble top counter. An ornamental Peranakan canopy is on the top pediment, but the other carvings are in the European style.

INSET: Detail of phoenixes and peonies on the top pediment carved in wood and decorated in brown and gold (gold leaf gilding).

Art of boat building

As a nation surrounded by water and with vast river systems, control of the seas and waterways ensured sovereignty, particularly so when the interior of the land was largely inaccessible. In Malaysia, this was an impetus for the building of a large and varied number of boats or perahu, *which plied the waters of the region. The indigenous peoples of Borneo have a long history of boat building, as do the Malays of the east coast of the Peninsula, renowned for their colourful and decorative traditional vessels of which, unfortunately, few are seen sailing today.*

The houseboat of the Perak British Resident J. W. W. Birch (pictured here with F. A. Swettenham in 1874) plied the waters of the Perak River.

Boat building—traditional east coast style

1. Selecting the wood and erecting the framework

An appropriate wood, depending on the availability of sawn timber and the type of *perahu* (boat) being built, is selected, such as *cengal* (*Neo*alanocarpus heimii*), *meranti* (*Shorea parvistipulata sp. albifolia*) or *cempedak air* (*Artocarpus teysmanni*).

Next, the *linggi* or prow is put in place. The major elements of a *perahu*—keel, stem and stern—form the basic framework of any boat. The keel is the structure to which every other part will be attached. The stem (carved in some cases) and shape of the stern depend on the type of boat to be built.

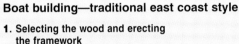

2. Shaping or bending (melentur)

The hull boarding (*papan lepang*), strakes, and, later, the threshold beams (*bendul*), are coaxed into the correct shape. To do this, the boards are tied to the keel at one end and at the opposite end, then heated by coals until the desired shape is achieved. The beams are shaped similarly, except that they are not connected to the keel but placed at the upper edge of the topmost hull boarding.

3. Setting the ribs

When the first boards of the hull have been shaped, the ribs (*kun*) are fitted. They are fastened to the keel and parts of the hull using the traditional hold-and-peg (*tebuk pasak*) method, with the pegs (*pasak*) holding the ribs in place.

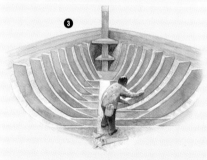

4. Making the hull

Boarding (*papan lepang*) and strakes are used to make the hull. The *papan lepang* become the skin (*kulit*) which is fastened by pegs to both the right and left sides of the keel. Layers are added, attached to each other and the ribs by the pegs. To leak-proof the hull, the bark of the *gelam* (*Melaleuca leucadendron*) tree is placed between each *papan lepang*.

5. Mast, spars and forming the bangau

For the mast (*tiang layar*) and spars, a number of woods are used, including *medang* (*Litsea spp.*) and *mentangor* (*calophyllum spp.*). Characteristic of an east coast fishing *perahu*, a *bangau* is a carved and painted decorative board on the port side designed to hold the sails and mast when taken down.

6. Caulking and painting

Every joint of the hull is sealed with a gum made from resin (*damar*) that had been extracted from certain trees. When the gum dries, the boat is painted. Some boats, in particular the inshore Malay fishing boats such as the *sekochi* (small boat), are very colourful.

Ancient seafaring

The coastal people of Southeast Asia were capable seamen who established trade links with India and beyond. In the first century CE, Malay sailors had already mastered long sea journeys. Ptolemy's knowledge of the Malay Peninsula, or what he called the Golden Khersonese, surely came from these seamen. His map of the Peninsula included two places in the northeastern state of Terengganu, Perimula and Kole, known today as Kuala Terengganu and Dungun.

In the 19th century, Malay sailors from Terengganu and Kelantan made substantial fortunes trading with neighbouring places such as the Riau Islands, Borneo, Cambodia and southern Thailand. Up until World War II, Malay sailing ships regularly plied a route from Thailand to Kuala Terengganu, bringing salt and sometimes Singhora clay roof tiles (*atap batu*), and returning to Thailand with charcoal.

Traditional vessels of the Peninsula

Basic dugouts (*jalor*) were used by the Malays before they began to build more complex *perahu* (boats). Riverine people relied on them for fishing, catching crabs and prawns as well as for ferrying goods.

A more sophisticated form later emerged where the sides of a half log were hollowed out until they were thin enough to be opened out by the careful application of heat by means of burning embers. The fore and aft parts were shaped with an adze. Then the hull was soaked in water for as long as a month, after which the *jalor* was opened out again by filling it with water and heating it from below with embers. This would open out the sides sufficiently to take the ribs, knees and crosspieces.

Besides the functional *perahu*, there was a whole range of royal *perahu* which were used mostly in the *istana* (palace) in Kelantan. Each royal boat had a specific use. For example, one might receive visiting royal dignitaries, while another would carry the sultan, accompanied by musicians, during water festivals. Unlike normal *perahu*, the royal *perahu* were rowed. Types of royal perahu included the *petala indera*, *petalawati*, *seneng* and *tedong sela*. They tended to be elaborately decorated with *awan larat* (see 'Techniques, forms and motifs of Malay woodcarving') and other carvings.

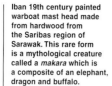

Because of the problem of sandbars, due to the main ports in the Malay Peninsula being largely located at the mouths of rivers, both east and west coast boats were designed and built with shallow draughts, V-shaped sections and sharp floors, an important characteristic. However, there are differences between *perahu* from the west and east coasts. First, on the west coast, the additional problem of strong tides, often varying by as much as six metres, and light winds meant that boats were traditionally oar propelled. However, on the east coast, stronger and more regular winds allowed for propulsion by sail and, hence, much larger boats. Second, the ornamental *bangau* was a strictly east coast development.

Only a handful of skilled craftsmen still build boats traditionally anymore and calls for the old types are few and far between. Terengganu and Kelantan are two places where traditional boat-building techniques are both famous as well as still in use, a particular location being Pulau Duyung in Terengganu. These craftsmen use neither plans nor blueprints, which does not detract from their precision and attention to detail. Interestingly, their techniques are even being applied in the construction of modern yachts and fishing boats.

Many parts of Semporna Bajau *lepa* (boats) are adorned with beautiful decorative carvings.

Indigenous Bornean vessels

The people of Borneo living near the coast and internal waterways obviously made and used boats for activities such as fishing as well as for transport, particularly to remote inland areas. On the whole, these were functional rather than decorative.

Because of their seafaring traditions, the Bajau people of Sabah have a particular affinity with with water and an established history as skilled boat-builders and mariners, especially the Bajau Laut (Sea Bajau) who make their homes on houseboats. The artistry of the Bajau of Semporna is displayed in the carved decoration applied to their boats (*lepa*).

In Sarawak, the traditional bark longboats of indigenous groups are still used in some places. Longboats created for special purposes, such as the Kayan, Kenyah and Iban war boats of old, were elaborately decorated with carvings. Kayan and Kenyah boats often featured a carved animal head at the stern.

Iban 19th century painted warboat mast head made from hardwood from the Saribas region of Sarawak. This rare form is a mythological creature called a *makara* which is a composite of an elephant, dragon and buffalo.

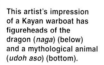

This artist's impression of a Kayan warboat has figureheads of the dragon (*naga*) (below) and a mythological animal (*udoh aso*) (bottom).

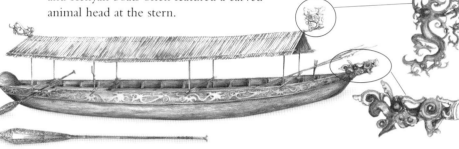

Ornamental embellishment of perahu

The *bangau* is a decorative guard found on traditional Malay fishing boats (*perahu*) on the east coast of Peninsular Malaysia; none has ever appeared on west coast boats. It is placed on the port side of the boat, almost appearing as if it has grown out of the vessel.

The function of the *bangau* was to provide a support for the sails and fishing nets when the boat was not in use, but traditionally it also had another less tangible purpose—it was believed to be the place where the spirit (*semangat*) of the boat resided which assisted the catch and protected the fishermen from the vagaries of the sea or sea demons that might throw the ship off course. It is not known exactly when the graceful shape of the *bangau* first appeared. While it is named for a common white cattle egret of the paddy fields and was often carved in the likeness of birds, and sometimes figures such as seahorses, dragons (*naga*) and shadow puppet characters, over time it became more stylized with typical Malay meandering *awan larat* designs being favoured. Similarly carved and decorated, the shorter *okok* or *ongkak* lies across the bow and is attached to the keel, acting as a prop to secure the anchor and counterbalancing the *bangau*.

Bright multi-colours are another trait of east coast traditional boats. This decoration ranges from simple coloured stripes (yellow, red, blue and green) to very elaborate designs featuring Malay motifs that may be painted on prows and hulls. As an example of the skill of the craftsman, the designs would usually be painted directly without the need to trace the pattern first.

TOP LEFT: Fishermen in Terengganu bring in their colourful and elaborately painted fishing boat. Such boats are still in use today.

LEFT: The decorative *bangau* has long been a feature of the fishing boats of the east coast of Peninsular Malaysia, as can be seen in this picture, probably taken c. 1890.

RIGHT: An artist's impression of carved wooden *bangau* that are crafted on the prows of many Terengganu Malay fishing boats.

Wood and other carvings

There is a long and proud local tradition of working with wood and other natural raw materials such as bamboo, coconut shell, bone, horn, deer antler, boar tusk, hornbill ivory and occasionally stone. In the past, most of such works were either made by craftsmen for their own use or were commissioned by wealthy patrons. Then, as now, a high level of skill coupled with patience and sophistication was needed to generate objects of great artistry and beauty—be they humble domestic utensils or rare majestic structures of monumental proportions.

Various masks from Sarawak:

1. *Hudok* masks are used by the Orang Ulu in rituals and festivals.
2. Orang Ulu mask of the protective sun god (Henry Bong Permanent Collection).
3. Iban elder mask for protection (Henry Bong Permanent Collection).

Wood—a favoured choice

Wood has been the most favoured raw material for carvings and sculpture due to a few factors. It is relatively easier to obtain due to the numerous quality heavy and medium hardwoods as well as some select softwoods available from the rain forest in Malaysia. As such, it is less costly than rarer materials such as ivory or precious materials like silver or gold. Wood is also easier to work on through carving, compared to tooling on metals. Early animistic beliefs accorded wood special qualities of spiritual strength (*semangat*) dependent on the species, location and even orientation of the tree from which the wood had been extracted—for instance, timber from tree trunks facing the rising sun was preferred, being deemed to be purer and with greater strength. These pre-Islamic notions are largely not emphasized by Malay carvers today, but Orang Asli carvers still hold them dear, crafting products from certain species of plants as part of their handicrafts.

Local carving traditions

Carving has long been a tradition of the peoples of Malaysia, passed on from one generation to the next, and a visual manifestation of their culture, customs and beliefs. Over centuries, Malay craftsmen have used wood for their creations, although forms and motifs were modified with the coming of Islam (see 'Techniques, forms and motifs of Malay woodcarving'). The Mah Meri and Jah Hut carvers from the Orang Asli groups of Peninsular Malaysia also create carvings and masks in wood which tell of their people and beliefs. These have received international attention and are now sought after works of collectable art. In Sabah and Sarawak, an age-old carving history provides varied examples of both utilitarian and decorative woodcrafted items including musical instruments, walking sticks, carved embellishments on rafters, walls, doors and posts of longhouses, ritual masks, burial poles and huts, sickness images and carved sword handles and sheaths. Other materials—hornbill ivory, bone, horn and bamboo among them—were also carved

ABOVE: 18th century sandstone carving by the Seru tribe of Sarawak (now extinct) (Henry Bong Permanent Collection).

BELOW: Orang Asli Mah Meri carver creating a *moyang harimau berantai* (spirit of the tiger with chain) carving.

Masks

Among many local indigenous groups, masks sculpted from wood play an important part in traditional dances and rituals. A number of groups in Sarawak use masks for special occasions. The Kayan and Kenyah celebrate the harvest festival with a ritual dance in which face masks are worn. As such masks are to keep away evil spirits from the longhouse and to guard crops, generally the visage portrayed is evil-looking with protruding eyes and fangs. Iban masks (*indai guru*, literally 'mother teacher') are worn by a woman to deter children from misbehaving. They are made out of gourds or wood and painted. However, in the past they were stained black with soot with the eyes, forehead and mouth outlined with white lime.

Masks are also a distinctive cultural feature of the Orang Asli groups of Peninsular Malaysia. In Mah Meri culture, masks (*topeng*), of which there are many, are not considered objects, but rather *moyang* (ancestral spirits). It is believed that through these masks one can communicate with the *moyang*—hence the common hinged jaws for the spirit to speak through—and that whoever wears it will be filled with that particular spirit. Some are worn in ceremonial dances. The masks are elaborately carved and may be male or female. Each one has a story associated with it, frequently relating to water. Similarly, Jah Hut masks reflect that community's beliefs and environment, especially the forest where they live.

Mah Meri mask dancers.

for jewellery, ornaments, hairpins, bottle stoppers and weapon decoration, in the case of ivory, bone and horn, and containers, smoking pipes and blowpipe dart holders, from bamboo. Often, a material would be crafted on its own, but was sometimes further embellished with other materials, for example, silver worked in repoussé was often used to further enhance the wood carved hilts or sheaths of Malay and Iban swords.

Orang Ulu hairpin made from a boar tusk and carved with the traditional *aso* (dragon-dog) motif.

Carved bird cages and traps

Trapping quails was a popular pastime among the aristocracy, but today is mostly carried out by Malay men from the East Coast of Peninsular Malaysia. Elaborately crafted cages are delicately woven from various fern ribs and fibres around slender bars of rattan or *nibang*. Most traps sport superbly carved pediments or *gunungan* (cosmic mountain), and the front panels are embellished with openwork carvings.

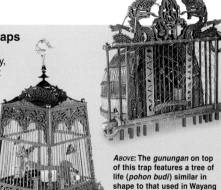

ABOVE: The *gunungan* on top of this trap features a tree of life (*pohon budi*) similar in shape to that used in Wayang Kulit, and is flanked by two *naga* (dragon or serpent) heads.

LEFT: Ornate birdcage showing a Thai influence in the elaborately formed hook and carvings.

LEFT: The base and corners of this East Coast birdcage are decorated with floral motifs in white, yellow, red, green and black.

LEFT : Unusual quail trap from Sarawak. The top and side panels are carved with typical Sarawakian motifs such as stylized dragon-dogs and geometric motifs. Strips of rattan interlace the bars of cage at the back.

BELOW: A coconut has been hollowed out and pierced with holes to provide ventilation for this quail trap.

A variety of carved forms over time

Some of the earliest surviving examples of woodwork are grave goods in the form of burial boats found in the Niah Painted Caves (Gua Kain Hitam) of Sarawak, where the earliest excavated settlements of man have been dated to about 39,000 years old and the 'death ships' themselves carbon dated to between 1 and 780 CE. Similar burial coffins have been found in the Kinabatanganarea of Sabah with carved buffalo heads as their mast heads.

While the earlier influences of the Hindu and Buddhist eras continued in the artistic expressions of some of the Bornean indigenous peoples, the Malay Muslim artistic expressions, from the 14th century onwards, became more focused on the world of floral expressions and moved away from the depiction of animals and humans (see 'Techniques, forms and motifs of Malay woodcarving'). Today, one seldom encounters direct bird/animal representations in the Malay Muslim milieu, rare examples of which include the hilt of the Kelantan-Patani *keris tajong* in the form of the head of a *pekaka* (kingfisher) (see 'Metalworking and weapons'), the royal giant ceremonial barge with the *burung petala-indra* sculpted in the round (see 'Carvings and sculptures: From cradle to grave') and some *congkak* board games in bird form. By the late 19th century to the present day, vestigial animal and bird forms remain only in simplified abstract forms like the decorative *bangau* (egret) of the fishing boats of the east coast of the Malay Peninsula (see 'Art of boat building'), the abstracted horse in the shape of the coconut scraper (see 'Carvings and sculptures: From cradle to grave') and the *jawa demam* (Javanese in a feverish fit) style of kris hilt (see 'Metalworking and weapons'). Most Malay woodcarvings are of modest size, being generally architectural embellishments like ventilation vents (in carved panels), decorations in bas-relief either cut through or in 1–3-layered carvings (see 'Techniques, forms and motifs of Malay woodcarving') or domestic implements.

End of a Sabah log coffin carved in the shape of a wild ox (*seladang*) head.

The Bronze Age influence of the Dongson era on Iban artistic expressions allowed the elaborate evolution of the archaic *naga* (dragon) foliated forms and others such as the *aso* (dog) spirits and those of other guardian spirits. Notable examples of statues sculpted in the round are the Iban *kenyalang* (hornbill effigy of the God of War), Iban and Orang Ulu *hampalong* (guardian figures), the *aso* table legs of the Kayan, *naga* (dragon) effigies as mast heads for war boats of the Iban, Kenyah and Kayan, as well as the *belum* (healing figures used by shamans) and fish charms of the Melanau of costal Sarawak.

Impressive carvings are found in old Kelantan in giant gateways called *pintu gerbang*, some reaching 3.5 metres high and 2.7 metres wide. Other spectacular carved edifices stand more than 9 metres high in the form of Sarawak burial poles, some dating back to the 17th century CE. The *jerunai*, also known as *kelidang*, of the rich Melanau was a single tree trunk carved and hollowed at the top to create a chamber to hold the interred body of the deceased in a big jar, and had mostly deep bas-relief work and some cut-through work at the top. According to traditional sources, the erection of a *jerunai* was carried out by dropping one end into a pit where a female slave was sacrificed alive by the burial process of the base of the pole, while another was tied to it after that and left to waste, both slaves accompanying the noble deceased into the realm of the dead (Likou Matai). The double-trunked *tiang kelirieng* of the Kayan aristocracy is the monument erected by Ayun Dian of Ulu Belaga in Sarawak in 1870 CE for his favourite daughter's tomb. It now stands outside the Sarawak Museum Annexe Building in Kuching, towering more than two storeys high. This majestic monument, and the smaller *jerunai* burial poles, stand out as masterpieces of wood.

Today, carved crafts still exhibit a high level of technical perfection and skill despite having to adapt to the encroaching elements of mass consumerism and the tourist market.

ABOVE: The Iban of Sarawak use carved *kenyalang* (hornbill effigies of the God of War) as a trophy for outstanding achievement.

BELOW: Melanau single trunk burial pole (*jerunai*) in its original location at Dalat in Sarawak. It is now in the Sarawak Museum.

Carvings and sculptures: From cradle to grave

Through carving and sculpture in various materials and forms, and in accordance with age-old traditions, skilled Malaysian craftspeople create almost every conceivable object that can be used in important cultural rites of passage as well as the cycle of life. From these works, a 'cradle to grave' continuum can be observed.

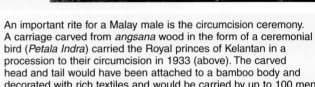

Infancy and childhood

The Kenyah and Kayan people of Sarawak craft baby carriers (right) from hardwood which may be adorned with beads, shells, bells or woven rattan. In the past, the Malays made a wooden pavilion (*wakaf*) from *cengal* wood for the ceremonial cutting of a baby's hair seven days after birth.

An important rite for a Malay male is the circumcision ceremony. A carriage carved from *angsana* wood in the form of a ceremonial bird (*Petala Indra*) carried the Royal princes of Kelantan in a procession to their circumcision in 1933 (above). The carved head and tail would have been attached to a bamboo body and decorated with rich textiles and would be carried by up to 100 men.

Adult Years

Across multi-cultural Malaysia, a wide and diverse range of carved and sculpted objects are relevant to a person's adult years, including weapons, items for body adornment, objects for entertainment, weaving implements, utility items, architecture and furniture, religious items and the effigies, guardians, charms, healing and spirit figures of indigenous peoples.

Weapons
In most cultures, traditional weapons are synonymous with manhood. The hilt and sheath of the revered Malay kris (right) (see 'Metalworking and weapons') were carved from materials such as wood (for example *kemuning*, *keruang*, *sena*) and ivory which might be embellished. The indigenous Bornean people, particularly the Iban, Kayan and Kenyah of Sarawak, also commonly utilized wood and other materials for their weapons, for instance, the *kelewang* hilt (*kemuning* wood), the *parang ilang* hilt (*sena* wood) and sheath (*cengal* wood) (see 'Metalworking and weapons'), and shields (*belian* wood).

Body adornment

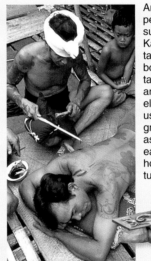

Among the indigenous people of Sarawak, such as the Kenyah, Kayan and Iban, tattooing is a form of body adornment. The tattoo imprint blocks and implements are elaborately carved, usually in *ramin* or *meranti* wood. These groups also used various materials such as bone, horn and hornbill ivory to create earrings, ornaments and decorative hairpins, hornbill casques to make earplugs and boar tusks and shells for bracelets.

Orang Ulu hornbill ivory earrings with the *aso* motif (left) and arm bracelet carved from a giant clamshell (right).

Apart from body adornment, tattooing (far left) has other functions, such as protection from malevolent spirits. This may also be reflected in the carvings decorating the implements (left).

Weaving implements
The weaving accoutrements of Sarawak, not only serve a functional purpose but are also beautifully carved and ornate. The implements for weaving the sacred Iban *pua kumbu* are made from wood (usually *belian*), deer antler, coconut shell and bamboo (see 'Cultural significance of textiles: Sabah and Sarawak'). Wood is used for the Iban spinning wheel (*belian*), backstrap loom (*ramin*) and the shuttle. The looms used by the Malays to weave their beautiful textiles are made of wood (*cengal*), as is their spinning wheel. Bamboo is used for thread bobbins as well as the slats (*lidi*) and needle (*cuban*) that are used to separate threads and weave in gold threads for the beautiful *kain songket* (see 'Malay woven cloth').

Iban wooden beaters with carved handles featuring plant, animal and bird motifs. Apart from their practical use in the weaving process, they also protect the weaver's creation and are a measure of her status.

Effigies, guardians, charms, healing and spirit figures
Many objects of a spiritual nature are produced by indigenous people, for example, Iban hornbill God of War effigies (*ramin* wood) and *hampalong* guardians (*belian* wood); Bidayuh guardian figures (*belian* wood); ceremonial masks (see 'Wood and other carvings') of the Orang Asli of the Peninsula and the Iban, Bidayuh and Orang Ulu of Sarawak (wood); Melanau *belum* healing (sago pith) and fish charm figurines (deer antler); and the spirit carvings of the Mah Meri and Jah Hut Orang Asli groups (*rengas*, *mempetir*, *tembusu* and other woods).

RIGHT: As part of the traditional rituals of the Iban Gawai Kenyalang ceremony, revered hornbill effigies adorned with jewellery, money and other gifts were paraded up and down the longhouse verandah before being installed on tall poles at the end of the festival.

LEFT: The carvings of the Orang Asli commonly depict the spirits they believe in.

Utility items

A multitude of wooden and carved objects have long been used for daily life by various ethnic groups. The domestic implements of the Malays include carved cake moulds, ladles and bowls, coconut scrapers, quail traps and cages (bamboo, cane or wood) (see 'Wood and other carvings'), fishermen's tackle and lunch boxes, *pisau wali* knife handles (*kemuning* wood and ivory), *sirih* (betel) sets, and ploughs. Indigenous Orang Asli and people from Sarawak and Sabah have many objects made from bamboo including blowpipe dart holders, tobacco and other containers and pipes.

Malay cake moulds with rooster, elephant and horse shapes.

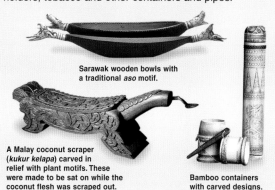

Sarawak wooden bowls with a traditional *aso* motif.

A Malay coconut scraper (*kukur kelapa*) carved in relief with plant motifs. These were made to be sat on while the coconut flesh was scraped out.

Bamboo containers with carved designs.

Sarawak Kayan men carving a longboat which has ornamental decoration. Longboats are still used for transport in Sarawak and Sabah.

Boats, prows and decorative features (such as the Peninsular east coast Malay *bangau* and the war boat mastheads of Sarawak), were created from various woods, including *medang hitam*, *cengal*, *white seraya*, *belian* and *meranti*, by the Malays, Chinese and people of Sarawak and Sabah (see 'Art of boat building').

Islamic

Wooden carved panels and objects with Islamic calligraphy and motifs have long been exquisitely made by the Malays (see also 'Islamic design principles and motifs').

Gilded 19th-century Malay Qur'an box carved with motifs from nature and a prayer seeking Allah's assistance in the quest for knowledge.

Architecture and furniture

Traditional Malay and indigenous architecture (see 'Traditional wooden architecture' and 'Techniques, forms and motifs of Malay woodcarving') has been skilfully carved from wood (especially *cengal*) over hundreds of years. Examples from the Malay community include palaces and gateways, houses, wall ventilation and carved panels and other decorative embellishments, pulpits (see 'Islamic design principles and motifs'), pavilions (*wakaf*), and shadow puppet theatres (see 'Puppetry'). In Sarawak and Sabah, longhouses, ladders, doors and storage barns are all made of wood, usually *belian*. Sarawak *aso* dog and *naga* tables were made of *belian* or *tapang* wood and were previously used by Chiefs but are now made as household furniture. Classical Peranakan and Chinese furniture and decorative pieces were crafted from various woods, both local and imported (see 'Peranakan and Chinese woodcarving).

Elaborate Peranakan wooden gilded lantern with a strong neo-colonial influence (Henry Bong Permanent Collection).

Entrance gate of Istana Jahar, Kelantan.

Objects for entertainment

A large variety of musical instruments (see 'Traditional musical instruments') consist of wood or other carved natural materials. Examples include the Malay *serunai* flute (*cengal* wood); Malay, Indian, and other indigenous string instruments (wood, bamboo); Malay gong and *gamelan* stands (*cengal*); Malay and Indian drums (*cengal* and other woods); Orang Asli, Sabah and Sarawak and Chinese pipes, flutes and other wind instruments (wood, bamboo); and Sarawak and Sabah xylophones (wood, bamboo).

Traditional games using wood include the Malay *congkak* board game and *gasing* (spinning tops) (see 'Malay kites and tops'). The shadow puppets for Wayang Kulit performances are carved from hide (see' Puppetry').

Wooden carved *congkak* board game in the now rare form of a *burung pertalawati* (mythological bird).

Burial structures

Among the most impressive carved works are those that serve as a memorial upon death. Malay grave or tomb markers carved from *cengal* wood or stone and royal *kacapuri* (see below) to embellish the sides, beautified resting places with intricate designs and motifs, which, after the coming of Islam, featured Islamic calligraphy (see 'Islamic design principles and motifs').

Secondary burial huts or *salong* were created from *belian* wood by the Kayan and Kenyah of Sarawak to store the belongings of deceased aristocrats. These lofty structures, standing on top of posts, could be as high as six metres and were elaborately carved. Usually, a carved hornbill figure woudbe placed on the roof looking downstream to indicate the journey to the next world.

Magnificent decorated burial poles such as the *jerunai* or *kelidang* single-pole structure of the Melanau and the *kelirieng* double-pole structure of the Kayan (right) are also found in Sarawak (see 'Wood and other carvings').

1. Mats, baskets, food covers and walls, all made from fibres, feature heavily in the interior of this Kadayan house in a Charles Hose photo taken in the early 1900s.

2. Women in Terengganu creating handicrafts as a cottage industry. After *mengkuang* fibres have been dried they are woven into items such as mats, bags and wall hangings.

3. Malaysian fish trap made of bamboo strips with a coconut shell opening to release the fish.

4. Penan carry baskets with a wide range of motifs.

5. A colourful Kenyah sunhat, measuring up to a metre wide, decorated with beads, sequins, coloured fabric and a bamboo or palm leaf strip tassel.

6. Mat made using natural and black dyed rattan strips by a Penan woman from Long Abang, Akah River, Baram. It has (from left to right), diamond cut, bird and teeth motifs.

7. Rattan basket used by farmers to store fish (in water) caught from rivers and rice fields.

8. Lundayeh *wakid bakang eet* (back carrier) made from rattan and attached to a wooden board for stability.

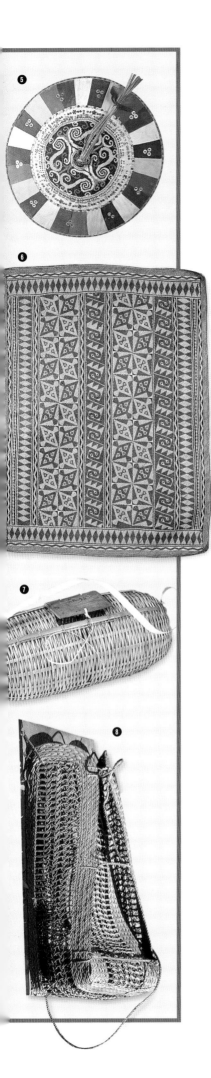

PLAITING AND BASKETWARE

The plaiting of leaves or reeds is one of the earliest crafts practised by mankind. It may have begun when leaves were piled up to sleep on, or used to protect from the cold and rain. It was found that interlaced leaves provided more efficient protection against the elements. Leaves and reeds were also easier to obtain than animal skins. Prehistoric evidence of mat-making in Malaysia is scanty; vegetable artefacts do not last in an equatorial climate. Nevertheless, impressions of plaited wrapping materials were identified in some Neolithic burials in the Niah Caves, Sarawak. These traces of pandanus mats date back to 200 BCE–400 CE—not very old in a site where human occupation goes back 35,000 years.

In the Malay Archipelago, the basket-weaving, mat-plaiting people, primarily women, worked fibres mainly for domestic consumption; selling only surplus production to itinerant traders. Explorers, adventurers and colonialists of the past 200 years seldom mention the homely art in their writings. Instead, they noticed the splendid *songket* worn at the Malay courts, and few omitted descriptions of artistically finished, but deadly, weapons. But local traditions then did not permit a strange man much access to an ordinary family's living quarters—the soldiers and traders who travelled in the Malay Peninsula hardly glanced at the mats that must have been spread for them to sit on. However, Hugh Low, a colonial administrator whose career started in Sarawak in 1846 and ended in Perak in 1889, noted the plaiting traditions. The women of Sarawak, he wrote in 1848, sometimes embroidered the corners of mats bought from the Natuna Islands (located between Terengganu and the Borneo coast) with a 'border of open work of pretty patterns round the edges, and which is larger as the mats decrease in size, they being always made in sets, until the smallest one, which lies above, is formed entirely of open work.' This description also fits some mats made in Terengganu.

Mats were not the only objects woven from leaves and reeds. In the days of open boats, travellers wore hats made from palm leaves on a rattan frame and carried their personal belongings in baskets, for example, a small basket to hold their smoking and betel-chewing ingredients. Pandanus mats were used to wrap goods, to line the floors of boats for people to sit on, and to spread over the heads and outstretched arms of deck passengers if a squall sprang up. Until the early 20th century, rural households owned very little wooden furniture. Mats were used for sleeping and sitting on, for covering and wrapping things, and for partitioning dwelling space. Goods were gathered, carried and stored in baskets, some of them fitted with lids. Maybe a sandalwood storage chest stood against the wall, or a wooden rack beside the clay hearth held dishes, but generally only the rich and members of the nobility patronized the cabinetmaker's art. The common man and his family lived on mats.

Malay craftswoman weaving colourful baskets.

Working with indigenous fibres

Forests and seashores have always provided the raw materials for basketry and matting. Some of the reeds, leaves and creepers are cultivated, but most are obtained from the forests. In most communities, it is typically the women who work these indigenous fibres into useful and attractive everyday objects. Screwpine leaves, such as mengkuang *and* pandan, *and rattan cane provide basic raw materials for most mat making and basketry work. Mats and baskets are decorated by using dyed fibres and variations of the plaiting technique.*

This early 20th-century picture shows an open-air rattan factory in the Malay Peninsula where rattan was sorted, straightened, stripped and prepared for delivery to manufacturers of furniture, mats, hats and similar items.

Preparing the fibres

The most common plant fibre used in mat-making and basketry is screwpine (*Pandanus* spp). Two varieties of screwpine—a coarser one known locally as *mengkuang* and a finer variety called *pandan*—typically provide the basic raw material for most of the weaving and plaiting needs. Some species of palm fronds are also used, either on their own or combined with other materials, to make rough mats, but little artistry is lavished on these objects.

Matting and basketry materials are seldom plaited fresh. Their preparation is as time-consuming as the working itself, but it requires less skill. In a work group it may be relegated to inexperienced hands, under the eagle eyes of skilled workers, usually older women.

Gathering screwpine leaves is a tedious job as the collector has to be careful of the thorns on the spine and sides of the leaves. Preparing the leaves for plaiting and basketry work is labour-intensive.

Rattan is also used in mat-making and basketry. Collecting rattan is commonly carried out by men as it is hard physical work. Some rattans, which belong to the palm family, are found in primary jungle, but they grow best in denser secondary growth which can be almost impenetrable. They can grow to more than 150 metres in length, and from three millimetres to four centimetres in diameter. Considerable strength is needed to get at the creepers, tear them down, strip them, and cut them into convenient lengths or coil and carry them out of the forest. The rattan is encased in a thorny sheath, and this sheath must first be stripped before the

Penan women making *ajat* (rattan baskets), common items in Sarawak, and popular with visitors too.

ABOVE: Rattan (*Calamus* spp.), a climbing species, has notoriously spiny stems to protect itself from predators.

RIGHT: Daun pandan.

desired inner smooth cane is revealed. Rattan cane may be used whole if it is very fine, or if the end-product has to be strong. For most uses, the canes are halved or quartered, or the shiny skin sliced off.

Plaiting

The term 'mat-weaving', while frequently used, is misleading; these materials are not woven on a loom or frame, but plaited. The mat-maker sits on the ground while she works; she uses her feet and toes to steady loose strands, particularly when a mat is being started. Once the fabric is established, the mat-maker works forward. If she is using the diaper technique common to the Indo-Pacific region, she holds a sheaf of diagonally opposed strands in each hand, and crosses them under and over each other in a constantly moving row.

Most Malaysian mats and baskets are worked diagonally, in a basic twill. Ornamental designs are achieved by variations in this 'two-over-two-under' (*anyam dua*) pattern. To strengthen the rim, the twill is transposed. Two of the hallmarks of a well-wrought mat are the straight edges and accurately right-angled corners.

The exceptions to the diaper weave rule are significant; most of them are found in Borneo. The Orang Ulu of central Borneo make a beautiful, very strong mat by placing pencil-thick lengths of rattan next to each other and threading them together at regular intervals, using an awl. The ends are bruised and scraped to expose the fibre, which is plaited at the edge. This mat is quite stiff—it can be rolled but never folded. The Lun Bawang and Lundayeh people of eastern Sarawak, Brunei and western Sabah, the Kadazandusun of Kota

Anyam dua (two-over-two-under) plaiting technique

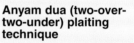

1. Simple mat-making technique using diagonal interlacing—starting a mat.

2 & 3. New strands are fastened by folding over the previous one.

4. Folding the strands at approximately 45 degrees to form the side.

5. The mat is finished by folding the strands to the back.

Source: Susie Dunsmore, 1991

Materials and their uses

Common name	Botanical name	English name	Use
Bemban	*Donax* spp.	arrowroot	sleeping mats
Buluh	*Bambusa* spp.	bamboo	baskets, walls, hats
Daun nipah/nyiur/mulong	*Nypa fruticans*	palm, coconut, sago leaves	mats, hats, walls, thatch
Pandan/mengkuang	*Pandanus* spp.	screwpine	mats, baskets
Rotan	*Calamus* spp.	rattan	baskets, mats
Tekalong	*Artocarpus* spp.		straps, lining
Various ferns, creepers			lashing, stitching, tying

Mengkuang (*Pandanus* spp.) is commonly found growing on beaches.

Belud and the Mount Kinabalu plateau make carrying baskets with vertical rattan supports held together by chains or interlacing of finer strips; these are usually reinforced with palm spathe between the carrying straps to protect the wearer's back from the rough weave.

Besides the basic diaper and cross plaiting, there are a few special techniques, mostly for baskets. Heavy-duty carriers with an articulated rear panel, used for big loads, are often made of honeycomb weave for lightness, strength and air circulation.

Decoration

There are three main ways to decorate a mat: the use of colour, variations in the plaiting technique to produce figures, eyelets or contours, or combinations of both.

Most Peninsular Malaysian mats are bi-coloured. An enterprising craftswoman may decide to use a wide range of colours for her work. Simple mats are plaid, using strips of different hues as warp and weft. Fancy ones are much more elaborate: by varying the number of strands to be crossed over or under, the worker can achieve any geometric design. Overall planning is important, and the mark of a good craftswoman—one small mistake at the outset will throw the whole pattern out of kilter. Beginners learn to make a plain fabric first, then stripes and plaid, then regular rows of squares or triangles, curves, full and hollow circles. Later they learn to combine and transpose these elements to make the full, traditional patterns.

From the east coast of Sabah comes brightly coloured plaid, underlaid with a plain layer to make a two-ply mat. More complicated designs are achieved by folding back the strands of one colour and continuing with another. These large, soft mats are much sought after by travellers; they can be folded up in both directions making them easy to carry. A type of sleeping mat, mostly found among the Iban of Sarawak, features intricate self-coloured patterns which only appear in oblique light.

A variation in the working which raises a plaited strip or knobs in the fabric is a much esteemed method of embellishment; mats with eyelet and openwork borders belong to this category. For practical reasons, this method is more commonly used for baskets; a corrugated mat might not be comfortable to sit or sleep on. It is in the three-dimensional craft of basketry that some of the most elaborate skills are displayed. Speciality techniques, with names like 'rice seed', 'mad plait', 'bird's eye', are not for the beginner. Some small baskets for personal use are minor masterpieces, executed with taste and skill and worn with pride, whether they are made of finely split rattan or of soft screwpine.

A good mat-maker takes pride in producing sturdy, neat edges. A number of different edgings are distinguished: the tucking-in, plaiting, indenting, raising of the ends of the working strips.

Mat edges have names like 'shrunk', 'shark teeth' and 'eel bones'. Large baskets suffer rougher wear than mats, so they may be strengthened with vertical struts of rattan and finished with a rim of rattan lashed on with a finer fibre. A basket for special uses may have a top rim of wood or palm spathe, decoratively stitched to the main fabric; Iban seed baskets are often finished in this way.

Sarawak hunter with an easily carried bark mat.

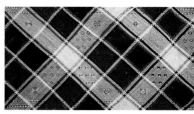

Pandan mat from Kampung Rusila, Kuala Terengganu, with a plaid pattern that incorporates small motifs.

ABOVE: Jangka, a wooden comb of fine blades set at fixed intervals, is used to cut leaves into strips which are then prepared for weaving.

BELOW: An example of *rombong*, a plaited multi-purpose basket with embroidered decoration.

From mengkuang leaves to a rombong basket

Illustrated is the traditional craft that uses plaited *mengkuang* leaves to make multi-purpose baskets with covers (*rombong*). The woven basket and cover is 'embroidered' with dyed strips of *mengkuang* to make *rombong* in a variety of patterns, designs and colours.

The method of dyeing the leaves by boiling in a pot has not changed greatly, as seen in this early 20th-century photograph.

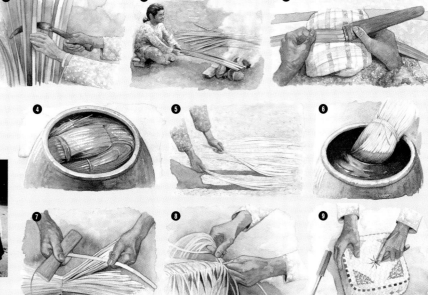

1. The central ribs and serrated edges are discarded.
2. The leaves are scorched over burning coal. This is done to strengthen the leaves and to prepare them for cutting.
3. The leaves are cut into strips of equal width using the *jangka* (cutting comb).
4. The strips are rolled into bunches and soaked in water for two days to bleach the original colour of the leaves.
5. The strips are dried to change the colour to yellowish white.
6. The dried leaves are immersed in the dye of the desired colour of the *rombong*, after which they are dried under the sun.
7. A *pelurut* (wooden smoother) is used to make the strips flat and flexible to facilitate weaving.
8. Plaiting starts by plaiting six strips together vertically and horizontally. The number of strips and plaiting steps determine the size of the *rombong*. The strips are woven to create a round base. The body of the basket is made by weaving vertically.
9. A piercer is used to insert dyed strips through the base of the *rombong* to make surface designs/patterns on the *rombong*. After the base is ready, a cover is made using the same process.

Variety in form and function

At one time, the typical Malaysian home was furnished with mats to sit and sleep on, and baskets for everything else. They continue to be made for new uses and markets. Although not durable, a well-made item is treasured and is sometimes made for special occasions. Baskets are used in all aspects of life, from carrying babies and produce to storing valuable belongings, while the use of mats ranges from being used in harvesting to wrapping corpses. Conical covers do double duty—as hats to protect against the elements and to keep flying insects away from food.

Variety of basketwork made by students at the Sultan Idris Teachers' Training College, Tanjung Malim, Perak, early 20th century.

Mats

Mats are ephemeral. There are no ancient heirloom mats, comparable in age to ceramic, glass and metal antiques; they would be in tatters. A fine mat spread for guests is a silent boast—the 'mother of the house' or her mother must have made it. Visitors admire it; their praise is modestly declined—this mat is the daughter's work; she's still a beginner, maybe, God willing, her skill will improve; one day, she may do as well as the visitor herself whose 'clove blossom' mats are famous from this village to the next.

A pandanus *kuih* (cake) cover with conical edges to accommodate pieces of cake stacked in a pyramid.

Mats used to be specifically made for special occasions. For instance, the mat on which the bridegroom sat to announce his commitment to marry the bride had to be very fancy, and preferably of the young lady's own handiwork. The rural Malays of Sarawak perform a pre-nuptial rite with the bride seated on a mat, holding a candle. After the ceremony, the mat and candle are required to go to the Mak Andam (the bridal lady-in-waiting). The plain pandanus mat on which a body lay prior to burial is neither buried nor discarded, but given away; the bereaved family cannot keep it.

Penan carry basket.

In urban Malaysia, plain sleeping and sitting mats are still in domestic use. But colourful mats no longer just serve traditional needs. They have become fashionable decor, both as wall hangings and on the parquet floor. Not many Malaysians sleep on a mat on the floorboards nowadays, but many place a mat on top of their mattress in lieu of bed linen, especially during hot weather.

Baskets

Baskets are used primarily to carry things, and for storage. They may have to 'carry' a hundredweight of rice, or betelnut chewing implements or a few cigarette papers. In fact, a wide range of baskets is fashioned to cater for a wide range of purposes and loads.

Malay weaver with an assortment of wares: bags, mats, hats and food covers.

Farmers carry a basket when they go to the fields: it holds their lunch, water bottle, knives and sickles. Vegetables for the evening meal are brought home in it. At harvest time, the precious grain is poured into a rolled-up mat stood upright inside a sturdy back basket. This more than doubles the carrying capacity, and literally dwarfs the man who is lifting his own body weight in rice. Many big baskets have an articulated back panel, fixed at the base but only tied at the sides, which serves to accommodate wide loads.

After the rice is harvested, it must be threshed and dried—large, strong mats are used for these operations. For storage, some communities construct enormous bins of tree bark with rattan supports; offerings for the good spirits are suspended above these containers in baskets.

Sarawak rattan baby carrier with shell, teeth and bead decorations.

Among smaller containers associated with agriculture, the seed basket is a particularly fine example. Worked two-ply for strength, the outer, decorative layer is plaited as finely as the craftswoman can manage. The base of some seed baskets looks like a protruding cone, using a technique similar to that used for ornamental baskets shaped to represent a fruit, or baskets with stubby legs resembling those of the Chinese 'lion-foot' jar. In Sabah and Sarawak, similar techniques are used to produce hats and receptacles to hold offerings for the animist gods.

One specialized basket, used in the high plateau of Borneo, is the baby carrier. This back basket allows a young mother to carry her infant with her wherever she goes, leaving her hands free to carry other things or to work. The beaded decorations on the carrier are an indication of the family's status; beads, hawks' bells and animal teeth were credited with powers to strengthen the young soul. Most of the carriers that are seen in handicraft shops are made for sale; very few families would dispose of one that had actually sheltered a baby.

Storage baskets are tightly woven, often lined with tree bark or animal skin, and have a closely fitting lid. Traders and raiders of old carried their travelling luggage in such a basket, which was almost waterproof. In a household without wooden chests, such baskets were used to store valuable belongings such as holiday clothing, carefully folded away with strips of dried fragrant screwpine (*pandan*) leaves and dried turtle egg shells to keep insects out of the precious cloth-of-gold, embroidered muslin veils, or powerfully patterned ikat textiles woven on the backstrap loom.

These days, handbags have taken over the function of small, intricately woven baskets, materially and symbolically. Both are used to carry the owner's personal belongings; both indicate status. The grandmother who once carried a betelnut basket decorated with beads and gold thread will have the equivalent of a granddaughter who carries a trendy leather or fabric handbag today. For everyday travelling, to the fields or to the market, a slightly larger, plainer carrier is used.

In today's modern kitchens, baskets for kitchen use are less visible as plastic has taken over. Large winnowing trays are still used, often to spread food for drying under the sun. And *ketupat* are still being cooked in little palm-leaf packets quickly plaited by skilled hands. A narrow basket is pushed into the fermenting mush of rice wine to form a well from which the liquor can be ladled out.

One type of carrier, manufactured by some Orang Asli tribes, is somewhere between a basket and a bag—it may be used as a back basket but it is soft, rather like a sack, and carried by back- and forehead-strap. Small versions of this bag hold personal belongings. In Sarawak, some Bidayuh make a very similar soft bag as an attractive wrap for the family's contribution to a communal feast but, as in the modern kitchen, plastic is more commonly used nowadays.

Some types of fish and animal traps are made from rattan and bamboo. These are either basket traps and fish weirs, or spring traps with a trip wire to trigger a spear set on a rattan or bamboo spring. Bird traps are still used in many areas, although with increasing population densities the spring traps for deer and pigs are considered too dangerous. In the old days of constant inter-tribal strife, the warriors' protective shields and war caps were worked out of strong rattan canes.

Hats and food covers

Malaysian hats are large, designed for shelter as much as for beauty. A flat conical hat, made of palm leaves on a circular rattan frame, is used by rural folk as shelter from the elements. Coloured fibres, cut-outs and rattan struts may be used as decoration. Some hats have a circular inset for better fit, while others are worn with a cloth wound around the head. Very few traditional hats have chin straps or ties, although a woman may throw a sarong over her hat for the sake of modesty as well as for extra shade.

Hats and food covers

1. Orang Ulu sunhat.
2. Melanau sunhat.
3. Sabah food cover.
4. Bukan-Sadong woman's hat.
5. Murut sunhat.
6. Kadazandusun hat.
7. Sabah decorative food cover.

Gaily coloured fans made from natural fibres such as bamboo.

One colourful, hat-like object sometimes seen in rural markets is not a head cover at all but a food cover. These have proved so popular with souvenir-hunters that miniature colourful versions are made for sale.

In Sarawak and Sabah, the various ethnic groups have their own characteristic hats. In the old days, the headgear of a traveller must have helped to identify him as friend or foe. Beautifully patterned hats are worked from fine rattan or bamboo strands, usually over a base of palm leaf. Hat decorations include cloth appliqué, cowrie shells and bead embroidery, with the modern additions of sequins and tinsel. A typical Central Borneo hat has a tall crown, and a bristly quarter-brim fore and aft; this is often painted or embroidered.

Housing materials

Plaiting is used in other things besides mats and baskets; it is used in construction too. On the high plateau of Sabah, for example, there is such a thing as a bamboo house—entire houses constructed of bamboo, with very few auxiliary materials. In other parts of Malaysia, timber houses may be lashed with rattan ropes, or walled with thick bamboos split open and flattened into cheap if not very durable planks. In Peninsular Malaysia, decorative walls may be woven of bamboo strips.

One type of house, fashioned of palm leaf, is used to shelter souls. The coastal Melanau of Sarawak hold funeral ceremonies for persons lost at sea whose bodies have not been recovered. Palm leaf effigies of the victims are placed in a little house, neatly made and decorated, which, after an appropriate farewell ceremony, is sent out to sea on small boats.

Penan headman wearing a traditional hat made from reeds.

Iban using rattan to build a wall in a longhouse, Sarawak, 1950s.

The artistic tradition

Mat-making techniques are traditionally passed down from generation to generation, from a skilled hand to an inexperienced beginner. In some communities, a woman's worth was once measured by her skill in the art of mat-making. It is hard to document exactly when a new mat design emerged, but what is known is that certain designs characterized a certain village, community, or even a person. Mat patterns are given names, too. The purposes for mats and baskets have remained consistent, but some traditional forms and uses have been modified to suit modern tastes.

Multi-coloured *pandan* mat made in Kampung Rusila, Kuala Terengganu that incorporates swastika and *pucuk rebung* (bamboo shoot) motifs.

Finely woven rattan food carrier.

Three-tiered rattan and bamboo food carrier.

Finely plaited rattan mats and baskets made by the Kayan, Kenyah and Penan of Sarawak.

Historical patterns and motifs

Much has been said and written about the Dongson influence on Malaysian design. Beyond a doubt, Indochina and the Malay Archipelago share in a larger, common culture, but trying to establish the exact descent of one or another of its aspects can be misleading, and tends to stray far from the mark.

Mat patterns are restricted by the technique of diaper-plaiting which favours straight and intersecting lines and oblique 45-degree lines. Curves are composed of angular steps. These limitations make the commonly recognized Dongson patterns eminently suitable for basketry decoration, but no older, indigenously Insulindian materials are available for comparison so it seems best to leave open the question of lineage.

Individual components of each motif are isolated and re-combined in many ways to make an endless variety of different but similar designs. Mat-makers generally pride themselves in copying old, complicated patterns from their elders' work, which argues for a continuous descent of ancient 'flowers', as they are called. Within a region the discerning eye can spot the characteristic designs of a particular village.

Considering the nature of basketwork, the only way we can know the really old patterns is from a long sequence

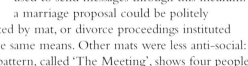

LEFT TO RIGHT: Melanau box made from rattan and sago palm bast; large carry basket from Sabah made with rattan and bamboo.

of good reproductions, and these have inevitably been filtered through the eye and mind of each succeeding craftswoman. But every generation gives birth to a few creative individuals who adapt and innovate. Each generation sees new things introduced from outside. The constant movement of trade brought new patterns and new mat-making techniques into the region to mingle with the old. A skilled craftswoman can copy any of these, or incorporate some parts of them in her own, traditional work; this creative innovation goes on to this day.

A pictorial tradition

Mat designs are repetitive, either in friezes and frames, or in overall patterns. If ever there was a picturesque tradition in mat-making in Peninsula Malaysia, several centuries of Islam might have eliminated it. In other parts of the Insulindies, mats were woven to tell of ancestors and their doings, to depict the underworld, to record current events that were considered important by the craftswoman. Such mats were never common, and they are very rare today.

An Iban weaver whose community had shifted from the highlands to the coastal region in the 1950s found the goats raised by her Malay neighbours interesting enough to depict one on a mat; the same lady also incorporated modern weapons and aircraft in her weaving. The Lundayeh of west Sabah, one of the few ethnic groups who do not consider fine mat-making exclusively women's work, used to send messages through this medium: a marriage proposal could be politely rejected by mat, or divorce proceedings instituted by the same means. Other mats were less anti-social: one pattern, called 'The Meeting', shows four people peaceably drinking rice wine out of one jar.

Naming patterns

Mat patterns have names, though not nearly every mat-maker knows them all. Most names are traditional, while a few are given by the creator of something recognized as new by herself and her group. A large number of patterns commonly used by the east coast Malays are named after species of flora and fauna that the weavers are familiar with, such as 'clove blossom', 'frangipani', 'eight petals', 'durian flower', 'bamboo shoot', 'elephant head', 'tiger's pad', 'pigeon's eye', 'shoal of fish'

and so on. Naturally patterned things are imitated, as in 'tortoise' or 'snake skin'.

Monochrome Iban sleeping mats tell tales of legendary heroes, particularly of the lady Kumang whose pet leopard forms an important part of sleeping mat designs; 'leopard claw stealing fruit' takes pride of place besides 'bird's nest fern', 'sunrise' and 'the man in the moon'. Only the person who made the mat can tell the entire story of how one part of the design relates to the other parts; this is gender-linked lore, mostly discussed among women. Penan rattan mats, woven so closely as to be almost waterproof, feature nature-based designs such as 'river fish' and 'palm shoot', revealing a nomadic people's main preoccupation in their precarious hand-to-mouth existence.

One patterned mat, restricted to the west coast of Sabah and becoming rarer, is decorated in a very unusual way—a plain *pandanus* base is completely covered with dark cotton material and the edge bound with a contrasting frame. The mat is decorated with cloth appliqué and embroidery, making free use of sequins, beads and metallic threads. The designs are partly ornamental, partly picturesque. They show botanical, human and animal figures, in elegantly balanced layouts, similar to those seen on some supplementary-weft textiles of Sulawesi. Such mats are not meant for sitting on, but form part of ceremonial presents, and are hung on the walls of a house hosting a festive event like a marriage.

The future of mats and baskets

Today, changing lifestyles have made mats and baskets redundant for many Malaysians who look for status symbols elsewhere. The survival of the mat-maker's craft is dependent on the tourist market. Miniatures of hats and household utensils are sold as souvenirs. The craft is unlikely to die out completely, as fortunately a number of modern designers have pioneered, and will continue to pioneer, new uses of an old skill. Dinner mats, table runners, wall hangings, rattan furniture and other interior decorations help to keep the skill of centuries alive.

Mat and basket superstitions

- Prepared mat-making and basketry material may not be left lying around; if people other than the craftswoman step on it, she will suffer from 'sore bones'.

- Matting materials must only be harvested at the time of the new moon. This one has scientific foundation: plant sap contains less sugar at this time, so the end product is less likely to be attacked by insects or fungus.

- A mat-maker must not stop work halfway through one row, nor may another person carry on the work.

- Ripping open the palm-leaf case of a steamed rice cake will cause the hasty eater to lose his way later.

- It is taboo to carry a cat or dog in a basket.

- Sleeping inside a rolled-up mat causes ringworm.

- Playing inside a rolled-up mat is taboo; in earlier times, corpses were thus wrapped for burial.

- Stepping over a fish trap renders it powerless to attract fish.

- Rice grain must be carried from the storage jar to the cooking pot in an attractive basket.

- People who stand or sit on a winnowing tray will lose their way in the jungle.

- If a man sets a fish trap and goes to harvest rattan on the same day, he will find a snake in the fish trap.

- Finding a snake inside a fish trap is a bad omen.

- The sleeping mat used by a mother and her newborn baby may never be thrown away.

- After a week-long Iban Gawai festival, some longhouses hold a rolling up the mats ceremony to signify an end of the celebrations.

Seated on mats with various motifs, a Murut craftswoman from Sabah weaves another mat, using her foot to secure her work.

Some Sarawak mat patterns

Buah bintang
Star

Buah tungku
Trivet

Buah kukut remaung
Leopard claw

Buah ruit
Fishing spear with barb

Source: Heidi Munan, 2005

Intricately patterned Penan mat.

Examples of Sabah mat motifs

'The quarrel' motif used in Murut baskets.

This pattern is so complicated to make it can frustrate the maker, hence the name 'mad pattern.'

'The meeting' motif to show four people drinking from one jar of rice wine.

'Coiled like a sleeping snake' motif.

Source: G.E. Woolley, 1929

Dusun hat weaving patterns.

1. Beautiful *songket* sarong, the golden Malay textile of significant cultural importance. Here, the traditional segmentation of the sarong into the body (*badan*), head (*kepala*) and border (*tepi*) is evident.

2. *Songket* weaver in Kota Bharu, Kelantan, in 1954. Such traditional weaving was once a family industry, young Malay girls learning the art from their mothers.

3. & 4. *Kain dastar*, which is folded and used as a headcloth by many indigenous groups in Sabah. The *tengkolok* is also folded and worn as a form of headwear by Malay men. This piece has *telepuk* gold foil embellishment.

5. Five-layered embroidered *tikar sila*, upon which a groom sits at his bride's house during the Malay/Muslim marriage ceremony (*akad nikah*).

6. Malaysia, as a multi-ethnic country, has a multitude of clothing styles utilizing textiles of many colours, type and design. Pictured are some traditional costumes of the Malays, Chinese and Indians, many of which are still worn daily, but have adapted to climate, fashion trends and, in some respects, the assimilation of other cultures.

7. Former Prime Minister Tun Abdul Razak Huss (left) wearing a batik shirt, which, from the 19 became popular as formal wear and office att for Malaysian men. Today, civil servants are encouraged to wear batik on the 1st and 15th of the month.

8. Women mixing salt, ginger and oil during the *Ngar* mordanting ceremony. This ritual is part the dyeing process for the yarn used to weav the sacred *pua kumbu* of the Iban of Sarawak

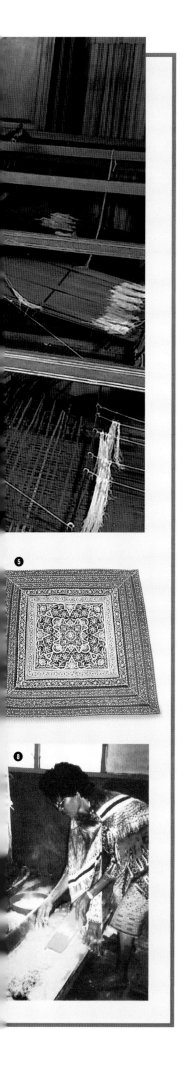

TEXTILES AND EMBROIDERY

Traditional textiles and embroidery in Malaysia are valued not only for their functionality, such as when used for clothing, but also for the beauty and status that they represent. The development of textiles and weaving techniques was in concert with the discovery and use of new materials: from tree bark and plant fibres in prehistoric times, to cotton, silk, gold threads and dyes. The Malay term *kain* (cloth) generally refers to any textile produced using the weaving technique.

Various textiles are produced from cotton using many techniques such as direct weaving (*tenun langsung*), single *ikat* (*ikat tunggal*) or embroidered weaving (*tenun sulam*). Of these techniques, single *ikat*, using a tie-dyed yarn, is one of the most familiar, and characteristic of some Bornean indigenous textiles. Silk textiles include those with gold thread or gold and silver yarn using the double *ikat* technique (*ikat ganda*). Today, the east coast states of Peninsular Malaysia are especially well known for *songket* and batik, and Perak for fine embroidery such as *tekat*.

Ikat textiles are now widely used to make lifestyle items such as cushion covers, purses and souvenirs.

Many textiles have cultural significance, for instance, *cindai* (imported from India) and local *kain limar* and *songket* have long held a place in Malay society, being used for important occasions and traditional costumes. Colours also played a role; it was recorded in 1405 that the ruler of Melaka was sent as a gift a suit of silk clothing and a yellow umbrella. The latter has been the emblem and colour of Malay royalty ever since. The *pua kumbu* of Sarawak also has spiritual significance.

Among the Malays and other indigenous peoples, abstract designs and motifs based on nature are the most favoured. The Malays use an interplay of geometric forms to pattern their sarong and *songket*, including interlocking chevrons and diamonds. Stylized designs such as *awan larat* (meandering clouds) and *pucuk rebung* (bamboo shoots) are two typical designs. The Iban of Sarawak use woven motifs to symbolize an event, thought or even a dream, with designs handed down from mother to daughter, while the people of Sabah prefer stripes and geometric designs.

The Straits Chinese are known for their embroidered *kebaya*, a long-sleeved blouse with characteristic intricate lacework worn with a sarong, and their highly elaborate beadwork found on accessories such as belts, slippers, handbags, tapestries and bedspreads. The products of these crafts are once again popular among Malaysians.

Some textile crafts continue to thrive partly due to prevalent fashion trends, but others have declined due to the laboriousness and intricacy, and thus cost, of production. For these latter crafts to survive, innovations are required, be they design, function or production techniques.

POS Malaysia stamps that feature distinctive Nonya embroidered blouses.

Development of local textiles

Prior to the arrival of Europeans in the 16th century CE, the early textiles and weaving traditions of the Malay Peninsula, Sabah and Sarawak were heavily influenced by trade with Indian, Chinese and Arab merchants of the 'water silk route'. Inspired by the foreign textiles imported in this way, unique indigenous and local textiles evolved and flourished.

RIGHT: A 16th century map based on Ptolemy's map of the 1st century CE of the Golden Khersonese.

Trade beginnings

The Malay Peninsula, Sabah and Sarawak, because of their strategic location and control of the passage through the Strait of Melaka and a large part of the South China sea, were involved in regional and international trade from an early date, particularly with India, China, Arabia and Indonesia. Numerous thriving trading entrepôts developed as a result.

One of the earliest references to this trade is in the 1st century CE map of the Greek cartographer Ptolemy, showing the Golden Khersonese (*aurea cherfonefus* or Golden Leaf), his appellation for the Malay Peninsula lying between the Indian subcontinent and the then unknown Chinese coasts. His map records various emporiums and ports on the Malay Peninsula such as the Tracola Emporium on the north west side of the Peninsula (site of the Bujang Valley in Kedah, where extensive Hindu temple ruins and Chinese ceramics dating back to the 10th century CE have been found), the Chrifoana Flu (Melaka River region), and the Sabana Emporium (site of old Johore at the southern tip of the Peninsula). Recorded locations on the east coast of the Malay Peninsula include

Influences on local textiles

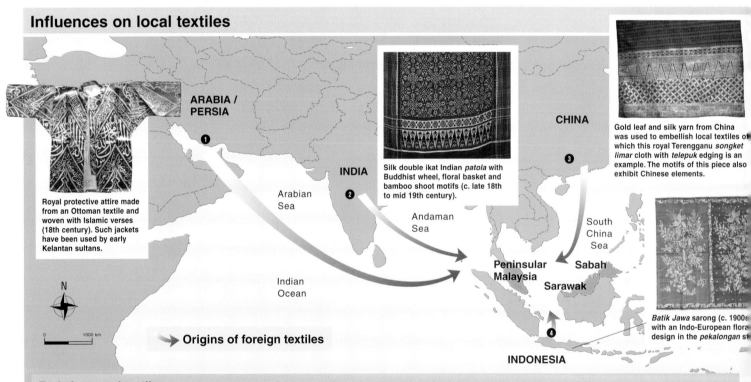

Royal protective attire made from an Ottoman textile and woven with Islamic verses (18th century). Such jackets have been used by early Kelantan sultans.

Silk double ikat Indian *patola* with Buddhist wheel, floral basket and bamboo shoot motifs (c. late 18th to mid 19th century).

Gold leaf and silk yarn from China was used to embellish local textiles of which this royal Terengganu *songket limar* cloth with *telepuk* edging is an example. The motifs of this piece also exhibit Chinese elements.

Batik Jawa sarong (c. 1900s with an Indo-European flora design in the *pekalongan* st

ARABIA / PERSIA

INDIA

CHINA

Arabian Sea

Andaman Sea

Indian Ocean

South China Sea

Peninsular Malaysia

Sabah

Sarawak

INDONESIA

N

0 1000 km

➤ Origins of foreign textiles

Early imported textiles

1. Luxurious Arab and Persian textiles were used in the 16th century by local courts and had talismanic value. Some forms of embroidery may also have derived from the Middle East. (See 'Malay embroidery and tekat').

2. Cotton brought by Indian traders in the early centuries CE, enabled local people to move away from wild plant fibres. Later, in the 15th century CE, the double ikat silk Indian *patola* (known as *kain cindai* here) was a premier court textile of the Malay Archipelago, and was believed to be sacred and embued with protective talismanic powers. It inspired the creation of local textiles including the exquisite *kain limar*, which is no longer woven, but is being revived. (See 'Cultural significance of textiles: Malay' and 'Malay woven cloth'). Indian royal textiles and arts may also have influenced local textile embellishment. (See 'Textile embellishment' and 'Malay embroidery and tekat').

3. Chinese silks and yarn were essential to the development of local textiles, such as *songket* (see 'Malay woven cloth'). Gold thread was also used for Malay embroidery (see 'Malay embroidery and tekat').

4. Javanese batik was initially imported and used in Peninsular Malaysia. The methods of producing it using wax and its designs and motifs inspired the creation of Malaysian batik in the early 20th century (see 'Batik craft and industry').

Perimula (the Kuala Terengganu area), Perimu (the Kelantan-Pattani area) and Samarade (the Nakhorn Si-Thammarat area in southern Thailand). In Borneo, the Sarawak River delta area of Bongkisam, known for its excavated artefacts, is shown as *Argentea metropolis* (silver metropolis), an obvious reference to the antimony smelting activities archaeologically evidenced by metal slags.

Apart from operating as thriving barter trade centres, these places would have provided safe havens for visiting traders and ships and fresh water for the long journeys of seafaring merchants. Cotton textiles from India and silk fabrics and yarn from China (see 'Malay woven cloth') would have been among the items that exchanged hands for local produce. Exports from Borneo included spices, rhinocerous horns, hornbill ivory, bezoar stones, aromatic resins, shells, kingfisher feathers, antimony and exotic marine products such as sea cucumbers and turtle eggs. From the Malay Peninsula areas, exports would have included elephant ivory and alluvial gold (see 'Gold jewellery and regalia').

Building on a tradition of fine textiles

Although artefacts no longer exist due to the perishable nature of fabrics, particularly in a tropical climate, there is a long established tradition of fine textiles being used and appreciated by royal courts and the affluent. For example, in 607 CE, during the Buddhist Langkasuka kingdom (c. 2nd–14th centuries CE), a Chinese envoy to Chi tu ('Red Earth Land'), believed to have been located in Kelantan, documented the wealth of the local kingdom and the grandness of its king who was described as sitting on a 'three-tiered couch, facing north and dressed in rose-coloured cloth, with a chaplet of gold flowers and necklaces of varied jewels'. The use of luxurious court costumes and textiles are also recorded in the *Sejarah Melayu* (Malay Annals), Chinese Ming Annals and the *Suma Oriental* of Tome Pires as being used by the Melaka Sultanate in the 15th century.

From the initial importation of textiles and yarns as trade goods from India, China, Arabia/Persia and other parts of the Malay World, evolved quintessential indigenous and local fabrics, among them the *pua* (see 'Cultural significance of textiles: Sabah and Sarawak' and 'Textiles of Sarawak'), *kain dastar* (see 'Textiles of Sabah'), and the Malay *kain limar* and *songket* (see 'Cultural significance of textiles: Malay' and 'Malay woven cloth') and batik (see 'Batik craft and industry').

Malay textiles

Early importation of cotton from India was an important textile advancement. The later availability of silk thread from China from the 13th century, enhanced even more the development of local weaving traditions which were further revolutionized in the 16th century with the introduction of the frame loom from Europe which has been used ever since by Malay weavers (see above) to create their luxurious fabrics (see 'Malay woven cloth').

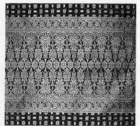

Above: Court *songket* (19th century) with a *gigi gergasi* (clenched teeth) formation of double *pucuk rebung* (bamboo shoots) and *lawi ayam* (chicken spur) motifs on the *kepala*.

Left: 19th century *limar* with a double row of *pucuk rebung* motifs and scattered flowers (*bunga bertabur*) on the *kepala* and interlocking bays (*teluk berantai*) adorning the *badan*.

Sarawak and Sabah textiles

The introduction of both cotton and the backstrap loom, probably via India through early maritime trade, had a huge impact on the indigenous textiles of Sabah and Sarawak. The backstrap is still used today by weavers there to create textiles distinctive to their particular group's worldview and beliefs. Most notable are the *pua kumbu* of Sarawak (see 'Cultural significance of textiles: Sabah and Sarawak' and 'Textiles of Sarawak') and the *kain pis* and *kain dastar* of Sabah' (see 'Textiles of Sabah').

Top: Contemporary 20th century *kain dastar* from Sabah with typical geometric designs.

Above left: Detail of *pua kumbu* woven by Siti Au Undom, entitled *Tangkar Lubong* (warrior who has died without burial). This design relates to a traditional Iban ritual for important men. Aniline and plant dyes were used.

Above right: Late 19th century Iban *kain kebat* skirt made with natural dyes on indigenous cotton and featuring stylized figures.

Left: Siti Au Undom, a weaver of the highest *Indu Nakar* status, weaving *pua kumbu* on the backstrap loom in her longhouse at Saratok in Sarawak.

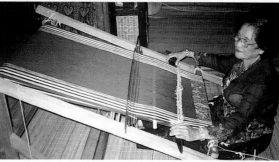

Cultural significance of textiles: Malay

Textiles and clothing play an important role as ritual paraphernalia in Malay culture. At one time, some of the more exotic and luxurious textiles, for example, yellow coloured textiles and those woven with gold thread, were exclusively used for the attire of royalty and the aristocracy. Cloth was not only made into blankets (ulas modom)*, infant carriers* (kain dukung) *and long shawls* (selendang panjang)*, but was also offered as ritual gifts.*

Coronation ceremony of the present Sultan of Selangor, Sultan Sharafuddin Idris Shah on 8 March 2003. Following the *bersiram tabal* or royal bathing ceremony which took place elsewhere, the prospective Sultan is wearing royal gold *songket* about the shoulders as he walks to the palace.

Qur'anic verses being recited during a hair-cutting ceremony. The child is lying on a *songket* hammock.

ABOVE: Ceremonial batik textile used during a funeral covered with the word 'Allah' in calligraphic writing

RIGHT: Kain limar decorated with calligraphy of prayers to Allah and the Prophet Muhammad. This late 19th-century example demonstrates the lime squeeze colouring effect exemplified by the Malay limar.

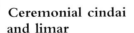

Ritual cloths

Among the western Bajau people and the Brunei, Sarawak, Sabah and Peninsular Malays, woven cloths—especially *cindai, limar* and floral *songket penuh* (see 'Malay woven cloth')—were very important ritual paraphernalia and cultural items and an integral part of traditional society and family institutions for these groups.

Such items had a specific place in rituals and cultural practices, commencing from the birth of a baby through to wedding ceremonies and the royal installation or death of a ruler. For example, textiles were an essential requirement in Malay ceremonies such as *melenggang perut* carried out in the seventh month of pregnancy to welcome and safeguard the arrival of a baby, in the *bercukur jambul* hair-cutting ceremony for a baby, in a *bertindik telinga* or ear-piercing ceremony to mark a forthcoming betrothal or wedding day, in *bersiram tabal*, a royal bathing ceremony preceding the *raja bernobat* or music played during a ruler's installation (see 'Traditional musical instruments'), in *mandi sampat*, a special bathing ceremony for a bride and groom and in the *berkaul* ceremony carried out upon the death of a ruler.

Ceremonial cindai and limar

In the Malay Archipelago, the cloth known locally as *cindai* originated from India (known there as *patola*), where it was used for saris. The Malays imported it in different lengths and used it as a ceremonial textile and as part of the attire of royalty and the aristocracy. Subsequently, to suit local preferences, this cloth inspired the creation of, and was superseded by, a beautiful indigenous prestige textile, *limar*. (See 'Malay woven cloth').

Cindai was once described in a Malay literary text as *cindai hikmat* (magical *cindai*), bestowing on the wearer the assurance that he would achieve safety and good fortune. Perhaps somewhat strangely, the cloth worn by members of royalty and warriors to protect themselves in battle was known as *cindai betina* (feminine *cindai*) and had fine floral patterns. The legendary Malay hero Hang Tuah was said to have worn 'seven twists around the waist'.

Conversely, women wore *cindai jantan* (male *cindai*) which had bigger, often yellowish, flowery patterns and was shorter in length than that worn by men. *Cindai*, and later *limar*, could be worn by women over the shoulder or around the waist and was normally worn as a shawl by female members of royal and noble families. Unsewn *limar* was reputedly worn by Che Siti Wan Kembang, the female ruler of the state of Kelantan (1610–63), wrapped around as a bodice with her outfit completed by a *limar songket* sarong and a *songket* stole.

The social and ceremonial significance of textiles such as *cindai* and *limar* was particularly evident during ceremonies for weddings, births and even deaths, especially for royalty and the nobility. By the 16th century such

Tuanku Abdul Rahman of Negeri Sembilan (1895–1960) and his consort Tuanku Ampuan Khursiah dressed in fine *songket* traditional outfits, taken in 1934.

textiles had an established ceremonial quality and were also given as gifts for royal weddings and might be bestowed on a person for strength or other blessings, or as a form of honour or reward. *Limar* decorated with calligraphic Qur'anic or Hadith verses was used during funeral ceremonies.

Songket and gilt textiles

Until about the early 20th century, gilt patterned fabrics such as *songket* and *telepuk* (see 'Textile embellishment') were exclusively used by royalty or the nobility and as essential items at customary ceremonies. They could only be used by commoners when given as a gift by the Ruler or by brides and grooms on their wedding day. In particular, according to custom, commoners were forbidden from copying the style and designs of royal garments and the excessive use of luxurious gold threads was expressly prohibited. One of the forbidden royal designs was the *songket teluk berantai* (interlocking chain loop *songket*). Thus, these rich and luxurious fabrics represented the social structure of the Malay elite.

This restriction of use to royalty and nobility was in place at least from the reign of Melaka's Seri

Fans like this, decorated with *tekat* gold thread embroidery, are a part of traditional wedding finery. In the past, objects and attire with such decoration could only be used by the noble class in Malay society (Henry Bong Permanent Collection, c. 1900s).

Costume symbolism

In Malay culture, textiles which were used as shawls or as a complete set of clothing carried a highly symbolic meaning. Such symbolic functions of cloths as described in some literary texts are based on their forms and styles. For example, in the tradition of Seri Maharajah Muhammad Shah of Melaka (1424–44), the use of the colours yellow (in all shades and tones) or textiles with gold threads or embellishment was completely forbidden to commoners until about the early 20th century. The wearing of silk sarongs with batik or special rainbow coloured patterns (see 'Textile embellishment') was also prohibited. A colour symbolism operated during this period which was generally white or gold for the ruler, yellow for members of the royal family, purple for members of the court, blue or purple for the Chief Minister (Bendahara), green for the Chief of Law and Order (Temenggong) and red for the Admiral (Laksamana).

Certain styles of headdress called *tengkolok* (see 'Malay dress'), also denoted rank and status lwith the styles varying between the nine states. According to tradition, the *tengkolok* was shaped and folded in layers according to the wearer's status: a Ruler had five layers, four layers for a Bendahara, three for a Temenggong and from one to three layers for commoners. These styles were sometimes named for a particular feature of the shape, such as 'chicken with a broken wing' (*ayam patah kepak*) for the ceremonial chief of Pahang, 'coffee plant leaves' (*cogan daun kopi*) worn by the Sultan of Pahang and many others like 'a flower in its sheath', 'nesting eagle' (*lang mengeram*) and 'the cock's comb' (*balung ayam*).

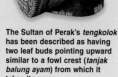

The Sultan of Perak's *tengkolok* has been described as having two leaf buds pointing upward similar to a fowl crest (*tanjak balung ayam*) from which it takes its name.

Meaningful motifs

The decorative patterns and motifs of Malay textiles evoke special meanings. Bamboo shoot motifs (*pucuk rebung*) (right), extensively used in Malay textiles, were arranged on the middle panel (*kepala*) of a sarong, at the corner of *tengkolok* or *kain destar* (Malay headdress: see 'Malay dress'), or at the *kaki* (the bottom edge) of fabric. Thus positioned, with the base of the shoots firmly placed on the bottom with their peaks pointing upwards, this motif was believed to bestow strength, confidence and power upon the wearer.

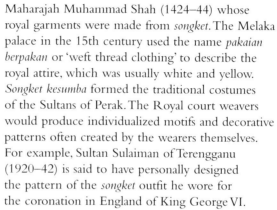

With the advent of Islam, motifs were modified and textiles were patterned with decorative Arabic calligraphy. It is said that during his legendary duel with Hang Jebat, warrior Hang Tuah wore a cloth tied around his waist (*ikat pinggang*) with boldly written Qur'anic verses, and that his headdress carried the following words:

Written with Arabic verses, a talisman for every corner, wisdom for every angle.

*Bersurat kalimah Arab
Tiap sudut ada azimat
Tiap segi ada hikmat.*

Maharajah Muhammad Shah (1424–44) whose royal garments were made from *songket*. The Melaka palace in the 15th century used the name *pakaian berpakan* or 'weft thread clothing' to describe the royal attire, which was usually white and yellow. *Songket kesumba* formed the traditional costumes of the Sultans of Perak. The Royal court weavers would produce individualized motifs and decorative patterns often created by the wearers themselves. For example, Sultan Sulaiman of Terengganu (1920–42) is said to have personally designed the pattern of the *songket* outfit he wore for the coronation in England of King George VI.

As for functionality, *songket* was most often used for sarongs, *baju kurung* or *kebaya panjang* (traditional dresses of Malay women), *selendang* (stoles), *destar* (male headdresses) and *bengkung* (worn tightly around the waist), especially in the Peninsula and Brunei (see 'Malay dress').

Old literary texts record the importance of *songket*. For example, the *Hikayat Malim Dewa* describes the gifts of Tuanku Malim Dewa to the princess Tuan Puteri Andam Dewi as including a piece of *songket* (*kain jong sarat* pattern) as a token of his love. According to the customs of the Johor-Riau Sultanate, in a royal wedding procession, *kain songket penuh* (full *songket*) is said to have surrounded the palanquin on which the bride and groom sat.

Produced in standard sarong lengths of 100 centimetres by 180 centimetres, *kain songket* still often forms part of the wedding gifts (*hantaran*) of a Malay couple and continues to be worn by them. The couple is considered as 'king' and 'queen' for the day (*raja sehari*). High-quality *songket* pieces are considered family heirlooms.

Young male members of the Terengganu royal family using *songket* sarong covers after their circumcision.

Purple *songket* cloth *hantaran* arranged as a peacock. Such beautiful designs were common in the old days.

Songket hantaran

Following Malay cultural tradition, *songket* may be given by either the bride or groom to the other as part of the items making up the traditional wedding gifts called *hantaran*. Usually it will be creatively and beautifully arranged and displayed.

Cultural significance of textiles: Sabah and Sarawak

The textiles of Sabah and Sarawak form part of the traditional costumes of the indigenous people of these states and are used for ceremonial occasions and special purposes. Of these textiles, those of the Iban, especially the pua kumbu, *have distinct religious significance—*pua kumbu *features in Iban myths, has traditionally been an important part of their ceremonies and rituals, and has symbolic designs and a creation process which are inextricably connected to their beliefs and the supernatural world.*

Above: Embroidered *kain pis* from Sabah, which is worn as a headcloth.

Below: Traditional Iban male loincloth (*sirat*).

Textiles of Sabah and Sarawak
The textiles of Sabah are not of a religious or sacred nature per se but are worn by ritual specialists such as the Lotud priestesses (*tantagas*) of Tuaran, by everyone as costumes for ceremonial occasions such as weddings, and for dance performances (see 'Textiles of Sabah' and 'Costumes and ornaments of Sabah'). The traditional motifs used on the *kain pis*, made by the Binadan of the Kudat District (a Bajau kindred group), are, however, drawn from their legends (see 'Textiles of Sabah'). In Sarawak, apart from use in the costumes of the various indigenous groups (see 'Costumes and ornaments of Sarawak'), the textiles created by the Iban, in particular the *pua kumbu*, reflect Iban beliefs and play a special role in many of their sacred rituals and ceremonies (see also 'Textiles of Sarawak').

Ceremonial and ritual uses of textiles
When woven as *pua kumbu*, ikat fabric assumes a sacred and protective role, being used by *manang* (healers) in healing ceremonies; as divine invocations in the form of flags and tied to the effigy pole of the Great Hornbill representing Singalong Burung, the god of war, at Gawai Burung festivals; as mats on special occasions replacing woven plaited mats, such as for the Gawai Piring (Plate Festival); as wall hangings and drapes at weddings and also special ceremonies, such as those related to crops; as a cloth to rub a pregnant woman to protect her unborn child; as wrapping for newborn babies before their first ritual bath; and as funeral shrouds to cover the dead. Its use literally spans all major rites of passage and important occasions deemed auspicious by the Iban community. *Pua* is also a treasured family heirloom.

Above: An Iban shrine associated with headhunting is decorated with *pua*, guns, spears, coconuts and areca nuts.

Right: Plates with offerings lined up on *pua* for the Gawai Piring festival.

Historically, women used *pua* to receive the head trophies brought back by their menfolk after war or a successful headhunting expedition. Headhunting was believed to help restore the balance of cosmic order and ensure fertility and had direct links to the harvesting

Weaving taboos and rules
There are strict rules and prohibitions related to weaving Iban *pua*. First, particular aspects of the weaving process and designs can only be done by weavers of a certain level of experience and status. This ensures quality and technical perfection, but also serves to protect the weaver as each *pua* is believed to contain a spirit of its own (*semangat*), which could overcome the weaver and cause her to become sick, or even die, if she does not have the required experience and spiritual strength. In terms of design, apart from the competence and category of the weaver to use certain motifs, clearance must be obtained through a dream, usually from the goddesses of weaving Kumang and Lulong. Exacting requirements also apply to the patterns which must be created layer by layer, starting with what is known as the 'food layer', for example bamboo or fruit motifs, so that any attack by the *pua* spirit will be directed there. For the same reason, the potent central panel of the *pua* is contained by vertical borders and bands on each side and horizontal border patterns at the top and bottom (see 'Textiles of Sarawak'). Thus, the structure of the *pua* design and the procedure for its creation serves to protect the weaver.

Weaving was closely associated with the role of female *bobolizan* (shamans) among the Rungus of Sabah. These women had special status as weavers of cloth for traditional rituals and ceremonial clothing. During the weaving process they stayed apart in their own room. Their belief was that failure to strictly adhere to special rituals was dangerous and could cause illness. The task of weaving cloth no longer has special significance; now anyone can weave.

Iban weaver tying the threads to create the *pua* pattern. Her tattooed hands indicate her weaving status.

Hierarchy of Iban weavers

Indu Nakar / Indu Gaar: The most powerful and accomplished weavers with full control of the process—dying and weaving. Can create the most spiritually potent designs such as human and ancestor spirit figures (*engkaramba* or *antu*).

Indu Nenkebang / Indu Muntong: Empowered to create her own designs, but weaves only.

Indu Sikat / Indu Kebat: Can only weave basic designs and copy.

Indu Temuai / Indu Lawai: Can weave only plant motifs and is restricted to the width of the cloth.

Indu Paku / Indu Tebu: Novice weaver.

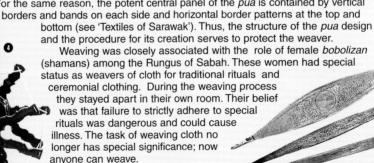

Traditionally, the role of Iban men in the weaving process was to create the carved implements—backstrap (**1**) and loom, spool (**2**), beaters (**3**) and spinning wheel (**4**)—used by the women. These implements were often ornamental and carved with designs that also served to provide spiritual protection to the weaver.

cycle. Headhunting was banned in different parts of Sarawak from the 1850s through to the 1920s. Women created the *pua* as part of their contribution to ensure success in warfare and struggles, weaving spiritually powerful designs. Even the yarn dyeing and preparation process requires special skill and powers and cannot be taken lightly. Offerings are made to the goddesses of weaving and certain steps in the dyeing process are especially perilous, thus earning them the appellation of 'the warpath of the woman' (*kayau indu*).

Pua is placed on the pole with the hornbill effigy during the Gawai Kenyalang festival.

Very old Iban *sungkit* is treasured and may also be used in a ritual way in the same manner as *pua*. The *lebor api* (blazing fire) was a potent *sungkit* cloth which was used to receive smoked trophy heads from warriors (see 'Textiles of Sarawak').

In Sabah, among the Lotud of Tuaran, the donning of the full elaborate ritual costume and accessories by their priestesses (*tantagas*) (left) in religious ceremonies is called *manarapoh*. This signifies the passage and entry into the presence of the principal deities, Kinohoringan and Umunsumundu, in the ceremony. A distinctive and important component of the costume is the ritual skirt (*sinugitan*), usually a heirloom item made of old Indian *patola* fabric or other similar imported trade cloth.

Iban textiles

Loosely translated, *pua* means blanket or cover. The fabric it is made from is produced by a technique of single warp *ikat* (called *kebat* by the Iban) on a backstrap loom (see 'Textiles of Sarawak'). One side of the vertical panel of a *pua* is created first, then a second panel is woven with the pattern in a laterally inverted image, reflecting the first panel. When the two panels are hand stitched together, the finished product is a bigger piece of textile with a symmetrical central pattern spreading out on both sides, which would otherwise have been impossible to achieve due to the size limitations of the backstrap loom technique. This fabric is also used to create the short Iban female skirt *kain kebat*

Iban girls wearing colourful *kain kebat* skirts. Unlike *pua* which is made the same way and belongs to a whole family, skirts are a personal possession.

Pua production

Pua are traditionally woven in two main Iban areas: Saribas and Baleh of the Upper Rejang (see map below). In the mid-19th century, Saribas *pua* started to use imported Chinese spun cotton threads and aniline dyes. Production was interrupted for two to three generations from the beginning of World War II, only recommencing during the 1960s–70s due to a renewed interest in Sarawakian textiles. Unfortunately, this meant that many of the traditional motifs and patterns of this region, and their significance, were lost. In comparison, *pua* continued to be produced in the Baleh region uninterrupted even during wartime, ensuring survival of their designs. These people have also continued to use mainly natural dyes and spin their own thread from the fibres of the native *kapok* tree (*Bombax valetoni*).

ABOVE RIGHT: Saribas 19th century *pua* using aniline dyes. It features anthropomorphic figures (*buah engkaramba*).

RIGHT: This 20th century *pua* from the Baleh region of Sarawak features fern motifs. Handspun *kapok* thread has been used.

(also known as *bidang*), where it is used in isolation as a smaller single panel that is draped vertically. In addition, it is the material used for tailoring the *kelambi*, an Iban jacket worn by males and females (see 'Costumes and ornaments of Sarawak').

The supplementary weft technique is used by Iban weavers to create colourful *sungkit* (see 'Textiles of Sarawak'), a cloth possibly influenced by the Indian *patola* (known as *cindai* in Malay: see 'Malay woven cloth'). It is not known when use of this technique began in Sarawak, but it is thought to have ended in the early 1900s, possibly earlier, before recommencing in the 1950s. *Sungkit* is not widely produced, being a technique predominantly used by weavers from the Ulu Ai area, who still make it.

Origins of pua in Iban mythology

The Iban 'Creation of Man' myth features a *pua*-covered wooden statue coming to life as the first man after three invocations by Raja Entala, related to Selanpandai, the god of creation. The sacred chants, including the *timang*, *pantun*, *sabak*, *renong* and *pengap*, of the *lemanbang* (bards) also tell of the origins of Iban culture. A story is told of a hunter, Menggin, who shoots a bird that falls to the ground as a woman's skirt (*kain kebat* or *bidang*). He takes the skirt home and is visited by a girl, Dara Tinchin Temaga, who is the daughter of the god Singalong Burung. The couple marry and she bears him a son, Surong Gunting, before returning to the celestial realm in bird form. Her husband and son follow her there using special jackets (*kelambi*) with bird motifs that she wove for them. It is there that her son inherits, on behalf of all Iban, the divine revelations of Iban *adat* (customary laws) which include bird augury for times of peace, agriculture and war as well as headhunting to avenge the dead and the use of *pua* to receive these offerings. From such myths, the important religious and cultural role of woven *ikat* textiles in traditional Iban society can be seen.

Iban child's *kelambi* vest woven with geometric and protective *engkaramba* spirit figures using the sophisticated *sungkit* (embroidery on the loom) technique (c. 1900s).

Malay woven cloth

The first textiles produced locally were woven from local plant fibres, which were later replaced by cotton. Early trade with merchants from India, China, Persia, Arabia and elsewhere introduced new textiles and materials and new dimensions of weaving, as did the introduction of the frame loom by Europeans in the late 16th century. Traditional styles of weaving are still practised today and there has been an increase in handwoven textiles such as songket.

Indigo plant leaves have long been used for indigenous dye colouring.

External influences

Southeast Asia has a long history of producing local vegetable fibre textiles and, later, locally grown handspun cotton textiles introduced by early traders from the Indian subcontinent. The evolution of Srivijaya into a maritime kingdom in the 7th century brought traders to the Malay Archipelago and an influx of foreign fabrics such as the *patola* from Gujarat, India and gold embroidered velvet and brocades from Arabia, Persia, India and China. These foreign fabrics enriched the unique variety of Malay fabrics that developed and were based upon them. Woven silk introduced by Bugis traders was very popular among the Malays from the 13th century. *Kain songket* and silk woven fabrics generally found wide application in the lives of the people in the Malay coastal kingdoms influenced by Islam and became a distinctive craft feature of the states of Kelantan, Kedah, Perak, Johor and Terengganu in the Peninsula and of Sarawak.

Malay dye colouring developed through combinations of naturally available materials such as *biji kemiri* (candlenuts), *akar murudu* (a type of root), *kulit sepang* (boiled *sepang* bark for dyestuff) and *daun tarum* (indigo plant leaves).

Cindai

Kain cindai (known as *patola* in Hindi), originating and imported from the Gujarat district of India, was very popular in the Malay Archipelago during the 15th century and was widely used during the time of the premier cultural tradition of the royal courts in the Malay kingdoms of the Peninsula, Sumatra, Brunei, Java and Bali. The cloth was brought to the Malay-Indonesian region by Muslim merchants from India and was very well received in local markets. Owing to its beauty, *cindai* became a very lucrative and important barter trade item in this region. Malay rulers desired it for their customary attire and it became an important ceremonial textile (see 'Cultural significance of textiles: Malay'). *Cindai* was, at one time, worn by males around the waist and by females as head coverings or shawls. It was made using the double ikat technique. Both the weft and warp threads were tied and dyed separately with various colours, thus enabling various patterns to be produced when woven.

RIGHT: Kelantanese *songket limar* (19th century CE) with persimmon fruit (*tampuk kesemak*) motifs.

BELOW: Example of *kain cindai* (*patola*) with geomtric patterns.

Limar

Malay expertise in weaving was demonstrated, and their production tradition further varied, with the development of the single ikat Malay *kain limar*, a textile with distinctive characteristics inspired by *cindai*. *Limar* was actually the name of the bound thread dyeing process. The parts of the threads which were not exposed to the dye would produce a floral pattern when woven. Malay *limar* also came to be more unique when further decorated with Arabic calligraphy and became an important item in ceremonial events (see 'Cultural significance of textiles: Malay'). Although only produced until the early 20th century, there are plans to instigate a revival of this craft.

Cotton and silk woven fabrics

Men in Kelantan wearing colourful checked cotton sarongs.

Cotton

Cotton woven fabrics were mainly worn by commoners. Attractive patterns were produced by weaving with coloured warp and weft threads. For instance, a beautiful *hujan emas* (golden rain) pattern was created by inserting silk or gold threads between cotton threads. Whether running at width or at length, other pattern designs created included *kain Rawa Bugis* designs, Muar designs, Samarinda designs and Palembang designs. Some traditional styles are preserved even today in plain woven cotton fabrics. A fine cotton plaid fabric, known as *kain pelikat*, imported from India, is commonly worn by men as a sarong and as part of their attire to attend prayers at the mosque.

Silk

Silk materials were first introduced to this region by Chinese merchants. Through past experience of weaving pineapple and wild orchid fibres, Malay weavers used silk to produce exquisite fabrics. Silk weaving was practised in the Malay World from the 13th century. Within the region, in the 14th century, production of silk woven fabrics is recorded in Kediri on a large scale and in other places such as Terengganu. Groups of Bugis people settled in Pahang during the 17th century, and, as a result of their guidance, Pahang became famous for silk products and fine Bugis silk fabrics (*kain Bugis*). The fabrics were exported by Bugis traders to all corners of the Malay Archipelago and became widely used as they were worn by males as daily clothing and were also the customary Bugis wedding gift from a bride to her groom.

Silk was originally woven using the direct weaving technique, using coloured weft threads interlaced with warp. Two different thread colours determined the fabric patterns. Usually Bugis designs had smaller patterns of small, dark squares using colours such as maroon, azure blue, violet, dark green, brown and dark brown. Colours and patterns were adapted to suit the male wearer.

Kain tenun Pahang

The colourful checked plaid patterns of *kain tenun Pahang* are distinctive. It can be silk or cotton and sometimes gold threads are woven in or the tie-and-dye technique (ikat) might be used. Usually it is not decorated with any additional motifs. It is believed to have come to Peninsular Malaysia in the 16th century from either the Riau Archipelago or the Celebes. It is recorded by anthropologist Dr W. Linehan that a Bugis aristocrat called Tuk Tuan (Keraing Aji) introduced a hand-woven fabric, made on the Malay frame loom, to the local people of Pahang. It is often made into sarongs and *samping* (see 'Malay dress').

Women weaving *kain tenun* in 1978 (above) on the flying shuttle loom (*kek siam*) and detail of a checked piece of the fabric (left).

Songket

Cloth of gold

The origin of *kain songket* is uncertain, although Indian and Chinese influences are evident in the materials used. *Songket* is a rich textile, its creation involving the weaving of gold, and sometimes silver, threads into silk or cotton cloth to form decorative motifs. Until the 20th century, *songket* epitomized the social structure of the Malay elite as its use was primarily restricted to royalty or the nobility (see 'Cultural significance of textiles: Malay'). In the past, palaces had resident master weavers and the royal courts controlled the textile trade.

The fabric has variously been known as *kain teluk berantai* (chain of bays cloth), *songket penuh* (full *songket*) in the Peninsula and *jong sarat* (fully laden ocean junk) in Sarawak and Brunei. The word *songket* is derived from the verb *menyungkit* meaning 'to lever up', perhaps because the textile is made using an intricate supplementary weft technique whereby a small bamboo slat (*lidi*) is used to separate threads so that gold threads can be woven in between the longitudinal warp threads of the background cloth. The Bajau and Iranun peoples of Sabah also refer to the addition of cotton threads to cloth as '*songket*'.

The centres for *songket* production in Peninsular Malaysia are the east coast states of Terengganu and Kelantan. Since the 1980s, *kain songket* has been introduced to a wider audience. Apart from being worn by Malay brides and grooms for their *bersanding* (sitting-in-state) ceremony, sometimes *songket* is given as part of the Malay marriage gifts (*hantaran*). It is also purchased by textile collectors, sold to tourists as a handicraft, used for high quality home and lifestyle decor items, and is displayed in museums and some government and commercial buildings as a typically Malaysian cultural work of art.

Antique *songket* from the collection of Tengku Ismail, Terengganu.

A flat needle (*cuban*) is used to weave gold weft threads into the *songket* fabric, thereby creating the intricate motifs.

Today, computer technology is utilized to design the *songket* patterns and motifs which are then woven into the finished product.

Decorative patterns of songket

Generally, Malay weavers still weave traditional decorative patterns, especially in the placement of motifs, at the head, foot and body of the textile (see 'Textiles and embroidery'). Arranged at the head and foot are usually bamboo shoot (*pucuk rebung*) or cock's tail (*lawi ayam*) motifs. Other common plant and animal motifs used include eight-petalled flowers, mangosteens, crocodile claws, butterflies, peacock feathers and shark's teeth. These motifs are arranged in three styles:

1. *Full floral arrangement*
   Motifs are embroidered in gold or silver thread to fill up the head, foot and body of the fabric. They are interlinked, roped or chained together, popularly known as *teluk berantai* (chain loops). The usual motifs are floral in a mesh formation. The background is usually silk or cotton in dark hues of black, dark blue, blood-red or maroon.

2. *Random floral arrangement*
   The random arrangement saves on the usage of gold thread. Motifs are embroidered some distance apart from one another and are not necessarily located parallel to one another. They are often arranged opposite to each other using slightly different weaving techniques.

3. *Patterned arrangement*
   Patterned arrangements are similar to random and full floral arrangements, but individual motifs are not arranged in isolation or tightly clustered together to cover the surface, but fall vertically according to a standing pattern or are laid across as a horizontal pattern.

Malay *songket* traditional outfit.

Examples of songket motifs:

Central star flower fenced in by an eight-pointed star.

Pucuk rebung (bamboo shoot) used on panels.

Tempuk manggis

Butterfly motif usually used as a border design with striped patterns.

Bunga tampuk pedada in the shape of an open corolla with petals. In the centre is a star-shaped flower. It is flanked by a floral pattern.

The frame loom

The availability of silk, after the lifting of restrictions that had previously been imposed by the royal courts (see 'Cultural significance of textiles: Malay') and the later adoption of the frame loom (*kek tenun*), introduced by Europeans (probably from western Europe) in the late 16th century, were significant advances for local weaving traditions. The frame loom differs from the older backstrap loom, which continues to be used in Sabah and Sarawak (see 'Textiles of Sarawak'), as a frame is used to support and maintain the tension of the warp instead of the weaver's body. A modification by local Malay weavers was a fine comb through which the warp threads could be separated and kept evenly spaced. The frame loom allowed greater control of fine silk warp and a better ability to create patterns with the weft threads, thus making it more suitable for silk weaving and particularly for *kain songket*. While *songket* is still woven on the frame loom, some weavers now use the flying shuttle loom (*kek Siam*).

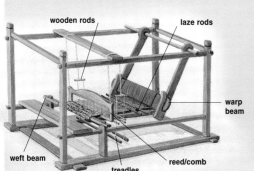

wooden rods

laze rods

warp beam

weft beam

reed/comb

treadles

Weaving songket

1. Hanks of raw silk or cotton yarn are dyed several times to ensure colour evenness and fastness then immersed in boiling water, rinsed with cold water and hung to dry.

2. The threads are separated from the hank before being wound onto a bamboo stem bobbin (*pelting*).

3. Warp threads are gathered from 80 bobbins suspended on a bobbin rack then stretched full length and wound on a warping board (*papan gulung*).

4. Warped threads are inserted through the reed of the batten before fixing them into the loom.

5. The weft thread is contained in the shuttle. During weaving, the weaver will move the treadles with her feet.

6. & 7. *Songket* patterns are made from an extra weft of metallic thread interwoven during the weaving of warp and weft. First, bamboo sticks (*lidi*) are placed within the warp to pick out the patterns, line by line. These can either be brought across three or five warp threads (*tekat tiga* or *tekat lima*). The *lidi* are then removed when the songket is tied and gold thread is sewn in to create the motif using a flat needle (*cuban*).

8. The gold threads are pressed into place by the batten.

Source: Kraftangan Malaysia publication.

Batik craft and industry

The word 'batik' in Malaysia generally describes the process of decorating cloth using the block printing (cap) or hand-drawn (canting) techniques, or a combination of both. The method of dyeing and colouring varies with the use of material of various textures, such as cotton, silk, rayon and organza. It may also be identified by the range of traditional designs and motifs used. Batik has become a symbol of national pride and a form of attire for all races. It is now distinctly Malaysian.

Models parading modern *batik tulis* silk fashions with the essence of traditional styles.

Patterns and motifs

Malaysia's tropical forests, flora, fauna, vegetal and plant life, have inspired designs represented in stylized form on batik fabrics. Marine life and geometric patterns are also part of the repertoire of batik patterns and motifs. In addition, sometimes company logos, association emblems and special commemorative designs are also incorporated.

Popular batik motifs include:
(1) the national flower, *bunga raya* (*Hibiscus rosa-sinensis*); **(2)** *bunga kenanga* (*Canadium odarata*); **(3)** *bunga cempaka* (*Magnoliaceae*); **(4)** *daun keladi* (yam leaf); **(5)** *burung* (bird) and *akar-akar* (creepers); and **(6)** *sirih emas* (golden betel leaves).

Development and forms of batik

The vision and entrepreneurial spirit of Haji Che Su of Kelantan and Haji Ali of Terengganu laid the foundation for the local production of the batik sarong in the 1920s—prior to this, Javanese batik was available in the Peninsula from the early 19th century. These entrepreneurs were also behind the first early local attempts to produce batik-type cloth, creating experimental textile prints without wax with patterns stamped on the cloth using wooden blocks. This was commonly known as *batik pukul* (stamped cloth), but has also been called *kain batik Kedah* due to its popularity in that state. Haji Che Su and his sons later utilized the stencil or silkscreen process to produce batik sarongs with motifs reproduced in the *pekalongan* style of Javanese batik, characterized by large floral bouquets with intricate geometric background patterns, usually consisting of traditional motifs of central Java. The business of making and exporting this form of inexpensive batik known as *batik Jawa* expanded with the formation of their family business SAMASA Batik—silkscreen batik is still made by the family today. Thus began the pioneering of batik-making as a cottage industry in Kelantan. Subsequently, in Terengganu, Haji Ali founded a family business making batik sarongs.

Sarawak Kenyah hand-drawn batik design entitled *Legendary Jar in Jungle*.

By the 1930s, batik makers on the east coast of the Malay Peninsula were already making *batik cap* (or *batik blok*) using wax and metal blocks. Initially, copper blocks were imported from Java. Later, brass and tin ones (recycled from old tin cans) were made locally. Motifs used were still closely akin to the designs of *batik Jawa*—for the central panel of the sarong designs would include floral bouquet and other motifs such as peacocks and ducks. During the Japanese Occupation (1941–45), batik production ceased. After the war, batik design changed to incorporate local themes and motifs.

In the 1950s, there were as many as 60 batik factories in Kelantan with several in Terengganu. Increased government support for the industry came with the establishment of the Rural and Industrial Development Authority (RIDA) in the mid-1950s to provide assistance to small rural cottage industries and then later Majlis Amanah Rakyat (MARA) in the early 1960s. These organizations encouraged the development of new uniquely Malaysian motifs as well as different production techniques. For instance, instead of the traditional two-metre batik sarong,

Timeline of the development of batik:

Pre-1920s

Stamped cloth with wooden blocks and no wax—type of 'imitation batik'.

ABOVE LEFT: Early 20th century stamped sarong. The *kepala* pattern has bamboo shoot and flowers-in-a-basket motifs.

ABOVE RIGHT: Carved wooden stamp from Terengganu.

1920s

Silk-screen process used.

An example of screen-printed batik with floral bouquet.

The silk-screen process uses large frames and a separate gauze screen for each colour to be printed. There are two forms: with and without wax. For the former, the design is created on the screen with wax. Dye is applied penetrating the unwaxed parts of the screen onto the cloth.

1930s

Batik cap (or *batik blok*) using wax and metal blocks was being produced in the east coast states.

ABOVE: Making a metal block. Strips of tin or brass are positioned over the design drawn on paper and then soldered together. A handle is mounted on the block.

LEFT: Although this piece with a floral and duck design was made in the late 1940s, it is typical of motif themes prevalent in the 1930s.

hand-printed batik by the yard was introduced. Later, innovations such as the 'crackle effect' and the discharge method of colouring were used. This style of batik became popular as it could be made into clothing and garments for casual, day and evening wear. It was hand-printed on different types of cloth such as cotton, lawn, voile and silk, and was ideal for use in the tropics.

The process of motivating change and product improvement resulted in the eventual adoption of the technique of hand-drawn batik known as *batik canting* or *batik tulis*, commercially produced from the 1970s. While the *canting* tool (a copper stylus with an attached container filled with melted wax) was used in accordance with the traditional Javanese method, experimentation in Malaysia led to new ways of applying colour (brushing instead of immersing in dye) on different types of cloth (voile, silk, cotton lawn and duck cloth).

The new-look batik

From the 1970s onwards, an explosion in the development of Malaysian batik is seen—the introduction of innovative techniques; the exploration of new expressions in design and the representation of traditional floral motifs, animal and plant life; the reinterpretation of colour application; the adoption of batik shirts as acceptable office and formal wear for men; and new uses for batik such as for furnishings and household items, souvenirs, fashion and art.

Batik designers, including Wan Nong, Ramli Malik, Fatimah Chik and Yusoff Fadzil Idris, played a major role in the revival of the batik industry and the creation of a new-look batik, renewing interest among batik enthusiasts and gaining new patronage from Malaysians, tourists and the export market. Enterprises such as Kutang Kraf, Aran Novabatika, Craftsmen Enterprise, Batik Malaysia Berhad, Sutrasemai, Azalea, Tjanting, Barakoff, Khadani, Jendela Batik, the Batik Guild and others, have contributed significantly over a period of time to the revamping of the batik industry. Research by organizations such as the Malaysian Handicraft Development Corporation and Bumiputra Batik Marketing Corporation as well as design competitions organized by the National Art Gallery (see 'National and state art organizations') have also been instrumental in inspiring creativity.

Batik techniques

Block-printing

Wax is melted in a large wok. The batik printer (*tukang cap*) dips the metal block into the hot wax and shakes off the excess.

The waxed cloth is then dyed by immersing it in a wooden trough, either in one, two, three or four layers of colour according to the design. A roller might be used to dye a large amount of cloth so that colour is applied evenly.

The cloth is laid on a table covered with damp banana trunk fibres (above). The cool fibres assist to solidify the wax when stamping the block on the fabric, making a clearer impression of the design. The block is stamped onto the cloth with a steady hand and meticulous care must be taken when stamping in order to obtain a continuous flow to the pattern (below).

Hand-drawing

The cloth is stretched across a frame to keep it taut. Hot wax is carefully applied to the cloth in fine lines to create the outline of the desired pattern using a copper stylus (*canting*) filled with melted wax.

Coloured dyes are applied to the cloth using a brush which requires care and skill. Background colours are applied first.

Finishing process

The following steps apply to both batik techniques:

FAR LEFT: The cloth is boiled in a large wok-shaped vat (*kuali*) of water to melt and remove the wax. It is then slapped against a smooth concrete slab to remove the last particles of wax.

LEFT: The batik is washed in detergent and hung out to dry completely.

Silk *batik tulis* shirts like this are worn by men as formal wear.

1940s / 1950s–1960s

No batik was produced during the Japanese Occupation (1941–1945). From the 1950s, there was an increase in batik production, the establishment of RIDA and MARA and development of new 'Malaysian' motifs and different techniques.

(1) Malay bamboo shoot (*pucuk rebung*) motif; (2) batik with crackle effect; (3) women buying sarongs at a RIDA mobile shop.

1970s to present

Adoption of batik technique using *canting*. Innovation of types of cloth, techniques, designs and uses. Production on a commercial scale.

aThe trend-setting hand-painted and block-printed designs by Wan Nong in the 1970s became known as 'alpha batik'.

Various batik handicraft items.

Malay embroidery and tekat

The art of gold thread embroidery has long been practised by Malay women. As it was originally a court art, such embroidery was traditionally associated with royal garments and court paraphernalia. In tekat embroidery, gold and silver threads are embroidered on a dark base fabric, usually velvet, and may be embellished with glass beads or sequins. It is now usually crafted for special purposes, such as to adorn the bridal dais and matrimonial bed, or to decorate food covers, pillow ends, bridal hand-held fans, betel sets, shoes and curtains.

Various household, wearable and ceremonial items decorated with *tekat bersuji.*

Malay woman with embroidery frame (c. 1924).

Embroidery craft

For a long time, Malay women have shown expertise in needlework and gold or silver thread embroidery. This traditional form of embroidery is known as *tekat* or *tekatan* and today takes two forms—*tekat bersuji* or *tekat suji timbul* (embossed or filled embroidery) and *tekat gubah* (compositional embroidery). Another variation is *kelingkan* (also variously called *keringkam* or *kelingkam*) using a flat metallic thread made of alloy.

As with *songket* weaving, the creation, composition and usage of the art of embroidery were initially a court art whose gold thread creations were used for customary and traditional occasions and for palace adornment and court regalia (see 'Malay woven cloth' and 'Cultural significance of textiles: Malay'). Then, as now, *tekat* objects were used during Malay wedding ceremonies to beautify the bridal dais and the matrimonial bed. Because of its royal usage, some commentators connected Malay embroidery with the royal embroidery art of Indian and Chinese courts. *Kelingkan* embroidery is thought to have Middle Eastern origins.

During the Melaka sultanate (1400-1511), gold thread embroidery from China greatly influenced local craftspeople in terms of decorative styles, materials and techniques. Even after Melaka's fall to the Portuguese in 1511, centres for the art of *tekat*

flourished in Perak, Johor, Selangor and Pahang in the new courts that were established there. In Perak and Pahang, the art prospered, particularly in areas surrounding the royal households, namely Kuala Kangsar in Perak, Pekan in Pahang, Kota Tinggi as well as Kluang in Johor, and Klang and Kuala Selangor in Selangor.

In the late 19th century, gold paper appliqué work developed among the Malays in southern Johor and the Johor-Riau area (see 'Textile embellishment'). Sarawak Malays were known for metal thread embroidery using thicker gold filaments worked on silk or georgette to make various traditional types of headgear such as scarves, stoles or veils, known as *keringkam* there. This kind of embroidery art also existed in Kelantan; on the Peninsula it was called *kelingkan* or *kelingkam*.

Fine gold thread embroidery was popular in Perak and in Selangor, which retained the technique of *tekat bersuji,* embossed embroidery covering an embedded core. In Sabah, the *kain dastar* of the Bajau-Iranun and the *kain pis* of the Binadan (a Bajau related group), both used for headcloths, sport gold embroidery along their edges. Brunei Malays in Sabah, on the other hand, combine their work with coloured threads.

The art of embroidery, especially *tekat*, eventually spread beyond royal circles and has now diversified from Malay royal and cultural artefacts such as sitting mats, pillow cases, fans, betelnut boxes, wedding equipage and royal garments to include handbags, shoes, food covers (*tudung saji*), wall decorations, all-purpose boxes and tablecloths.

Sarawak keringkam

Selayah keringkam embroidered shawls are culturally important to Sarawak Malays. They are traditionally worn by womenfolk to social gatherings and weddings, and in the past were worn by a bride when she visited her in-laws and served as a symbol of grief when a Malay women died—her shawl was placed atop one end of the coffin to be removed before burial and returned to her closest kin as a memento.

FAR LEFT: Malay woman wearing *selayah keringkam* in the traditional way as a head covering.

LEFT: A craftswoman embroidering a shawl with metal threads.

Designs and motifs

Malay embroidery favours plant and floral motifs and, to a lesser extent, bird elements (such as wings and feathers) in geometric form, and also Arabic calligraphy. Plant motifs include ferns, leaves of the bitter gourd, *taro* and *padi* (rice) and bamboo shoots. Floral shapes consist of cloves, hibiscus, sunflowers, orchids, chrysanthemum, cinnamon and herb flowers and climbing plants such as the *Telosma cordata* (Chinese violet), buds and flowers of the

Tekat embroidery

Tekat bersuji

The *tekat bersuji* decorative style is essentially needlework in relief, raised from the surface of the fabric, with gold or silver threads sewn over a template and anchored to the base cloth by silk threads. Plush velvet fabric in shades such as dark red, royal blue, dark green, purple, crimson and black, is usually chosen for this embroidery. From the front, none of the couching stitches are visible, and the gold thread looks as if it is sewn through the fabric. The beautiful luxurious finished embroidery has the appearance of shimmering gold precisely and dramatically outlined on a contrasting background.

In the past, the template (*empulur*) which forms the core of the design was sometimes made of *sega* rattan whittled according to the pattern required. Rattan was also used to reinforce or strengthen delicate work, for example, to wind round the edges of food covers as well as the surfaces of ornamental *suari* (marriage pillows), or *seraga* (elongated, round or square pillows with decorative end-plates). Thick paper or card is often now used as the core for very delicate work.

Embroidery process

Fabric (usually dark velvet) is tacked onto a white backing cloth of cotton or chintz which is tightly fastened on a wooden frame (*pemidang*).

The design template is usually made from thick white paper which acts as a core, a filling for the embroidery. The motif is drawn on the paper which is then cut and attached to the fabric (**1**).

Gold thread is wound around a *cuban*, a small bamboo or wooden cross and then sewn close together back and forth from right to left across the core until it is hidden (**2**). It is then fastened firmly underneath to the fabric by a separate thread stitched at the side to complete the embroidery (**3**).

Tekat gubah

Malays and Straits Chinese still actively create *tekat gubah*. This form of embroidery uses metal filaments (*kerikam*) of gold or silver thread, or other coloured threads, to create designs on cloth. Two or three strips of filament are couched onto the cloth of choice (usually velvet or silk) with red thread creating a contrasting pattern. Often, spangles, sequins or other embellishments are added to the design. Sometimes, this type of embroidery will be combined with *tekat bersuji* raised embroidery.

ABOVE: Floral motif early 20th century octagonal bolster end from Kuala Kangsar decorated with *tekat bersuji* on maroon velvet with a lace border (Henry Bong Permanent Collection).

LEFT: Combined *tekat gubah* and *tekat bersuji* Islamic inspired geometric design decorated with beads and baubles.

bitter gourd, as well as the fruit and flower of the pomegranate. Common geometric shapes include triangular bamboo shoots, squares, checks and plaids, lattice patterns or geometric shapes, such as the swastika, 'S' and double 'S' shapes and curves. Different motifs are combined harmoniously, for example, geometric or triangular patterns with foliage, plant or bird motifs, in different types of arrangement—single, sprawling or intertwining formations—usually depending on the purpose of the item being embroidered.

Although *tekat* embroidery lacks variegated colours, it remains outstanding in its use of graceful natural motifs. The sumptuous effect of gold thread against a dark-coloured (the most popular colours being maroon (*kesumba*), indigo blue (*biru nila*) or dark green) luxurious base embodies the rich aesthetic heritage of the Malay community.

Sultan Abdullah Muhammad Shah II (1874–1876) of Perak.

Perak royal tekat

In Perak, the art of *tekat* was originally the monopoly of denizens of the royal households and palaces. The Raja Permaisuri Perak Tua Uteh Mariah, consort of Sultan Idris Murshid al-Azzam Shah (1887–1916), was a renowned designer and artist who produced many beautiful *tekat* works including an angled throne mat, prayer mats, a five-sided mat, bolsters and cushions, ornamental cube-shaped marriage pillows, kris sheath holders, decorative or ornamental boxes and other royal paraphernalia such as the *cior*, a special three-layered mat or divan embellished with gold and silver embroidery, meant for the sultan. The sumptuous embroidered attire of the preceding Sultan Abdullah Muhammad Shah II (1874–76), adorned with gold thread embroidery in fern and dagger motifs, was also the creation of the Raja Permaisuri. The royal town of Kuala Kangsar is still known for *tekat bersuji* and is a recognized centre for this craft in Malaysia.

RIGHT: Gifts, including *tekat* mats and pillows, embroidered by the Raja Permaisuri and given by the Sultan of Perak to the Prince and Princess of Wales in 1901.

ABOVE: Prayer mat embroidered with gold thread, spangles and blue beads over red velvet and pink chiffon from Kuala Kangsar (Muzium Negara Collection).

This *tekat* wedding valance with beadwork trim from Kuala Kangsar shows classical Malay design elements (Henry Bong Permanent Collection).

Textile embellishment

Traditionally, woven fabrics were often embellished. Cloth was polished using cowrie seashells to produce a lustre (kain gerus) or gilded with gold leaf or foil (kain telepuk). Rainbow cloth (kain pelangi) was tie-dyed using the dye resistant technique or other types of decoration were applied, including gems, mirrors, beads, sequins and appliqué work. However, until the early 20th century, gilt decoration was solely within the province of royalty and the aristocracy.

Headcloth from the Kedah State Museum collection decorated with *telepuk*—short lines around the edge of the cloth and an organic motif in the centre.

The art of telepuk (gilding)

Eight-petalled floral stamp, carved in Terengganu.

Wooden block stamps carved in Pahang and Terengganu from the National Museum.

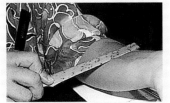

Gum arabic is boiled in water to dilute it then brushed on the underside of the arm with a wooden or bamboo spatula.

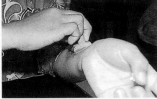

A carved wooden stamp with the required design is coated in the gum.

The stamp is applied to the fabric. A steady hand is required to ensure a smooth impression is made.

ABOVE: While the glue is still wet, gold dust is placed over the sticky cloth.

LEFT: The design is complete.

Telepuk (gilded cloth)

Kain telepuk (known as *kain perada* in Java and Bali) is woven cloth that is decorated with stamped gold leaf or foil, usually in a floral design. Technically, *telepuk* can be defined as a printed cloth. The base fabric is usually a dark coloured cloth which may have subtle designs or small checks like *kain Bugis* (see 'Malay woven cloth'). It is usually waxed and polished (*gerus*) first. From the 15th century, gold foil or gold dust was used.

A similar type of printed woven cotton textile from India known as *telepuk serasah* is said to have been introduced during the Melaka sultanate (1400–1511). The widespread use of *telepuk* decoration throughout the Malay textile region is included in classical Malay literary texts such as the *Hikayat Hang Tuah* and *Misa Melayu* which mention cloth sprinkled with golden droplets as background, cloth and waistcoats used by pilgrims sprinkled with golden droplets using the design of floating tinsel and decorative parasols stamped with glittering clinquant.

Historical references to '*telepuk*' could be construed as referring to any method of covering cloth with surface ornaments, including adornment with gold stamp as well as the sprinkling of gold powder or foil. Today, however, a differentiation is often made between various types of cloth that used golden hues with thread or tinsel in the form of *songket* (see 'Malay woven cloth'), waxed cloth and printed, floral-motif *telepuk* cloth.

An integral part of the process of designing *telepuk* is the use of printing blocks and flower matrices to achieve the desired patterns. A number of common floral motifs are carved onto the wooden printing blocks. Adhesive is spread on the surface of the block before it is stamped onto the cloth after which powdered gold or gold foil is applied to achieve the design.

Traditional *telepuk* designs consisted of mainly floral decorative motifs such as lotus, small hyacinths, water lilies, as well as leaf-type motifs. Some motifs were arranged in a particular way, for instance, bamboo shoots always adorned the cloth edges at both the head and base; lotuses in eight sections were either arranged in a dispersed mode or in a fully assembled mode very similar to *teluk berantai* (chain of bays motif); tendril or foliage motifs were

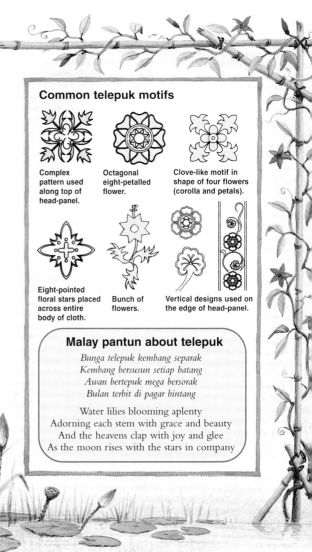

Common telepuk motifs

Complex pattern used along top of head-panel.

Octagonal eight-petalled flower.

Clove-like motif in shape of four flowers (corolla and petals).

Eight-pointed floral stars placed across entire body of cloth.

Bunch of flowers.

Vertical designs used on the edge of head-panel.

Malay pantun about telepuk

Bunga telepuk kembang separak
Kembang bersusun setiap batang
Awan bertepuk mega bersorak
Bulan terbit di pagar bintang

Water lilies blooming aplenty
Adorning each stem with grace and beauty
And the heavens clap with joy and glee
As the moon rises with the stars in company

printed either 'crowned' (coiled) or spreading like creepers across the base of the cloth or across the full width (lengthwise). Some textiles have incorporated calligraphic motifs with the Arabic script 'Bismillah' (In the Name of Allah), 'Allah' and 'Prophet Muhammad' inscribed in gold. The epic poem *Syair Siti Zubaidah* also recites how the *selawat*, the prayer for peace and prosperity to Prophet Muhammad, was 'written in gold tinsel'.

Kain gerus (polished cloth)

Kain gerus is fabric which was starched or waxed, to smooth it, and then burnished and polished (also called calendering) using wood or the glossy shells of molluscs (usually cowrie seashells) to produce a lustrous shiny effect. This polishing technique was usually applied to silk fabrics, but sometimes was also used on cotton fabrics. The polished cloth might also be gilded with gold foil using the *telepuk* method.

In the old days, particularly in Terengganu, Johor, Selangor and Pahang, the *gerus* polishing technique was sometimes used to rejuvenate royal *songket* clothing which had been washed, especially prior to important ceremonial occasions.

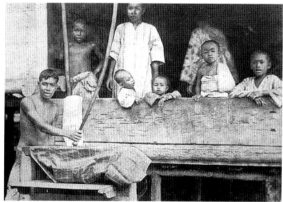

Malay man in Pahang polishing (calendering) cloth by pushing a cowrie shell which is attached to a flexible bamboo pole. The cloth was first starched then laid on a piece of smooth wood. Only narrow areas of cloth could be polished with each stroke of the shell.

Kain pelangi (rainbow cloth)

Kain pelangi held a very special place in Malay culture. It was worn by palace dignitaries and used in various ways—as fabric to complete one's attire, as a head covering, as a sash tied around the waist or as a wall decoration in royal bedchambers. Many of the costumes mentioned in classical Malay literature included *pelangi*, particularly as a headcloth, and emphasized its importance, the textile being variously described, including as 'magical' and 'princely'. The best known *pelangi* maker was a lady also called Minah Pelangi who lived in Terengganu during the reign of Sultan Zainal Abidin II (1793–1808).

Pelangi fabric was sometimes called *sutera perai* (dispersed silk) because of its fine texture. The technique for making it originated in Gujarat, India, especially in the provinces of Rajasthan and the Punjab, reputed for such textiles, where the cloth was known as *odhini* and *bandhini*.

Kain pelangi was created using the tie-and-dye technique on woven cloth, usually cotton or silk, rather than on unwoven threads, differentiating it from ikat textiles. The cloth was tied into knots then dipped in a dye solution. The dye would not penetrate the knotted areas thus creating patterns and the rainbow colours, from which the fabric obtained its name—the number of knots and dye baths determining the variety of colours and design. Sometimes the cloth was stitched loosely to produce dotted patterns across it. To the extent that the dye-resist technique is applied, this textile is similar to others such as *limar* (see 'Malay woven cloth') and batik cloth (see 'Batik craft and industry').

Other forms of embellishment

Sequins, beads and mirrors, imported from China, India and the Middle East, have long been forms of ornamental decoration for Malay textiles. These items were usually stitched onto the clothing, trousers or shawls of important people.

This is verified by classical Malay literary works. For example, textile ornamentation with mirrors is referred to in the *Hikayat Sri Rama*, where the hero Sri Rama is described as wearing trousers of velvet embellished with hundreds of mirrors around his waist, thousands along his legs and mirrors scattered all over his body. Beautiful sequinned clothes are referred to in the *Hikayat Hang Tuah*. In the Malay Annals (*Sejarah Melayu*), the Sultan of Melaka is recorded as rewarding Datuk Permadewan with a costume of trousers with gold, pearls and red gems hanging. Here, 'pearls' means the shine and glow from the ornaments themselves, which could have been sequins, beads or mirrors.

The use of sequins and beads on Malay textiles developed further with their addition to gold thread embroidery, such as shawls, pillows, fans and shoes ('see Malay embroidery and tekat'), and to the decorative costumes of performing arts such as Mak Yong and *gamelan*, for example, head gear, *gendek* (royal tiara) and chest covers. Contemporary fashion designers use beads, sequins, coloured mirrors, embroidery and lace to decorate Malay wedding costumes or high fashion *baju kebaya* and other outfits (see 'Malay dress').

In the late 19th century, a craft developed involving gold paper appliqué work (*tempelan bunga emas*) among several generations of Malays in southern Johor and the Johor-Riau area. It may have been inspired by Indian and Chinese work, although the motifs and designs are Malay. The technique was commonly used to decorate food covers (*tudung saji*). This kind of work on velvet or silk later became a craft feature of Kelantan and Terengganu.

Pelangi textile with pink, orange, white, yellow and red floral, bamboo shoot and other motifs on a deep purple background (Muzium Seni Asia collection).

Tray or dish covers (*tudung saji*) embellished with cut out gold paper stitched with gold thread onto silk, traditionally used on ceremonial occasions such as weddings or by royalty, particularly in Terengganu.

Straits Chinese embroidery and beadwork

The Straits Chinese heritage is reflected in a wide range of traditions and crafts, such as the contribution of Chinese embroidery and Malay costume embodied in the elegant Nonya kebaya, *traditionally worn by their women and now a fashionable form of attire for all Malaysian women. They were skilled at silk and metal thread embroidery and beadwork and, consistent with other heritage items, their motifs had predominantly Chinese and European influences.*

Beautiful embroidered Nonya *kebaya* tops (here the long *panjang* and typical short type) teamed with striking batik sarongs have stood the test of time and are still popular attire today, even among non-Straits Chinese.

Ancestral skills

Although they usually have Chinese names and speak a mixture of Chinese and Malay, the Straits Chinese or Peranakan, as they are also known, had their own customs and traditions assimilated from their Chinese and Malay ancestry. Among these were skills in embroidery and beadwork. Straits Chinese embroidery is older than their beadwork, as the latter only gained popularity during the colonial period when European beads were imported.

Needlework

As needlework using silk and metallic threads was costly, it represented the accomplishments of well-to-do Nonya women. They were taught the art of sewing and embroidery at an early age (usually from eight years) as talent for this craft was an eminent qualification for marriage apart, of course, from the traditional desired skills in cooking and housekeeping. Exquisitely handmade embroideries formed part of the marriage trousseau. While large embroideries were purchased from abroad, typical trousseau items included small personal articles such as costume accessories and intimate bridal chamber decorations.

Generally, embroidery by Peranakan in Penang tended to be more Chinese-oriented, preferring silk threads, while the work produced in Melaka showed strong Minangkabau influences, such as the use of couched metallic threads, known as *tekat gubah* in Malay (see 'Malay embroidery and tekat'). The most common embroidery technique involved two main types of stitches: satin stitch for a smooth surface in a single colour, and the contrasting Peking knot or Peking stitch to give texture. The cloth was usually fine cotton, silk or voile.

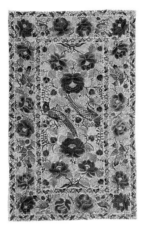

ABOVE: Nonya wedding panel (one of a pair) embroidered in satin stitch, Penang, late 19th century (Henry Bong Permanent Collection).

RIGHT: Embroidered ritual handkerchief of a Nonya bride (courtesy of the National Museum of Singapore, National Heritage Board).

18th century Melaka wedding shoe wraps with *tekat* gold thread embroidery and floral, fish and butterfly motifs.

Nonya kebaya

Nonya (Straits Chinese women) were traditionally easily identified by their embroidered *kebaya*, a version of the Malay *baju kebaya* (see 'Malay dress'). The *kebaya* design was developed by the Straits Chinese of Medan, Indonesia. Subsequently, Penang became the centre for the manufacture of this Nonya garment. The Nonya *kebaya* is a long-sleeved blouse fastened down the front with a set of three brooches called *kerongsang* and worn with a Malay batik sarong in cotton or silk.

Traditionally, the *kebaya* is made of imported Swiss voile, typically of the Robia brand, and is embroidered along the edge of the collar, down the front lapels, along the bottom hem and the sleeve-hem. The embroidery is mostly concentrated in broad areas on the lower front tapering corners of the blouse. A feature that is characteristic of *kebaya* embroidery is the lace-like cut-out work which is created by sewing a running stitch twice over to define the lace pattern; then a buttonhole stitch is sewn by hand to further reinforce the edges. The 'eyes', or holes, are then carefully cut out, leaving behind the intricate lace work. Cut-out embroidery is very time-consuming and thus more expensive than simple relief embroidery.

Motifs are usually highly stylized, and flowers such as orchids, roses and chrysanthemums are common. These are laid out among swirling tendrils and leaves. The design is first traced with pencil and carbon paper onto the fabric which is then stretched onto a wooden frame. The elaborate embroidery was traditionally done entirely by hand, but the speed of the process improved after the introduction of the sewing machine in the 1930s.

The Nyonya Kebaya, written by the late Datin Paduka Seri Endon Mahmood, wife of the Prime Minister, and published in 2002, showcased her personal collection of *kebaya* and drew local and international attention to this alluring and beautiful attire.

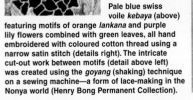

Pale blue swiss voile *kebaya* (above) featuring motifs of orange *lankana* and purple lily flowers combined with green leaves, all hand embroidered with coloured cotton thread using a narrow satin stitch (details right). The intricate cut-out work between motifs (detail above left) was created using the *goyang* (shaking) technique on a sewing machine—a form of lace-making in the Nonya world (Henry Bong Permanent Collection).

When silver appliqué was used, which was applied with stitching holes around the edge, velvet was the preferred cloth as it made a firmer base than silk. All of these expensive metallic decorations were seldom discarded even when the item had worn out, when they would be removed and recycled.

Beadwork

The earliest beadwork was stitched with silk threads on Chinese silk, also used for embroidery. Later, long-piled furry velvet was used as the base material. Subsequently, when metallic threads became scarce, beads were embroidered upon short-piled velvet on which the beads stood out better.

Originally, the beads used were of European manufacture, mainly from eastern Europe in the style of Venetian glass. Unlike the beadwork of many other cultures, traditional Nonya beadwork used glass beads ranging from 0.5 to less than 1 millimetre in diameter. These microbeads were threaded with waxed silk threads because no needle could pass through them. The types of beads varied—they could be translucent, opaque, faceted or even oxidized to a sheen. Victorian England excelled in beadwork; fashions travelled to other places, albeit with a time lag in styles. Unsurprisingly then, together with Venetian and Bohemian styles, Victoriana found its way into Nonya beadwork together with significant neo-Rococo and Art Deco flavours.

Foreign beads which were traded in Southeast Asia by West Asian, Indian and Chinese travellers in the earlier periods were generally large. These beads are sometimes referred to as 'trade wind' beads because the traders sailed according to the winds. With mechanization, tiny beads known as 'seed beads' became available. These small, hard perforated objects played an important role in world trade and have been the medium of transfer of art styles to faraway places. The Nonya used to purchase glass or metal beads from itinerant neighbourhood vendors who spooned out loose beads or offered them as threaded bunches. However, only plastic ones are now available unless old glass ones are recycled.

A major Peranakan beadwork item is beaded slippers (*kasut manik*). However, the highly intricate art of Nonya beadwork was not confined to slippers; other items such as handbags and belts, tapestries and bedspreads displayed a wider and more elaborate use of their skills. Baba (Straits Chinese men) had absolutely nothing to do with the manufacture of beaded objects.

Part of a long freize of faceted beadwork used to embellish the side of a Peranakan wedding mattress. French rocaille beads have been used. The colours and decorative stylized bird and peony motifs of this Penang piece are typical of local Nonya work (Henry Bong Permanent Collection).

Working with beads

Beaded slippers.

Beadwork methods
The Nonya employed three methods of beading: stringing, threading and stitching, the last being the mostly widely used. Beads were strung mainly for tassels and fringes. Threading beads was the most difficult, especially when executed without a supporting frame; considerable care was required in handling the beads, which ran along the threads unless knotted down. Almost like making lace, multiple threads were used simultaneously to form patterns and under an unskilled hand, the threads could entangle.

Beadwork was produced on frames that varied from simple wooden contraptions to elaborately lacquered devices, usually accompanied by a stand with drawers. For stitching, the backing material ranged from velvet to fine canvas, gauze and netting. Generally, all the beads were stitched down in the same direction so as to give a smooth surface. An even tension was needed, as beads may pucker if not anchored down properly.

珠子鞋

BEADED SHOES

Old poster outside a shop advertising beaded slippers.

Beaded shoes
Beaded shoes in slipper form (*kasut manik*) were worn by Nonya as part of their regular dress, whereas Baba only wore beaded shoes around the house. The number and exclusiveness of beaded slippers owned was one indication of a Nonya's wealth as mistress of the family. At one time, it was also the custom to present a pair of *manik* slippers to a marriage matchmaker. These slippers are no longer part of daily wear as they are too precious and fragile. However, they may be worn for special occasions and many women still embroider and collect them.

Beaded slippers crafted these days tend to be of a lower quality compared to those made by previous generations of Straits Chinese women—the beads tend to be larger, and thus the process of affixing them less demanding. Also, generally, velvet serves as a base and only the motif (instead of the entire slipper front) is covered with beads. Modern mass-produced slippers imported from Hong Kong also often reflect cruder techniques such as the combining of beads with sequins.

Common motifs still seen on beaded slippers include flowers, checks, diagonal patterns as well as images of small animals, of which squirrels, birds, ducks and rabbits are favourites. Sometimes other motifs may be encountered, reflecting the idiosyncrasies of individual designers. Older examples reflect the popularity of garden scenes which incorporate floral patterns and birds.

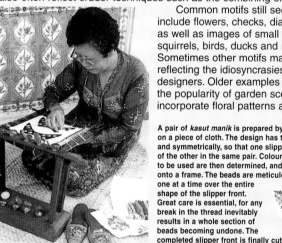

A pair of *kasut manik* is prepared by first drawing a design on a piece of cloth. The design has to be copied accurately and symmetrically, so that one slipper is a mirror image of the other in the same pair. Colours of the beads to be used are then determined, and the cloth fixed onto a frame. The beads are meticulously sewn one at a time over the entire shape of the slipper front. Great care is essential, for any break in the thread inevitably results in a whole section of beads becoming undone. The completed slipper front is finally cut out and affixed to the slipper base.

A Nonya did not adorn herself with beadwork as jewellery in the way women (and men) of many other cultures do. Beads were not used for rituals, bead types were not status symbols and beads were not believed to be imbued with magical powers. Nor did a Nonya's beads carry any status, sacred or otherwise, as in the sense of rosary beads. Indeed, beads had no ritualistic connotations whatsoever to the Straits Chinese.

While earlier embroidery techniques in silk or metallic threads feature Chinese motifs, bead embroidery which became popular later due to Western influence, tended to feature Western motifs. The mandarin duck motifs of traditional China, for example, were replaced by a pair of European bluebirds, while the crane gave way to the swan.

Small beaded or embroidered wedding purses were traditionally given to the bridal couple with a token sum of money.

Textiles of Sabah

Unlike other locations in the region, neither Hindu or Islamic cultures left a mark on the traditional material culture of Sabah, except for that of the coastal peoples. The production of indigenous textiles remained largely intact, although it is now a declining art. From intricate linangkit *panels to handwoven* dastar *headcloths and embroidered* kain pis, *the indigenous woven crafts of Sabah are worthy of admiration, and should be preserved.*

Kain dastar folded as a headcloth and examples of motif designs, the horse and rider common to the Bajau people and a stylized geometric pattern.

Woman weaving with a backstrap loom, on which traditional cloth is usually woven. The size of the woven cloth corresponds to the width of the loom and the length of the warp threads, so it is not generally very large. However, today, some weavers now use the frame loom to produce *kain dastar* to make its production more commercially viable.

Above: Colourful Bajau sash and pouches with the favoured horse and geometric motifs made using the supplementary weave technique (Henry Bong Permanent Collection).

Below: The Rungus costume worn for the *mongigol* dance features traditional *kain mogah* cloth.

Woven cloths

The intricate warp ikat technique used by many indigenous peoples in other parts of Borneo is curiously absent in Sabah. Traces of this tie-dye technique, in its primitive form, can be perceived in the handwoven textiles produced by the Rungus of the Kudat District. Rungus women are prolific weavers of handwoven cloth for *tapi* (skirt) or *banat* (bodice) made on the backstrap loom. They grow and process cotton to produce the threads for the textiles which they then dye, using locally grown indigo for their deep blue cloth interwoven with undyed threads. They also use commercially produced imported cotton threads to make cloth, not only for domestic needs but also for new markets created by the tourism industry.

A coarse cloth made from wild banana (*musa textilis*) fibre is becoming obsolete among the Dusun Tindal of Kota Belud. The cloth, dyed deep indigo blue, is made into the knee-length skirt (*gonob*) and the women's headwear (*sunduk*) which are then finely embroidered at the hem and edges (see 'Costumes and ornaments of Sabah'). The ensemble, comprised of heirloom pieces, is an integral part of a traditional Dusun Tindal female wedding costume, which includes a flared-sleeved jacket that is also worn as a ceremonial costume by the neighbouring Bajau and Iranun people. Elaborate additions of silver, cloth and bead accessories complete the attire.

The Kadazandusun of Kiulu, Tuaran District, also weave a coarse cloth processed from plant leaf fibres called *lamba* (*Curculigo latifolia*) to produce their headwear, called *sunduk*. This cloth has become rare as the few ageing weavers have stopped production altogether.

Originally woven from plant fibres and homespun cotton, the Iranun and Bajau of Kota Belud subsequently used imported threads called *gantian* which were home-treated to produce the well-known handwoven headcloths, variously called *dastar*, *tubao*, *tanjak*, *podong* and *sigal*, depending on the dialect and group, which are worn by almost all the indigenous people in Sabah who require a headdress for their costume. The way it is worn and tied on the head varies from one district to another. The Iranun traditionally produce two types of this metre-square of cloth, one using weft threads to create the common elaborately patterned piece on black warp threads called *tubao* (Iranun), and the other, a usually brighter and predominantly red piece using the more complex and difficult tapestry weave technique to create a more expensive cloth called *siambitan*. Folded and tied, it is worn on the head or as a waistband or shoulder scarf.

The *siambitan* is an integral part of the Dusun Tindal wedding attire, with pieces of the cloth folded diagonally over the chest and shoulders of the bride and groom (see 'Costumes and ornaments of Sabah'). The traditional motifs of *kain dastar* are mainly nature and geometry-based, but with a variety of colour combinations and styles. Given their tradition as horsemen, Bajau people often incorporate horse riders into their designs. Other motifs include tropical flowers, leaves and shoots (especially melon and cotton shoots), and common objects found in the environment around them.

Among the Iranun people, weaving is still a respected skill, with a number of women contributing to household income from the proceeds of the sale of their cloth. For this purpose, pedal-looms or frame looms (see 'Malay woven cloth') have been introduced to speed up and increase production. However, many types of cloth are still woven on the backstrap loom (see 'Textiles of Sarawak') to make traditional costume items. The Iranun have a rich glossary of distinctive traditional motifs derived from plants and animals which they weave into their textiles.

Iranun and Bajau woman also produce *kain mogah*, a long piece of black cloth made of cotton and patterned with striped bands of red or orange with small square and rectangular-shaped motifs. It is woven using the supplementary weft technique. This cloth is worn by Rungus male performers for the *mongigol* dance, by Lotud men and women as a long sarong for the dance performed during the *mangahau* (ceremony to appease the spirit of the jars) and as a trimming for a Bajau bridegroom's costume.

Embroidered cloths

Fine embroidery, often under-stated and unobtrusive, is a distinctive characteristic of the traditional embellishments on both handwoven and commercial cloth used for the traditional costumes of many Kadazandusun groups. The bright *kain pis* made by the Binadan and used for headcloths is rich in both colours and symbolism.

Heavily embroidered Lotud woman's jacket (*sukub kopio*).

Kain pis

The Binadan of the Kudat District, a Bajau kindred group, produce the *kain pis* which combines traditions of Chinese origin. This headcloth textile consists of two-facing metre-square pieces of contrasting coloured cloths embroidered with stylized motifs to produce a distinctive mirror effect for reversible use.

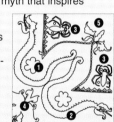
The *kain pis* headcloth, generally identified with the Rungus, is used as an integral part of their daily as well as ceremonial attire.

The two pieces of fabric, usually imported Chinese cotton, of black and red, black and orange, orange and red, or orange and yellow, were stretched taut on a square frame and extensively embroidered using an ancient Chinese technique, handed down from generation to generation. First, the desired pattern was drawn on paper with perforated holes which was placed on the fabric. A fine grey powder (crushed incinerated shell) was sprinkled onto it to create the outline of the design on the fabric. The design was created from the outside edges to the centre to ensure balance. Today, the pattern may be drawn with carbon paper or with a pencil by hand. The embroidery follows the pattern and is sewn so that the pattern appears on both sides of the cloth. Usually at least seven bright and colourful cotton threads are used, sewn in a dense satin stitch.

The motifs of *kain pis* traditionally represent the worldview, lifestyle and legends of the people who make it. Often, multi-coloured floral (**1**) and foliage patterns are intertwined with the mythical *kaliagah* water creature (**2**) (a fierce dragon-like creature from myth that inspires beauty) or spider (**3**) (according to legend, a spider assisted Prophet Muhammad to escape his enemies by spinning a web to hide him in a cave), bird (**4**) (the Agira, a double-headed bird, the foreteller of good or bad news, guards the corner of the *kain pis*), fish, seahorse and butterfly motifs (**5**) and other stylized animal forms.

Linangkit panels

Linangkit (sometimes called 'tapestry weave' in English) is a generic term used to describe a needle-worked panel of dense fabric that joins and decorates the seams of a number of the indigenous costumes of Sabah. The technique uses a needle and thread to create a system of tiny knots and demands patience, as it can take months to produce a piece, and good eyesight, as no loom is used. It is similar to the European technique of tatting. *Linangkit* is a unique feature of Sabah textiles, and appears to have originated from the southern Philippines where it has since become obsolete. Several western and northern coastal peoples of Sabah—the Kadazandusun, Iranun, Bajau, Lotud and Rungus—still use the *linangkit* technique to decorate their costumes (see 'Costumes and ornaments of Sabah').

Each group has its own collection of *linangkit* patterns and can be identified by the motifs and colours they use. Distinctive geometric patterns in predominantly bright orange and red colours are associated with the Lotud who use them as trimmings for their tube skirts, men's jackets and trousers. Panels are durable, usually outlasting the rest of the costume, and are sometimes recycled for the next one.

An array of Lotud *linangkit* on the *gonob* (sarong or short skirt) and the *kuluwu* (circular sash worn over one shoulder and around the body like a bandolier).

The Rungus also produce very fine, longer but narrower panels of *linangkit*, which they call *rinangkit* or *rangkit*, running the length of their tube-skirt, with smaller panels joining the seams of bodices, and larger panels for the back of men's trousers. Their geometric motifs are usually separated in boxes or compartments and are taken from nature and daily life—butterflies, pythons, leaves, stars, shells, stairs, the pattern of dog feet and the diagonal *pinakol* motif symbolizing the ceremonial chest sash worn by men. The Bajau and Iranun are less prolific in their production, but the few that do produce it create wide panels that intersect at the front of ceremonial skirts worn by women. The Bajau favour motifs representing the natural world and new life—stylized cotton flowers and bamboo shoots.

Interdependence—a means of survival

Mass-produced fabrics now provide the components of many indigenous costumes and are widely substituted for handwoven cloth. However, cloth production, especially of headcloths, is a symbiotic effort between the different ethnic groups as users do not always come from the community of the producers. This interdependence assures continued production and supplies, as long as these traditional textiles are still desired and used.

This Rungus woman is tying knots to produce a patterned segment of *linangkit/rinangkit* on a *sukolob* (sarong tube) using traditional motifs.

Linangkit on the sleeves of the traditional costume of these Dusun Tindal women. Men also wear jackets of similar design and use *linangkit*.

Textiles of Sarawak

The earliest cloth used in Sarawak was made of tree bark and formed the clothing of most of the state's indigenous groups. The subsequent introduction of the backstrap loom and cotton yarn, probably originating from India, led to the establishment of a continuing weaving tradition and the creation of woven textiles for clothing as well as ceremonial and ritual purposes. The most famous textile is the tie-dyed pua kumbu *of the Iban, whose weavers also produce a form of brocaded cloth and a striking supplementary weft textile called* sungkit.

Traditionally, for *pua kumbu*, prior to dyeing, raw yarn was treated with mordant for three days in a wooden trough (left). First, the ingredients for the mordant bath were measured (above) and mixed carefully during a special ceremony officiated by a qualified dye mistress.

ABOVE: Mid 20th century Iban *kain kebat* skirt woven in the supplementary weave technique with cotton and metallic thread. Also known as *kain kerab*.

RIGHT: The sacred *lebor api* (blazing fire) Iban *sungkit* cloth, was used to receive smoked trophy heads from warriors during former headhunting days. This picture shows a close up of the border detail (left) and the moving snake motif (right).

Weaving

Iban women are Sarawak's finest weavers, specializing in creating masterpieces on the backstrap loom. The most distinctive Iban textile, generally known in Malay as ikat (tied), is made by a technique which involves the tying and dyeing of the pattern into the warp thread prior to weaving; in Iban this is called *kebat* (tied). The spiritually powerful *pua kumbu* is of this type.

Weaving is a highly respected skill among the Iban; an expert weaver is entitled to a special 'praise name', such as 'She Who Knows how to Measure [the dyestuffs]' or 'She Who Knows how to Tie Patterns from her Own Mind', and occasionally had a mark tattooed on her hand. Her status approximated that of a male war leader, a successful headhunter. Not only was she able to tie and weave the intricate and powerful patterns which require strength of soul, but she could preside over the operation of preparing the mordant and dye baths for the valuable home-spun thread, and over the offerings presented to the female deities for protection, for which she was paid special fees.

After a beginner has learnt the technique of weaving on a backstrap loom—manipulation of heddles, shuttle and beater, regulation of weft tension to obtain a straight selvedge—she starts with simple pieces of cloth for everyday clothing. As she gains expertise, she is initiated into the secrets of tying patterns and attempts her first *pua kumbu*, a larger piece destined for decorative and ritual use during important festivals. As she gains confidence as a weaver, she begins to create potent patterns such as human figures, with permission from tutelage deities granted to her in a dream, with a possible penalty of madness for attempting a design beyond her power. Mastery is not usually reached until middle age. Every finished *pua kumbu* will bestow on her spiritual enhancement and improved status within the community.

Plain or ikat-patterned pieces are wrought in tabby weave, though it is possible to produce floating weft decorations with the simple backstrap loom. Instead of the pedal heddles of the cottage loom or frame loom (see 'Malay woven cloth'), the selected threads are tied to heddle rods which lie on top of the warp. The weaver lifts them up in the correct sequence to get the desired pattern.

Sarawak's Iban weavers produce a brocade cloth with silver and gold threads called *anyam*, similar to *songket* (see 'Malay woven cloth'). They also use the supplementary weft technique for a picturesque effect in the creation of a brightly coloured cloth which they call, somewhat confusingly, *sungkit*. Iban weavers make this by working threads in contrasting hues around the warp after each shot of the shuttle, using a hairpin or porcupine quill to manipulate the threads into intricate designs. The Iban still use the backstrap loom, although technically it would be possible to weave the traditional Borneo textiles on the frame loom. Handwoven cloth continues to be produced for ceremonial costumes, and for sale. However, everyday clothing is made from mass-produced fabrics.

Pua kumbu

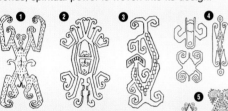

Pua kumbu is the most important of Iban textiles. It is one of their treasured heirlooms as are their brass gongs and hornbill carvings shown here.

Sacred and spiritual

In Iban, the word *pua* means 'blanket' and *kumbu* 'to wrap'. Together the words mean 'grand blanket', but the textile was not used as such. In some communities, it is still used today as a ritual cloth for sacred ceremonies and as a necessary adjunct to rites of passage and healing rituals—a newborn baby is wrapped in it for the ceremony of its first bath, offerings to the gods are placed on it, a corpse laid out in the longhouse before burial is covered with it, the shoulders of the sick are draped with it and shamans and others dealing with the supernatural use it to ward off evil. In the old days, womenfolk welcomed a successful war party by receiving the newly-obtained head trophies on their best *pua kumbu* and a girl had to weave at least one full-sized piece before she was considered eligible for marriage, in the same way that a young man had to take part in a raid and bring home one head as a trophy (see 'Cultural significance of textiles: Sabah and Sarawak'). Weaving is a task undertaken to establish womanhood and worth in the community.

As *pua kumbu* bridges the mortal and spirit worlds, spiritual power is woven into its design.

Examples of some of the numerous motifs used by the Iban for their *pua* designs: tiger (*remaung*) (1), Tiger Cat (2), Rusa Deer curled up (3), Bird (*burung*) (4) and White Shrew on a Bangkit Fruit (*Aji Bulan Buah Bangkit*) (5).

The weaving of human figures is not for novices. Attainment of this level indicates the spiritual strength of the weaver.

The Iban believe that every piece contains a spirit which must be tamed by the weaver, whose own spirit is in contention with it. For this reason, only experienced and powerful weavers may create the most sacred and potent designs—particularly those with human or spirit figures representative of ancestors (called *engkaramba* or *antu*)—and approval must first be obtained in a dream from Kumang or Lulong, the goddesses of weaving, or from a personal ancestor, for example, a grandmother. Even then, spiritual strength is required, and divine displeasure caused by weakness or transgression may cause a weaver to lose her skill, fall sick, become mad or in the extreme, lose her life.

The potency of a *pua kumbu* design is contained in the central panel confined by vertical borders (*anak*), the vertical bands (*ara*) on each side and the horizontal border patterns at the top and bottom (*punggung*). Traditional motifs include stylized plant (leaves, creepers, ferns and jungle flowers), human ('Man on the Moon', dwarves and elves) and animal figures (shrews (*aji*), lizards, frogs (*enkatak*) and other reptiles and insects). However, designs may feature anything that caught the weaver's imagination and was properly sanctioned in a dream, for instance, aeroplanes, machine guns and pressure lamps. Designs 'live', depicting tales and specific events and reflecting the spirituality and belief systems of the Iban. Established motifs are reused and reworked according to new interpretations while still resembling the original. However, only mature weavers would dare to create new original designs and motifs.

1. Crocodiles swimming among their prey with little spirits of the water world.
2. Ritual bamboo basket for receiving trophy skulls.
3. War shield pattern (*trabai bungkok*).
4. Blowpipe poison darts.

The backstrap loom

In the early centuries of maritime trading, it is likely that Indian traders brought the backstrap loom to Southeast Asia and introduced cotton as an alternative to bark cloth. The primitive, portable backstrap loom required little effort in setting up and, as there was no rigid framework, it could be set up anywhere so long as the warp beam was supported. There are three basic ways of setting up a backstrap loom—the breast beam is attached to the weaver's back by means of the backstrap that gives this apparatus its name, and the warp beam is either attached to a solid support (often a house pillar); weighted by a block of wood; or held by the weaver's feet. In all cases, warp tension is regulated by the weaver's body weight by leaning against the backstrap.

The weaving is done by interlacing threads at right angles to one another (the threads running the width, forming the warp and those running the length, the weft). The warp threads are looped through two beams, the breast beam and the warp beam, the weaver's body position keeping the warp threads taut. The weaver then moves a shuttle containing the weft threads back and forth through the warp.

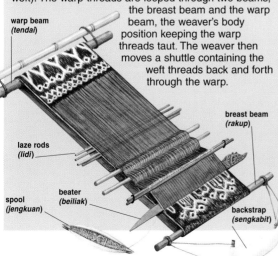

warp beam
(*tendai*)

laze rods
(*lidi*)

spool
(*jengkuan*)

beater
(*beiliak*)

breast beam
(*rakup*)

backstrap
(*sengkabit*)

Tie-dyed artistry

Pua kumbu is created using the tie-dyed warp technique called *kebat* by the Iban. Each segment of the pattern is tied off on the cotton warp with string or tough creeper fibre to protect the parts destined to remain white, before being immersed in the first, usually reddish-brown, dye bath. After drying and a second tying, a blue-black indigo dye is applied. The artist consults no patterns; she knows the whole design by heart. The complete pattern in russet, cream, blue and black is clearly visible when the threads are put on the loom prior to weaving.

1. White cotton threads are soaked in clean water overnight. Starch is used for strength.
2. The dry thread is spun into a ball.
3. The ball of thread is unwound onto the *tumpoh* loom to set the warp length, in a continuous upper and lower web.
4. The warp threads are moved to a wooden frame (*tangga ubong*) and small bamboo sticks are used to group three strands together across the width by weaving them under and over each group to facilitate pattern tying.
5. The designs are tied into the warp threads, here using raffia string, by preventing dye penetrating the tied strands.
6. After tying and removal from the frame, the threads are soaked in water then immersed in a dye bath.
7. When dry, the second tying occurs, leaving intact the first tied threads. The threads are dyed again and the process repeated for each colour desired. Once completed, the threads are untied.
8. The dyed threads are placed on the backstrap loom and weaving begins.

Source: Kraftangan Malaysia publications

Malay dress

The Malays have a long tradition of wearing elaborate costumes indigenous to their own culture, and have always worn them with pride. The rich colours, motifs, luxurious fabrics and the way clothes were worn displayed status and their celebration of beauty. Traditional styles are still worn today for everyday as well as more formal wear.

Malay family wearing traditional costume for their celebration of the Hari Raya festival. The girls and woman (wearing a *tudung* (head scarf) in front are wearing *baju kurung*, the other woman is wearing a *baju kebaya* with a *selendang* (shawl) and the man is weaing *baju Melayu* with songkok headgear.

Malay tailor is cutting the fabric for a *baju Melayu*.

Traditional style for men

The traditional outfit for Malay men is called generically *baju Melayu*. This generally consists of the *baju* (shirt), *seluar* (trousers), *samping* (short sarong) and *songkok* (brimless cap), sometimes a *bengkong* (waist band) and *tengkolok* or *destar* (headdress) will also be worn, the latter in place of the *songkok*. In the early days, the full costume was only worn by royalty and the nobility, but now it is worn by all sectors of Malay society, especially for official and formal functions.

Sarong and kain samping (waist cloth)

The sarong has long been worn by men and women in the Malay archipelago and is an important part of Malay dress. It is worn by men for formal wear and as attire for the mosque, by agrarian folk for daily wear and by city folk for home wear. Sarongs are tubular with the longer ends sewn together, are usually worn from the waist down, and are made from various textiles including batik, silk, cotton and *songket*. There are three distinct spaces which can be decorated on a sarong, the body (*badan*), the head (*kepala*) and the borders (*kaki kain*). These divisions determine the placement of the decorative motifs and patterns and also how the sarong will be worn, for example, the decorative head panel may be at the back.

There are many ways of tying a sarong. It may be wrapped around one's waist or chest by fastening it with a hitch or with a belt and letting it hang down to foot or knee level. The method of tying may be dependent on the region and the type of traditional costume being worn. When worn with *baju Melayu* the fabric is called *kain samping*, which is a shorter sarong falling to the knees worn by men tied around the waist over their trousers either on the outside or inside of the shirt (*baju*). Traditionally, the term *samping* was not mentioned in classical Malay literature but was instead referred to as *gaya dagang luar* (foreign trader style) when worn on the outside of the shirt or *gaya dagang dalam* (local trader style) if worn on the inside. In the past, the method of wearing *kain samping* indicated social divisions, as ordinary people visiting

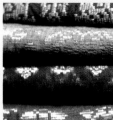

Songket samping for formal occasions.

the palace wore their *kain samping* on the inside while persons of noble ancestry wore it on the outside, a practice no longer followed today. When a *samping* is worn on the outside, a number of styles are available. For instance, It can be hitched to the left or right with three to five folds in the front or tucked at the waist. One style is the *ikat gombang* (handsome hitch) where the cloth is rolled and hitched on one side to form a wavy fold. Normally, the *kain samping* is worn by bringing both ends together in front. Where one end of the *samping* is worn at an angle instead of dropping straight down, the style is called *ikat kain berpancung* (cut-off), and was forbidden to commoners at one time.

Tying a samping

The most common style of wearing *samping* today is folded at the front and falling to the knees with a roll at the waist. This style is created as follows:

1. Step into the sewn fabric holding it a little above the waist. Fold the right side of the fabric into the centre, smoothing it down.

2. Fold the other side into the middle so that it is slightly overlapping while holding the previously folded half flat.

3. Roll the extra fabric down to the waist to secure.

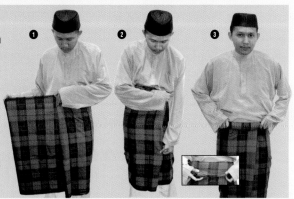

The collarless *baju kurung teluk belanga* shirt is a simple yet traditional style of *baju*. Another popular style is the *baju kurung cekak musang* with an erect round collar strip. Particularly worn in the 1930s, it is believed to date as far back as the 16th century. Today, *baju* may be made of silk, cotton or other fabrics, but rarely *songket* except, perhaps, for a bridegroom. Sometimes a *baju sikap* jacket is worn over the top.

Male headgear

The *tengkolok*, variously known as *bulang hulu*, *kain kepala setangan* (headkerchief), *tanjak*, *semutar* or *destar* in different parts of the country, is the traditional headdress that completed a Malay man's attire. These names referred only to the Malay headdress in relation to customary events and ceremonies, and when describing a groom's attire and royal apparel. The status of a *tengkolok* wearer is apparent from the textile, the manner in which it is folded and any other decorative item used. In the old days *kain pelangi* (rainbow cloth) that was sprinkled with gold dust (see 'Textile embellishment'), was the textile used for the *tengkolok*, such gilded cloth being forbidden to commoners until the 20th century (see 'Cultural significance of textiles: Malay'). The shape and decoration of the *tengkolok* is three-dimensional. The designs of its folds frequently draw inspiration from natural surroundings, for instance, animals (fowl, eagles, lions) and plants (coffee plant leaves, bouquets of flowers, coils of rattan). Some are named after individuals or outstanding statesmen such as *dagang sakit dirantau* (ailing traveller) for the usage of Datuk-Datuk Terengganu (nobility of Terengganu), *Datuk Bija Sura* used by commoners in Terengganu, and *ikatan Temenggung*, the *tengkolok* worn by the Terengganu crown prince. More often than not, the descriptions were in the superlative and related to the spiritual and mythical value of the *tengkolok*.

The *songkok* is a brimless oval shaped cap worn by men with *baju Melayu* and *samping* costume, mainly for special occasions. A simple white *kopiah* skull cap may be worn daily by men, particularly those who have completed the Haj pilgrimage.

The Royal *tengkolok* of the Yang di-Pertuan Agong, the King of Malaysia, is made from *songket* and adorned with a headpin of gold and diamonds. The fold design from Negeri Sembilan is called *ikatan dendam tak sudah* and remains a popular style even today.

Different baju styles

1. Style similar to *baju Kedah* with a short top, flared sleeves and sarong skirt. This outfit is made from hand-drawn silk batik (*batik canting*) fabric with geometric designs.

2. Contemporary designer *baju kebaya* with an embroidered gauzy top and a fashion skirt.

3. Caftans are commonly worn by women for home wear. This designer piece is made from silk.

4. Traditional *baju kurung*.

5. Designer *baju kurung* with a short top embellished with embroidery and beads and a fishtail-style skirt.

Traditional dress for women

There are a number of different styles of traditional dress for Malay women in Malaysia, often varying from state to state. Any fabric may be used but the most common include cotton, silk, voile, organza, velvet, chiffon, lace and *songket*, depending on the purpose or occasion. A *selendang* (shawl) may also be worn over the shoulder on one side or slung from the back over the arms to the front.

One of the most popular everyday garments worn by Malay women today is the *baju kurung* which is beautifully feminine but at the same time modest. It originates from Johor and comprises a loose knee-length long-sleeved top with a round neck that has a small front slit fastened with a button worn over a sarong which is sewn with folds on one side known as *ombak mengalun* (rolling waves). A similar type of costume is the *baju Kedah* which has a shorter top with three-quarter length sleeves, originating in Kedah, as its name suggests.

Malay woman and child (c. early 20th century) dressed in *baju kebaya labuh* with a batik sarong and traditional jewellery and ornaments.

A *baju kebaya* has a long-sleeved top which is split in front, usually joined by a set of three gold or silver brooches joined by a chain called *kerongsang*

(see 'Silverware'). It has different forms—*kebaya labuh* (long *kebaya*), which is one of the oldest and is still worn today; *kebaya pendek* (short *kebaya*); and *kebaya Bandung* (*kebaya* with a joining centre piece). The skirt is in a sarong-style overlapping in the front to display the decorative panel. *Baju kebaya* is worn throughout the country, but especially in Melaka, Perak and Penang. Nonya women wear it with a batik sarong and a delicate embroidered top (see 'Straits Chinese embroidery and beadwork').

One of many small family-run shops which sell a multitude of colourful fabrics for ladies' *baju*.

Royal dress

Costumes worn by royalty and the nobility are quite unique to particular states and are not commonly worn today—for instance, the Minangkabau-based costumes of Negeri Sembilan; the Perak 'princess-style' costume with *songket* trousers, sarong and shawl; and the Kelantan regal costume worn by Che Siti Wan Kembang, a female ruler during the 17th century, consisting of a long silk cloth wrapped around the breasts, a *songket* sarong worn around the hips with folds arranged in front and a long *songket* stole worn over the shoulders, all unsewn.

Female headgear

In days past, a shawl (*selendang*) might be drawn loosely over the head as a covering. In particular, the Malays in Sarawak wore fine embroidered shawls in this way, called *selayah keringkam* (see 'Malay embroidery and tekat').

Today, Malay women generally wear a head scarf called a *tudung*, which is worn in a variety of ways, including some styles with Middle-Eastern influences. The designs and patterns of the *tudung* range from simple and plain through to boldly floral to those embellished with sequins, beads and the like. Cotton, silk and chiffon fabrics are commonly used.

Selayah keringkam shawls worn by Sarawak Malay women are embroidered with metal threads.

Tying a simple tudung style

1. Fold scarf into a triangle then pin together under the chin.

2. Take one corner across and pin to the left or right shoulder so that the edge angles down.

3. Take the other corner across to the opposite shoulder and pin neatly on top of with a brooch.

4. The *tudung* is complete.

71

Chinese and Indian dress

The rich and vibrant costume traditions of the Chinese and Indians of multi-ethnic Malaysia are evident not only in their everyday life but also on religious, festive and formal occasions. The traditional cheongsam, embroidered kebaya *and sari are the costumes most embodying the style and essence of Chinese, Straits Chinese and Indian women respectively. A wide variety of textiles are utilized including sumptuous brocades, velvet, satins and silks, gauzy chiffons, delicate lace and simple cottons.*

For important occasions, for example weddings or festivals such as Deepavali and Chinese New Year, Indian and Chinese children may be dressed in their traditional costume.

Chinese dress

Traditional style garments may be worn on festive occasions such as Chinese New Year, but mainly by women and children as is evident in this picture. Chinese men today tend to wear western clothing.

Female wear

The traditional dress worn by Chinese women is commonly known as cheongsam which means 'long dress' in Cantonese (in northern China, it is known by the Mandarin word *qipao*). Typically it has a high neck with a closed collar, is buttoned on the right side near the shoulder, is fitting to the body and has slits on the sides, all of which combine to emphasise the female shape. The sleeves and length of the cheongsam itself may be short (knee-length), medium (mid-calf) or full length. Function and the type of occasion for which it is being worn may determine the fabric used—for formal occasions a long cheongsam of expensive brocade, shimmering silk or embroidered satin is usual, compared to less formal or daywear, where more simple fabrics such as cotton in a knee-length style may be preferred.

The sam foo (Cantonese name), a waisted blouse and trouser suit, was once a common form of attire for working women, although it could be worn as more formal wear. Now, it might be worn by elderly women or girls in either cotton or silk. Sometimes a Shanghai-style high necked top with a long flared skirt was also worn by women and girls, usually made of embroidered satin or silk.

The Nonya *kebaya* worn by Straits Chinese women is a costume that has blended Chinese embroidery with the Malay *baju* and sarong (see 'Malay dress'). Usually tailored in Swiss muslin, voile, silk or cotton, the richly embroidered blouse (see 'Straits Chinese embroidery and beadwork') is worn with a batik sarong in a bold floral pattern. The hemline of the blouse is usually hip-length, but may be shorter, and is fastened with brooches. The Nonya *kebaya* has become fashionable among other races with the blouse even being worn casually over a pair of jeans or trousers.

Male wear

Until at least the 1920s, early Chinese leaders wore full-length, embroidered silk Mandarin robes, while merchants wore similar robes in cotton. Traditional attire is still sometimes worn by Chinese men for special occasions and comprises the *gua* (shirt with high collar and long sleeves, with fabric buttons), or the *pao* (loose long gown with collar and long sleeves) with long trousers.

The attire of Straits Chinese men (known as Baba) was originally a frog-button tunic worn over loose trousers and mandarin gowns, but later, apart from wedding garments, they often followed Western fashion.

Auspicious motifs

Intricate beadwork and gold thread embroidery of phoenix and dragon motifs are dominant in the design of Chinese costumes, particularly those worn by the well-to-do or for special occasions. The male dragon is the symbol of the Emperor and of supreme power which is frequently used on the clothes of Chinese Mandarin people. Traditionally there were rules about the orientation of the dragon depending on the status of the wearer. The female phoenix symbolizes the Empress, beauty and purity and was a frequently used motif on ladies' clothing within the Chinese imperial family.

Phoenix and bat (1), bamboo (2), peony (3) and butterfly (4) motifs. Other typical motifs include the chrysanthemum (longevity), lotus (beauty and purity), fish (wish for a future full of prosperity), the Five Blessings motif, the Longevity motif, the Eight Happiness motif and the Cherry Blossom.

Embroidered shoes

Tiny silk embroidered shoes were used by women in China from the 10th century when it became customary to bind their feet, considered a mark of beauty and breeding. Although the practice was banned in mainland China in 1911, it continued in other places, including Melaka, but is not followed today. The shoes are still made in Melaka, but are now sold as souvenirs for tourists.

Melaka craftsman making silk shoes, which are only about 10 centimetres long.

Above: This tailor has been sewing *cheongsam* the same way for 50 years.

Left: A Straits Chinese family: the young girls are wearing embroidered long skirts and tops with high-necked collars, the older ladies are wearing their distinctive Nonya *kebaya* and the men, Western attire.

Chinese and Indian costume traditions

Dating from the 14th century, the first Chinese immigrants to this region came to Melaka, Penang and Terengganu. They brought with them their costume traditions from China, particularly the clothing styles of the Qing dynasty, sometimes evident still in wedding attire. Some married locally, adopting local customs, their descendants becoming known as Peranakan or Straits Chinese and their attire a hybrid of different influences. Today, Chinese traditional costumes are worn by men and children mainly for special occasions,

if at all, compared to the contemporary styles that are often favoured by women for everyday wear.

The rich and age-old costume traditions of the Indian community in Malaysia come directly from India and are very much influenced by trends there with respect to fabrics, styles and design. Traditional attire is worn by many Indians, particularly women, on a daily basis and not just for ceremonial and formal occasions, reflecting its versatility and practicality, and also assuring its survival. This is enhanced by the worldwide popularity that Indian fashions and styles are presently enjoying.

Indian dress

Female wear

The ubiquitous traditional sari worn by Indian women measures one metre wide and five to seven metres long. It is typically of cotton or various kinds of silk, although chiffon, georgette and synthetic fabrics are also common now. The sari may be worn in many ways; the most common in Malaysia is the South Indian style in which the fabric is wound around the waist, pleated in the front with the decorative end (*munthani* or *pallu*) thrown over the left shoulder to the back, either draped loosely or pleated neatly. In comparison, North Indians wear their sari drawn from the back to the front over the right shoulder. The sari is tucked into a long petticoat (*pavadai*) and worn with a short tight blouse which leaves the wearer's waist bare. Brightly coloured bold saris are generally favoured, although pastel shades popular in North India and Indian Bollywood films have become fashionable, as have filmy embroidered or sequinned chiffon and crepe fabrics. Traditionally, white is worn by widows. Expensive silk saris are often embroidered with gold or silver thread.

Women also wear the *salwaar khamez* which is a long or knee-length tunic (*khamez*) over trousers (*salwaar*), which may be wide and loose (called pyjamas) or tight-fitting to the leg from the knee down (*churidaar*). A shawl (*dupatta*) worn over the shoulder or around the neck complements the outfit. These suits can be made from any fabric ranging from simple cotton to glamorous and decorated beaded or sequinned chiffon. A shorter top, no

This family celebrating the Deepavali festival of light are wearing colourful traditional costumes—women in sari, girls in *pavadai thaamani*, man in the centre of the picture in *veshti* and *jibba* and boys in a long *kurta* over pants with a shawl.

longer than mid-thigh length, is the *kurta*, generally made in colourful cotton and worn either with *churidaar* or as casual wear with jeans or pants. For special occasions, young girls wear either a *salwaar khamez* or an ornamental waist-length top and long flared skirt (*pavadai*). A similar outfit is the North Indian *lengha*, also with a tight blouse and long skirt.

Male wear

The dhoti (*veshti* in Tamil), an ankle-length rectangular white cloth tied around the waist, is worn by Indian men. Usually hanging down to the feet, it is sometimes worn with one end pulled up between the legs and tucked into the back of the waist. For ceremonies, a silk dhoti with embroidered borders is used. The *lungi* or *kaili* is a similar more informal outfit which might be worn by men around the house and for sleeping. With a dhoti, traditionally a piece of cotton or silk fabric (*angavastram*, also known as *thundu*) is draped around the shoulders like a stole or used as a scarf around the neck or tied around the waist over the *jibba*, a long loose cotton or silk shirt. Generally, headwear is not worn, but sometimes a type of turban is worn when the *angavastram* is wrapped about the head (known as *mundacu*), particularly when certain tasks are carried out or by those playing an important role in religious ceremonies.

North Indian influenced styles are popular for formal wear, consisting of an embroidered long shirt (*kurta*) with a Nehru-style stand-up collar and fitting *churidaar* pants. A shawl may be worn over the top.

Above: Girls buying saris prior to the festival of Deepavali when new clothes will be worn.

Left: This couple is dressed in typical south Indian attire for a ceremonial occasion (here a temple wedding). The groom is wearing the traditional *veshti* and *jibba* in silk and the bride, an elaborate silk sari embroidered with gold thread.

Examples of sari embellishment

Beads/sequins

Copper work

Gold embroidery

Tying a sari

One of the most common ways of tying a sari is this South Indian style.

❶

❷

❸

❹

❺

❻

1. Wear the blouse and the petticoat tied tightly.
2. Tuck the sari into the petticoat from right to left all the way around.
3. & 4. Make about 5 to 7 pleats of about 4 centimetres width.
5. Tuck the pleats firmly into the petticoat a little to the right of the navel.
6. Bring the sari one more time around the body from the back to the front, under the right arm and then over the left shoulder.

Costumes and ornaments of Sabah

The population of Sabah is heterogeneously and culturally diverse, as are its equally varied range of traditional costumes. These are relatively plain and simple, but are enhanced by an array of jewellery and ornaments. The need to meet new modesty standards, to establish identity and differentiate between the ethnic groups and the growing emphasis on cultural tourism and the attendant economic benefits have led indigenous craftsmen to reinvent and modify inherited artistic traditions and styles of costume and ornamentation.

Egalitarian character

A salient feature of Sabah's costumes and textile traditions is their relative lack of attachment to social status and the value of textiles. Clothes serve the basic function of covering the body rather than providing a means to manifest class distinctions. However, more ostentatious clothing is reserved for special occasions to distinguish the wearer from others, such as for weddings and other important rites of passage in a person's life. Some perceptible differences in rank and position are, however, apparent in some communities. The motifs on the *sukolob sinombitan* (a needle–worked panel on a cotton tube) worn by a Rungus headman's wife are more elaborate than those of other women in the longhouse or village to indicate her position. The Iranun people of Kota Belud and some of their Bajau neighbours wear and use colours during weddings to indicate their ancestral lineages, but these are more for sentiment rather than to establish social status. Descendants of the Datu class wear and use green with other colours for weddings and funerals, with yellow for the Sharif descendants.

Ritual specialists who officiate at traditional and religious ceremonies enjoy special attention and are usually attired in garments and accessories which distinguish them from others at these events. For instance, the *tantagas* or Lotud priestesses of Tuaran wear elaborate costumes, sometimes with frequent changes in costume paraphernalia, to illustrate the progress of some aspect of the ceremony, for example *manarapoh* (see 'Cultural significance of textiles: Sabah and Sarawak').

Use of ornaments

The extensive use of jewellery and various cloth, metal, organic and inorganic ornaments by the peoples of Borneo usually make up for their costumes' lack of colour and perhaps plain appearance. The recent additions of glittery trimmings are designed to create and amplify visual impact (see 'Jewellery and ornaments of Sabah and Sarawak').

Lotud ritual jewellery

An array of Lotud ritual jewellery and ornaments is illustrated by the female priestesses (*tantagas*) of Tuaran (above) when they perform important religious ceremonies. They wear colourful ritual paraphernalia with ornaments and accessories which reflect a matrix of craftsmanship and traditions of various origins. A bunch of brass bells (*giring-giring*) is carried. Brooches of dried rhizome beads (*kamburongoh*) are pinned to their blouses while a bundle of these beads tied around a jarlet (collectively called *pilamong pilopi*) hang around their wrist or arm during ceremonies to mediate with the spirit world. On their heads is a row of four hair ornaments made of black chicken feathers, red cloth and turquoise-coloured beads (*siwot*), and, around the crown, an embossed patterned gilt or gold circlet on a red rattan band (*sigar*) (see 'Jewellery and ornaments of Sabah and Sarawak').

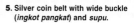

Traditional costumes and ornaments

Bajau

Male
1. Headdress of folded *kain dastar*.
2. Brightly coloured shirt (*badu*) with flared sleeves (worn for formal occasions) and a different coloured undershirt which is visible underneath. *Betawi* buttons may decorate the front and sleeves.
3. Contrasting trousers (except black, which is for weddings) with red trim (*suar*).
4. Sash (*selendang*) tied around the waist.
5. Silver coin belt with wide buckle (*ingkot pangkat*) and *supu*.

Female
6. Bright long-sleeved blouse (*badu sipak*), usually yellow.
7. Full length black wrap-skirt with a wide vertical panel of *berangkit* in front (*olos berangkit*). For weddings, a long handwoven skirt with horizontal stripes, usually red and black may be worn (*kain mogah*) (see 'Textiles of Sabah').
8. *Mandapun* collar.
9. Silver bangles (*galang*).
10. Silver coin belt with a wide buckle (*ingkot pangkat*).
11. Two-piece silver head decoration in the shape of a ship (*sarempak*) with dangling ornaments (*garigai*).

Supu, a round silver engraved tobacco case worn by men attached to their belt.

Murut

Male
1. Sleeveless jacket (*babaru puputul*) made from bark of the *puputul* tree (*Artocarpus kunstleri*) decorated with simple beadwork.
2. Bark loincloth (*aba puputul*) about two metres long, commonly in red symbolizing bravery, and wound between the legs and around the waist.
3. Headband decorated with pheasant feathers (*tupi' sinulatan*).

Female
4. Short black cotton sleeveless blouse (*babaru linantian*) decorated with colourful beadwork.
5. Long wrap skirt (*tapi' linantian*) decorated with colourful beadwork.
6. Silver dollar coin belts (*pipirot*).
7. Beads and necklaces of varying lengths.
8. Strands of tiny, usually antique, shell beads (*bungkas*) worn about the hips in several rows, tied at one end (usually family heirlooms).
9. Beaded cap headdress (*salupai*) made of carnelian beads.
10. Set of hairpins with dangling beads (*sinikot*) worn in the hairbun.
11. Pair of shell bracelets (*holong*).

Kadazandusun

Papar Kadazandusun

Female

1. Short jacket (*sia*) made of black cloth (usually velvet) with gold trimming and brass *betawi* buttons along the neck and cuffs.

2. A white blouse (*sia id saahom*) is worn underneath the jacket.

3. Knee-length skirt (*gonob*) with a horizontal and vertical strip of cross-stitch (*langkit*) lined with gold thread.

4. Conical hat (*siung*) made of bamboo strips with decorative red and black panels and tufts of coloured feather down (indicates woman is single) or artificial flowers (indicates woman is married). A scarf (*soundung*) is worn underneath the hat.

5. Silver dollar (British trade dollar) belts (*rupia* or *lupia*). The number worn indicate marital status—four for unmarried, two for married, and one for widows or elderly women.

6. Flat spiral silver bangles (*bolilit*) on arms.

Male

7. Long-sleeved black jacket (*sia*) with gold trimming.

8. Trousers (*souva*) with gold trimming.

9. Folded cloth (*kain dastar*) headdress (*sigal*) (see also 'Textiles of Sabah').

Lotud

Female

1. Black cotton blouse (*sukub kopio*) with red *tinobogi* at the seams; cuffs decorated with a bamboo shoot motif with sequins and gold thread.

2. Ornamental collar (*mandapun*).

3. Knee-length dark skirt worn by priestesses (*sinugitan*). Other women wear a black cotton tube skirt (*gonob*) decorated with a strip of *tinobogi* embroidery around the hips and a panel of *linangkit* needle-woven cloth from the waist down.

Penampang Kadazandusun

Female

1. Black blouse (sleeveless (*sinuangga*) for young unmarried women; three-quarter sleeves (*sinompukung*) for middle-aged women for daily or casual use; and a different type (*kihongon*) worn by elderly women and priestesses). Gold coin brooches (*paun*) may also be worn on the blouse.

2. Long black cylindrical wrap skirt (*tapi*), often decorated with gold trimming (*siling*).

3. About the waist and hips, Straits silver dollar coin belts (*himpogot, tinggot, simpogot* or *botungkat*).

4. Belts of brass rings with engraved motifs strung on rattan straps (*tangkong*), sometimes with white shell rings (*husau*) in three layers on the hips.

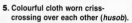

5. Colourful cloth worn criss-crossing over each other (*husob*).

6. Brass or silver bracelets, earrings (*simbong*) might be worn as well (see 'Jewellery and ornaments of Sabah and Sarawak').

LEFT: Priestess wearing ritual costume and accessories

Dusun Tindal

Male

1. Velvet shirt (*sinipak*) with flared sleeves slashed at elbows over a long sleeved undershirt.

2. *Lolopot*, two sashes of handwoven cloth (*kain dastar*) folded diagonally over the chest.

3. Trousers (*soluwar*).

4. Sash (*pomohorot do tawak*) and silver coin belt (*simpogot*).

5. Headdress of traditionally folded handwoven cloth (*sigar*).

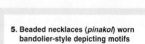

Female

6. Black velvet long-sleeved blouse (*sinipak*) with flared, slashed sleeves decorated with *linangkit* (panel made using a needle weaving technique (see 'Textiles of Sabah') or gold trimming on the upper sleeves.

7. *Lolopot*, two sashes of handwoven cloth (*kain dastar*) folded diagonally over the chest.

8. Scarf (*solindang*) folded across the shoulders.

9. Knee-length indigo skirt (*gonob*) with embroidered hem.

10. Hood (*sunduk*) made of *pisang lanut* (*Musa textilis*) with embroidered border.

11. Chained silver coin belt (*simpogot*) worn around the hips, usually under another silver belt (*baratina*).

12. Several strands of coloured beads (*kinokogis*) are worn around the hips by Dusun Tindal women of Kota Belud.

4. Small nickel coin belt (*loti*), joined in a row to a rattan hipster girdle (*lilimbo*), made of thin strips of rattan, dyed red or black, tied together.

5. Bead necklace with silver cones (*karo, kamuggi* or *lontugion*).

6. *Siwot* (four hair ornaments of black chicken feathers tied together with red cloth), *sigar* (headband made from the frond of the *nipah* palm and inlaid with embossed strips of silver, gilt or gold).

7. Hollow embossed silver rings worn on the upper arms (*simpai*) and around the ankles.

Male

8. Black cotton shirt (*sukub*) decorated with *tinobogi* needle embroidery or stitchwork and *linangkit* needle-woven cloth panels.

9. Trousers (*binandus*) with a square piece of *linangkit* at the back under the waist.

10. Folded *kain dastar* headdress (*sundi*).

11. Silver chain with an attached round silver tobacco container (*supu*) around the waist.

5. Beaded necklaces (*pinakol*) worn bandolier-style depicting motifs taken from Rungus folklore.

6. Shell disc worn around the neck (*sulau*) and a single-strand beaded necklace (*litai*).

Male

7. Long-sleeved handwoven shirt with geometric motifs (*badu'*).

8. Baggy trousers with wide waistline decorated with a large panel of *linangkit* (see 'Textiles of Sabah') on the back and seams (*soval sarabulu'*) and waistband (*hokos*) made of red, green and yellow cotton strips.

9. Two folded lengths of printed fabric (*sandai*) worn from each shoulder to the calves and narrow handwoven circular sashes with geometric motifs crosswise over the chest.

10. Headcloth of *kain pis* (see 'Textiles of Sabah').

11. Two bands of beadwork (*pinakol*) with geometric and human figures looped across the shoulders.

Male

7. Black long-sleeved shirt (*gaung*) decorated with gold trimming and buttons.

8. Black trousers (*souva*) with wide indigo blue waistband and gold trimming along the seams and black sash (*kaking* or *toogot*) tied at the waist.

9. Handwoven cloth (*kain dastar*) (see 'Textiles of Sabah') folded or twisted into shape (*siga*) and supported by a circular hat of coiled string (*tupi' sinikat*).

Rungus

Female

1. Below-the-knee tube-skirt (*tapi'*) with fine, long narrow panels of *linangkit* needlework running its length (see 'Textiles of Sabah').

2. Tight bodice (*banat*) with small panels of *linangkit* needlework joining the seams.

3. Band of beads (*sisingal*) worn on the crown of the head.

4. Around the arms (*saring*), legs (*lungkaki'*), neck and hips (*orot*) are worn tight spirals of coiled brass wire; *orot* are interspersed with strands of beads.

Costumes and ornaments of Sarawak

The traditional costumes of the peoples of Sarawak are adorned with distinctive beadwork and needlework, a variety of metal objects, feathers, animal teeth, claws and tusks. Jewellery and ornaments including resplendent headdresses, colourful pompoms, and unique rattan and silver corsets are also worn. The prevalence and importance of beads in Sarawak, as decoration and as part of animist rites, continue even today.

Kelabit family in traditional costumes and ornaments.

Colourful jacket and skirt decorated with beadwork.

Simple costumes, elaborate ornaments

To be comfortable in an equatorial climate, a minimum of clothing is required. The men of Sarawak traditionally wore a plain loincloth, and their womenfolk a short skirt; young children generally went naked. Jackets and hats were worn as protection from the elements. The traditional costumes of the indigenous population were thus quite simple, made for the most part of home-processed natural fabrics. These were enhanced by beadwork and elaborate ornaments made from silver, gold, brass, beads, organic materials and objects.

New styles and items were cheerfully adopted when and as they suited the wearers' tastes; ethnic groups borrowed sartorial ideas from neighbours.

Costume styles have changed with the availability of materials, contact with other cultures, and fashion. Each ethnic group has evolved certain typical forms, made and worn with many regional and personal variations.

Beads as adornment

In Sarawak, and also in Sabah, the craft of working with tiny rocaille or seed beads is alive and thriving. The technique used is threading

Old Kelabit earrings of carved hornbill ivory with beadwork embellishment.

Iban costume

Female

A short handwoven skirt of *kebat* (ikat) or *anyam* cloth (see 'Textiles of Sarawak') used to be the Iban woman's everyday costume. A sash crossed over the breasts, or a jacket, might be worn at festival times. Today, a sleeveless bodice, often complemented by a narrow ornamental sash, is the norm. For festival wear this is topped by a beaded shoulder yoke finished off by wool pompoms, or a stiff velvet cape encrusted with beadwork and sequins.

Traditionally, silver is preferred to gold for personal ornaments; considered 'cool' and therefore promoting health. A woman wears a simple head-comb or an elaborate headdress including coils and dangles (*sugu tinggi*). Silver armlets and anklets, a silver 'corset' of tiny rings strung on rattan hoops (*rawai*), silver belts composed of mesh work or chained coins complete the gala dress (see also 'Jewellery and ornaments of Sabah and Sarawak').

Silver *sugu tinggi* and beaded shoulder yoke.

Male

A loincloth measuring 4–5 metres by 50 centimetres of red or blue calico is embellished by handwoven, embroidered or beaded 'tails' fore and aft. A jacket decorated with *sungkit* or *kebat* (see 'Textiles of Sarawak'), needle-weaving or beadwork is worn, today often over a cotton shirt. The headdress may be a turban or a rattan cap, studded with argus pheasant feathers. Men may wear heavy bangles and anklets, and sometimes silver belts, or necklaces of large glass and semi-precious stone beads.

Orang Ulu costume

Female

The typical Orang Ulu skirt was an oblong piece of textile fastened at the hip; often two such 'aprons' overlap, one tied at the right and one at the left side. The modern costume consists of a long skirt and tunic, heavily sequined or beaded, and worn with belts and necklaces of ancient value beads or modern replicas. A beaded or plaited headband tops off the costume; for outdoor wear a wide hat with a beadwork central blaze is worn. Heavy brass earrings were traditionally worn (see also 'Jewellery and ornaments of Sabah and Sarawak').

Male

A bark or calico loincloth is topped off by a jacket of decorated bark cloth (see 'Textiles of Sarawak'), or a stiff cape of goat skin—only the high-ranking chiefs dared to wear leopard skins! The war bonnet resembles a beaded helmet, decorated with tufts of hair, chips of mirror, animal teeth and hornbill feathers. Orang Ulu men reserve the best, most valuable beads for their own use.

Orang Ulu woman doing beadwork, which has many uses, including clothing and ornament embellishment as well as headwear worn by men and women.

on crossed strands, not mbroidery or bead-weaving. Today's palette is brilliantly varied; traditional beadwork colours were muted red, white, black and yellow, turquoise and orange.

The Iban work elaborate sword belts and necklaces out of seed beads. Traditionally costumed young women wear a colourful bead cape, possibly derived from the over-dress composed of beads which is still used in the upper Rajang area. The Melanau attach a beadwork inset to the top of their 'bead blouse'.

The Orang Ulu people are Sarawak's recognized beadwork experts. They seldom make whole garments, but apply decorative beadwork panels to jackets, skirts and loincloth tails, baskets and baby carriers. In the past, status decided who was allowed to wear which design: the human figure was reserved for the aristocracy, while 'lesser' motifs were carefully graded down the social scale.

The Kelabit and Lun Bawang (Murut) women of eastern Sarawak (and related groups in Sabah, Brunei and Kalimantan) wear a skullcap strung entirely of antique beads, while other related peoples make headdresses and caps of seed beads and animal claws worked on rattan frames.

FAR LEFT: Various healing and protective beads.

LEFT: Late 19th century photograph of the value bead collection of a Kayan chief's wife.

RIGHT: The eye bead (indicated) in this Orang Ulu necklace is of the kind found at the Sungai Mas historical site in the Malay Peninsula.

BOTTOM LEFT AND INSET: Melanau woman tying beads for new daughter-in-law on arrival at her new home. Beads would also sometimes be tied around the wrists of sickly persons as a way to strengthen their soul and improve their health.

Trade and value beads

Beads were traded to the Malay Peninsula and Borneo in exchange for valuable jungle produce and gold for over one thousand years. Over the centuries, traders brought the treasured beads to Borneo from China, India, North Africa, West Asia, Italy, the Netherlands, Bohemia and England.

Apart from the locally made bone and tooth beads of prehistory, stone and glass beads have been imported and produced in southern Thailand and Peninsular Malaysia since the beginning of the 8th century, as archaeological sites in Sungai Mas and the Bujang Valley in Kedah prove. Two very ancient types continued in production for several thousand years and are still popular: the long, hexagonal faceted brownish red carnelian bead from northwest India, and the barrel-shaped deep blue glass bead from China, which was still made in Java by migrant Chinese artisans in the 16th century.

Beads were essential to animist rites to strengthen an officiant's soul in his or her dealings with the spirit world. A few 'strong' beads and brass bells were attached to the top of an elaborately beaded baby carrier to protect its occupant; toddlers wore beads to keep them safe and healthy. The Melanau bride received beads from the groom's family, commensurate with her family's status. Beads were needed for house-building and housewarming rites; as protection for the artist or the sword-smith, and as provision for the last journey. For these purposes, only old beads were considered powerful enough.

However, new beads—no more than 200–300 years old—are undeniably beautiful, and valuable in themselves. An expert Orang Ulu woman can name up to a hundred types of beads accurately, and value them in terms of farm produce, livestock (one Kelabit bead cap for two buffaloes) or in monetary terms. Bead customs vary: among some people they are simply value objects, to others they still carry the nimbus of spiritual power and must be handled with care, preferably by those connected with religious practices.

The bulk of today's heirloom beads reached Borneo within the last 200–300 years, though some are older. Collectors are attracted by the polychrome splendour of Venetian, Dutch and Bohemian beads; their entry into what used to be a closed market within Borneo has certainly driven up prices and encouraged the production of replicas.

Bidayuh costume

Female

Short skirts and jackets of black calico, faced with red, are worn by all Bidayuh groups. Festive headgear varies— the Jagoi women use a flat, coloured cap made of black, red and white calico with streamers at the back; their Biatah and Ulu Sadong sisters prefer a tall conical hat of finely woven bamboo or beadwork topped off with a flat palm leaf 'umbrella'; the Selakau and Jagoi Singgai wear a black headcloth trimmed with silver coins. Silver or brass chain belts and silver bracelets enhance these sombre outfits, as do carefully strung bead neckpieces, formerly only worn by ritual specialists.

Male

The loincloth, made of bark (see 'Textiles of Sarawak') or calico, started to give way to the plaid-weave cotton sarong in the early 20th century. By some Bidayuh groups, a sarong is worn over a set of rattan waist hoops by men performing the 'eagle dance'. For formal occasions Bidayuh men prefer long black trousers and gold-trimmed tunics, topped off with a red-white-black headcloth; this outfit is enhanced with a set of powerful blue glass beads strung with bear claws, boar tusks and leopard teeth which, in the past, was confined to warriors and shamans.

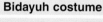

Necklace of glass beads, bear claws, brass bells, ancient Chinese coins and brass wire coil worn by a priestess.

Melanau costume

Female

The coastal Melanau, having lived alongside the Malays for a long time, have more or less adopted their neighbour's fashions. For formal wear the Melanau womens' black tunics or blouses are hemmed with dainty, ancient beads; the over-long, slit sleeves are looped back to display sets of heavy silver-gilt buttons. The preferred colour for the gold-brocaded (see 'Textiles of Sarawak') sarong skirt is maroon or pigeon's blood red.

Male

Melanau men wear black tunics and trousers, with a dark red gold brocade sarong decoratively fastened around the waist. The headcloth may be of matching fabric, or batik; it is tied without protruding peaks and wings.

Side view of the type of button which adorns a woman's sleeves.

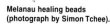

Melanau healing beads (photograph by Simon Tchee).

1. Elaborate jewellery is worn by a Straits Chinese bride. The pieces would usually be family heirlooms.

2. This type of European-style silverware was part of the silvercraft revival efforts in the 1930s by the Kelantan Malay Arts and Crafts Society.

3. Rungus woman in traditional costume wearing coiled brass ornaments (c.1940s).

4. Malay weddings are occasions where heritage items such as *kris* (worn by the groom) and traditional gold jewellery are still used.

5. Heavy brass earrings are worn by women and men of the Sarawak indigenous peoples.

6. Craftsman in Terengganu making the clay moulds into which molten brass will be poured.

7. Gold jewellery has traditionally reflected status and position and is particularly favoured by the Indian and Malay communities. The industry comprises large and small local manufacturers and retailers, some of whom export their products, and jewellery importers. Goldsmiths and small gold shops can still be found in towns and cities.

METALWARE

Metalworking, from heavy weaponry to the most delicate jewellery, has been an established industry in all parts of Malaysia for several centuries, though it is unclear when it first began here. Some archaeological evidence appears to support an indigenous Iron Age and local bronzeware production in the early Bronze Age.

Advertisement for a 1957 promotion of Malaysian pewter in Canada.

Iron ore is mined on a very small scale in parts of Pahang, Kedah, Perak and Terengganu, and has been used for tools and weaponry in Malaysia for several hundred years. The weapon that most epitomizes mystique, tradition, culture and identity is the Malay kris, a unique dagger that has mythically been credited with supernatural powers. The kris is no longer used as a weapon, but it is still a collectable work of art, also serving a ceremonial function on occasions such as weddings and as a part of court regalia.

Base metals such as copper, lead and zinc have been found in Kelantan and Pahang. Copper mining was once a large industry in Sabah. However, Malaysia ceased copper production in 1999. In Peninsular Malaysia, the art of casting brassware (an alloy of copper and zinc) originated in the states of Terengganu and Kelantan around 1700, and was probably introduced from Thailand. Terengganu 'white brass' is particularly famous.

Malaysia has no silver mine, but silverware of religious significance from the first millennium CE has been found here. Silversmithing began as an offshoot of the established gold-working tradition. It served the needs of the nobility and was a substitute for more favoured but expensive gold ornaments. The areas of Malaysia most often associated with silverwork are Kelantan, Melaka and parts of Borneo.

The most abundant metal found in Malaysia is tin. In the late 1840s, rich deposits of tin ore were discovered in the Kinta Valley, Perak, and in the Klang Valley, Selangor. Chinese immigrants journeyed inland to work in the mines and to prospect for new fields. A thriving pewter (an alloy of tin and other metals) industry became established and Malaysian pewterware is highly acclaimed internationally.

Small veins of gold exist in Malaysia, though the country imports large amounts to make jewellery and other objects. Gold mining ceased at the end of the 1800s. Historically, aside from its use as currency, the crafting of ornaments and jewellery developed during the 17th and 18th centuries, largely due to the patronage of Malay royal courts. Today, the sale and manufacture of gold jewellery is a large industry in Malaysia.

For all types of metalware, early local master craftsmen achieved high standards of workmanship, although often using simple homemade tools. Metalware craftsmanship suffered a recent decline. However, the government and the Malaysian Handicraft Development Corporation, among others, encouraged a revival of classic forms of metalworking and the reinvigoration of traditional crafts.

The 500 year-old Taming Sari kris is part of the Perak royal regalia and was once owned by the famous warrior Hang Tuah. Its handle and sheath are made from gold leaf and the blade from an alloy of 20 metal composites.

Metalworking and weapons

Weapons in Malaysia were traditionally crafted from iron. Production techniques have largely remained the same, although modern bellows and more sophisticated tools were introduced in the 20th century. Of the variety of traditional Malaysian weaponry, the most unique, mysterious and legendary is the Malay kris, a dagger initially used as a thrusting weapon for fighting at close quarters. The kris later became a symbol of status, a ceremonial icon and a prized work of art.

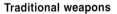

Iron

Harder than bronze, iron's strength and magnetic properties make it a suitable material from which to fashion weapons. It is probable that the first iron used in Malaysia was meteoric iron, which differs from smelted iron as it usually contains a small amount of nickel. The first smelting in Malaysia is unrecorded. Archaeological evidence of iron slag debris intermixed with dateable finds of earthenware and ceramics indicates that the manufacture of iron was carried out in Santubong, Sarawak, from about the 10th to the middle of the 14th century CE. Smelting may also have been carried out in the Tembeling region of Pahang.

Since iron ore has never been locally mined in quantity, historically, local blacksmiths bartered for iron slabs from foreign traders. From the 20th century onwards, metal supply came from scrap such as old car springs and vehicle parts.

This swivel gun (probably from Borneo) has simple decoration on the barrel and pointed foot. A twisted fluted pattern was a common design.

Traditional weapons
Common traditional weapons include: (**1**) *kerambit* or *lawi ayam* (cock's tail feather), a narrow bladed claw-shaped dagger designed for ripping; (**2**) *badik*, a short-bladed stabbing weapon with a tabular hilt; (**3**) *tumbuk lada* (pepper crusher), a slightly curved single edged blade; (**4**) the *lembing* spear which was usually fitted with a wooden shaft about 120–180 centimetres long; (**5**) *lading*, a short stabbing spear fitted in a dagger-type hilt and used with an underhand thrust; and (**6**) *keris sundang*, a broad-bladed sword for cutting or slashing which was either straight or wavy.

Weapons

Malay blacksmiths forged a number of traditional weapons which included cannons, spears (generally called *tombak* or *lembing*), slashing weapons, swords and short daggers of various shapes and sizes. Of all the Malay short weapons, the kris is the best known and most significant.

In Sarawak, the ornate *parang ilang* was originally used as a fighting weapon, especially for headhunting, but today it serves as a home decoration or is given as a gift to mark a special occasion or event. Like the kris in Peninsular Malaysia, it is considered to have hereditary supernatural powers and is most prized. Generally, the wooden sheath is decorated with carved bones lashed to the side with plaited fibres or brass wire. The hilt is made of hardwood or deer horn elaborately carved with stylized figures. In the past, sometimes both would also be adorned with human hair, now substituted with dyed tufts of goat hair. The Bajau people of Kota Belud in Sabah also have a traditional ornamental blade called *parang gayang* which sometimes had patterns etched into the metal. The hilt was carved from wood or horn.

Imported foreign weapons after the fall of Melaka in 1511 included lightweight iron and brass cannons and swivel guns which were later manufactured by the Malays, but declined at the end of the 19th century.

Parang ilang blade with fretwork of spirals and tendrils inlaid with brass circles and a carved and decorated hilt.

Ironworking and blacksmiths
By about the 16th century, it was common for most rural villages in the Peninsula to have a domestic forge where blacksmiths worked when not occupied in the fields or with fishing. Manually operated bellows (still used in Terengganu) were used to fan the fire in the forge. Bellows consisted of a pipe or a long box from which air was pumped by a piston into the furnace or hearth pit in order to produce a continuous stream of air.

Iron was melted and shaped into tools or weapons. When the desired shape had been achieved, it was plunged into cold water to harden it. Blades were forged by repeatedly heating and folding red-hot slabs of iron and hammering them into blades. Some weapons were made of composite elements, such as wood or ivory for handles. Also, depending on their intended use, decorative elements employing brass, silver and gold, or a hilt and scabbard, might be added.

As the craft of ironworking developed, master blacksmiths, *pandai besi*, came to be, and are still, highly respected. The most skilled and well known blacksmiths in Peninsular Malaysia, descendants of a long line of master craftsmen, live in Terengganu and Kelantan, where they still produce iron crafts, particularly kris, for collectors, tourists and a small domestic market. Likewise, in Sarawak, the Kayan and Kenyah people are renowned for their superior ironworking tradition and expertise, particularly in the forging of swords.

Artist's impression of a small Malay village blacksmith.

Right: A blacksmith in Sarawak using a piston-bellows.

The Malay kris

A cultural and historical icon
The kris is more than a weapon; it is symbolic of Malay culture and heritage, tradition and spirituality. Myths, superstition and history surround it. It has been used by Malays for more than 600 years, and is widely believed to have originated in Java between the 9th and 14th centuries; most Western scholars place the modern kris prototype in the 12th century. Early depictions of the kris are contained in temple wall carvings in Java dated to the 14th century.

A Kelantanese style early 19th century *keris tajong* hilt example carved from wood with silver embellishment.

Making a kris
Since the early days, a Malay kris was valued mainly for its blade and every Malay royal court had its own blade maker. Although some kris blades are made solely from iron, most are alloyed with another metal, usually nickel or steel, which is placed on either side of the iron and pounded repeatedly to produce a damasked dark and light effect called *pamur*. The *pamur* is etched out by washing the finished blade in a solution of arsenic and lime juice, which reacts with the base iron, turning it black and leaving the nickel or steel unaffected.

A good blade is often made up of several layers of metal. The typical wavy edge of the kris blade is achieved by repeatedly reheating the metal and hammering the edges of the blade against the side of the anvil. Once the maker is satisfied with the blade, it is then fixed into the hilt (*hulu*). This is usually done by forcing the hot pointed tang into the hole already prepared for it and then cementing it with locally made glue of *damar* (resin) and oil. The grip of the handle or hilt is often curved to be at right angles to the line of the blade, thereby adapting the weapon for a forward thrust.

Master carver, the late Nik Rashiddhin Nik Hussein, carving a *keris tajong* hilt. The aggressive power of the *keris tajong* as a warrior's kris is reflected in its fierce facial expression and the dark wood. It was also used by royalty.

The kris as a weapon
The kris stands apart as a unique weapon. It is highly developed for thrusting or for piercing flesh and penetrating vital organs. The blade is edged on both sides as well as pointed at the end, its main function being to severely wound the victim, and to render easy withdrawal of the weapon during an encounter with the enemy. Kris blades are either straight or wavy. Both types were used for fighting, but only the former was used to carry out death by execution.

Hilts
Traditionally, most kris hilts are normally fashioned from hardwood, ivory, bone, horn or a composite of these elements fitted together to form the shape required. Before the coming of Islam, the hilt was usually shaped to portray a Hindu deity. After the adoption of Islam, the Hindu-inspired hilts were modified to a simple standard and more practical shape known as *Jawa demam* ('the fevered Javanese')—so-called, as it resembles a stylized figure of a man in the throes of a fever—also known today as *keris semenanjung*. The east coast areas of Malaysia are recognized for other forms of kris hilt, namely, the *keris tajong* and *keris pekaka* ('kingfisher') The differences between the two, if any, are a matter of debate.

A hilt ferrule made from brass, silver or gold, is placed between the hilt and blade. It may be either simply engraved or an elaborate piece of jewellery.

Sheaths
The sheath of a kris is generally made of wood pegged together and glued in place. Across the top of the sheath there is a crosspiece (*sampir*) often in a boat-like shape. The sheath is frequently made from polished fine-grained ornamental wood, sparingly decorated with perhaps silver or ivory trim, although there are examples of kris sheaths and hilts encased in intricately worked silver and gold, especially in the case of kris belonging to royalty or the wealthy.

Pamur patterns
The striking *pamur* or damascene pattern distinctive of kris blades was in the early days of talismanic importance—some markings were considered lucky for a particular person or a specific purpose, such as trade or war. The creation of individualized *pamur* is no longer practised in light of the present-day purely ceremonial function of kris. There are numerous recorded *pamur* motifs and designs, most described with fanciful names such as 'fish navel', 'grasshopper's legs', 'embedded rock', 'water hyacinth', to name but a few. *Pamur* patterns were categorized as either *pamur mlumah*, where the lamination lies parallel to the flat surface of the blade and *pamur miring*, where the lamination is aligned perpendicular or diagonal to the flat of the blade. In addition, designs could be pre-planned and 'willed' (*pamur rekan*) or left to chance and 'fated' (*pamur tiban*). The latter usually had more spiritual significance, and sometimes manifested as unexpected shapes such as animals, stars, circles and, the most powerful, a human figure.

Examples of different *pamur mlumah* patterns: (top) stripe design running vertically down the blade; (above) wavy line design; (right) central layered large circle design.

Mystical kris
The kris has long been, and still remains, a mystical object. It has been attributed with spiritual and supernatural powers, including the ability to protect its owner from physical harm and misfortune. Traditionally, its very creation was enveloped in elaborate rites and rituals to appease the spiritual elements believed to inhabit the weapon, which, if ill-treated or neglected, might depart, leaving the kris powerless. It was also so closely identified with its owner that, at one time, on certain occasions it was considered a legal proxy for the owner, for instance, where a bridegroom did not personally attend his wedding.

Historically, there were a number of accepted factors by which the superiority or luckiness of a kris might be judged, as it was believed that the kris must be compatible with its owner otherwise misfortune might befall him. These included the number of times it had shed blood, the fame of its maker, its alleged magic powers, the pattern of its *pamur*, the quality of the alloys used and the blade length.

There are many systems of kris measurement; some are based on comparative measurements in relation to the blade itself, and others combine the blade measurement with a personal measure of the owner, such as the width of a thumb joint or the distance from nipple to nipple, and a formula.

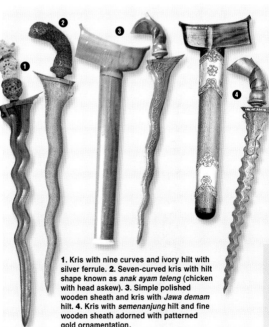

1. Kris with nine curves and ivory hilt with silver ferrule. 2. Seven-curved kris with hilt shape known as *anak ayam teleng* (chicken with head askew). 3. Simple polished wooden sheath and kris with *Jawa demam* hilt. 4. Kris with *semenanjung* hilt and fine wooden sheath adorned with patterned gold ornamentation.

Evolution
The kris has evolved from a sacred and royal fighting weapon to a standard part of Malay dress and an indication of social position for the rich and powerful, before assuming its present-day role as a ceremonial symbol, a cultural icon and a collector's item or family heirloom. The kris is included in the royal regalia of most of the Malay rulers as well as that of the Yang di-Pertuan Agong (see 'Gold jewellery and regalia').

81

Brassware

Malays have long used fine brassware in daily life, this custom evolving due to a need for an alternative to silver and gold, usually reserved for royalty and the aristocracy, for use by ordinary villagers. Items such as dulang *(large trays),* sirih *(betel) sets, kettles, pots, spittoons, oil lamps and incense burners are now entrenched in traditional Malay culture. The brassware of Terengganu artisans, particularly white brass, is renowned. Brass cannons, gongs, kettles and adornments are also highly prized by many of the indigenous peoples of Sarawak and Sabah.*

ABOVE LEFT: Undated bronze socketed implements known as celts found in Sungai Jenera, Kelantan.

ABOVE RIGHT: Dongson bronze bell found near Muar, Johor, believed to be dated at 150 CE.

Early bronzeware

Decorated bronze drums, named after the Dongson area of North Vietnam where they originated, and similar large bells are the most notable ancient bronzeware found in Malaysia, and are believed to have been imported during the late Bronze Age, approximately 2,500 years ago.

Other smaller bronzeware items were also thought to have been imported, until the discovery in Gua Harimau, Perak of a socketed bronze celt (a type of adze) and a casting mould dated to the earliest period of the Bronze Age. This, as well as similar discoveries in Tapadong, Sabah, suggests that bronzeware might have been produced here during the Bronze Age. Ancient bronze objects including a knife, bowls, figurines and turtle-shaped belt toggles have also been found in Peninsular Malaysia and Sabah and Sarawak.

Ancient turtle-shaped bronze belt toggle, an heirloom kept by the Kayan people of Sarawak, and believed to have been made locally.

Origin

The origin of brass (an alloy of copper and zinc) in Southeast Asia can be traced back to the earlier art of casting bronze, a mixture of copper and tin. Bronze work in Southeast Asia has been dated to 3000 BCE based on archaeological finds in northern Thailand. It spread to other parts of Southeast Asia during the Dongson period (c. 500 BCE). It is widely believed that the art of casting brass was first introduced into Kuala Terengganu and Kelantan from Thailand about 300 years ago.

Development of brassware and uses

The brass industry owes its initial development to ordinary villagers who began using simple objects made from brass—serving trays, kettles, cooking pots and heavy buckets. Over time, brass casting evolved into a craft industry producing smaller domestic pieces of traditional design for decorative and social use, and for the religious ceremonies of the ordinary Malay household. Such items included candlesticks, ashtrays, scented water dispensers and *sirih* sets, which came to be passed down from one generation to another and closely guarded as valuable heirlooms.

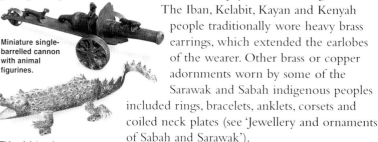

Miniature single-barrelled cannon with animal figurines.

This miniature brass cannon in a crocodile form symbolized strength and power.

In Brunei, the Malays developed an artistic flair for decorating bronze cannons with intricate local motif designs and other beautiful patterns along the muzzles. Their work was imported into the neighbouring districts of Borneo. Much later, the Iban, and to some extent other ethnic groups, began to learn casting methods and created their own styles—cannons with dragons, crocodiles and other similar designs—for their own purposes. The large plain ones were actually used as weapons. Miniature brass cannons were made as a form of currency, were given as an exchange of gifts, and were also kept as pieces of art.

Among many Borneo peoples, bronze and brass gongs, cannons and kettles were highly prized as family heirlooms and were often presented

Brass kettle from Sarawak decorated with a dragon spout and lion handle.

Ornamental Sarawak brass gong featuring dragon, fish and crab motifs. Apart from being used for musical accompaniment, signalling and summoning, gongs play an important part in ceremonies and rituals.

during betrothals as bridal gifts, and used for religious ceremonies and social occasions. Brassware generally had many functions, aside from practical household uses, including forming part of bridewealth or burial or funerary goods, and as a traditional form of payment for transgressions.

The Iban, Kelabit, Kayan and Kenyah people traditionally wore heavy brass earrings, which extended the earlobes of the wearer. Other brass or copper adornments worn by some of the Sarawak and Sabah indigenous peoples included rings, bracelets, anklets, corsets and coiled neck plates (see 'Jewellery and ornaments of Sabah and Sarawak').

Ornamentation style

Over the past 200 years, ornamentation on Peninsular brassware has remained limited to a small number of designs and motifs, the most common being floral and vegetation motifs within geometric motifs or short excerpts from the Qur'an. Alternatively, craftsmen left their work completely devoid of decoration, apart from perhaps some scalloping along lips and edges, as seen in the polished shiny brasses of Terengganu. Brassware from Terengganu is markedly different in form and style from that made in neighbouring Southeast Asian countries and Sarawak, which display an intricacy and elegance of form, with fine designs and patterns of various elements. The products from Peninsular Malaysia are relatively plain and simple, the emphasis being more on the functional shape of the object rather then on the decorative pattern. In comparison, Sarawak brass objects are usually decorated with figures of real or imaginary animals like the dragon or crocodile, similar to Brunei brassware.

Making a brass cooking pot

The following illustrates the production of brassware using the 'lost wax' or *ciré perdu* process.

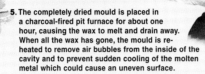
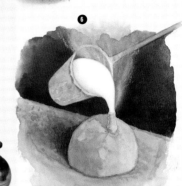

1. A model of the item, or a section of it, is created from fine clay, plaster of paris or wood and dipped in cold water, then molten wax, several times. It is allowed to cool between each application, until the correct thickness and density of wax is reached.

2. The wax-coated model is turned on a foot-operated string lathe. Then the model is separated from the wax mould—depending on the shape, the wax may be cut into two halves then re-joined—and immersed in water.

3. The wax mould is coated on the outside with three different layers of fine clay: (1) unadulterated clay as a base to retain a clear impression from the wax mould; (2) a mixture of clay and fine beach sand to offset shrinkage in the final layer when it is fired; (3) clay mixed with rice husks to prevent cracking when the clay dries out. It is dried in the open for a couple of days between each application.

4. A casting funnel made of wax is made, coated, and attached to the bottom of the mould.

5. The completely dried mould is placed in a charcoal-fired pit furnace for about one hour, causing the wax to melt and drain away. When all the wax has gone, the mould is re-heated to remove air bubbles from the inside of the cavity and to prevent sudden cooling of the molten metal which could cause an uneven surface.

6. A mixture of brass is melted in a crucible and then poured carefully into the hollow mould through the attached funnel, ensuring every part of the cast object is reached and that it cools as evenly as possible. Any leaks in the clay are immediately sealed with fresh wet clay.

7. Once the mould has cooled, and the brass has hardened, the baked clay is broken off. The cast brass is examined for any flaws, which are removed and filled with tin or lead solder. To disguise any repair work, a mixture of gold and aluminium crystals in varnish is rubbed into the spot.

8. The object is polished manually on a simple string lathe. The beautiful shine on white brass is achieved through the use of fine emery paper.

Source: Kraftangan Malaysia publication.

The industry

During the 20th century, the use of brass items as domestic ware fell increasingly into decline, particularly because of the import of alternatives such as iron, steel, aluminium and plastic. Other factors contributing to the industry's decline included the importation of cheaper brassware from Thailand, India and Burma, the irregular supply of raw materials and the laborious and outmoded technique of local manufacture.

Specialized brass kitchenware still has a market today, as do high-value craft objects such as *sirih* sets, candlesticks, ritual washing equipment, incense burners and vases, and in Sarawak, betel boxes, gongs and kettles. Craft items are usually made to order.

In recent years, the craftsmen of Terengganu have also been sought out by cultural groups to produce sets of brass gongs for the *caklempung*, a percussion instrument which forms part of the orchestra used by local *gamelan* groups (see 'Traditional musical instruments'). With the encouragement of the Ministry of Culture, Arts and Heritage and the Malaysian Handicraft Development Corporation, these craftsmen have been led into a new era, and given new challenges. This new demand will perhaps open a new horizon for an age-old tradition to be continued.

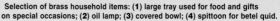

Workers at Pusat Kemajuan Kraftangan Malaysia (Malaysian Handicraft Development Centre) in Kuala Terengganu inserting funnels into items for the lost wax process of brass manufacture in 1978.

Types of brassware and casting techniques

Brass casting is still an important village industry, especially in Terengganu. Utilitarian pieces, such as cake moulds, cooking pots and vessels, large bowls and kettles, are generally made from yellow brass. White brass, with a mirrored finish, is mainly used to create more exclusive decorative objects such as *sirih* sets, trays, ashtrays, perfume sprinklers and gift items that are made to order. Both types of brass are usually cast in the *ciré perdu* or 'lost wax' method. This process is common for all types of casting where moulded wax is replaced by metal.

The formula for the composition of local brass varies between craftsmen, from between one and four parts of brass to one of nickel and one part of zinc. Yellow brass is composed of one part zinc to eight parts of scrap brass. White brass contains a higher proportion of zinc than normal brass, and contains approximately five parts of brass to two parts of nickel.

White brass incense burner at Abidin mosque, Kuala Terengganu.

Selection of brass household items: (1) large tray used for food and gifts on special occasions; (2) oil lamp; (3) covered bowl; (4) spittoon for betel quid.

Silverware

Silver has been used in the creation of a wide range of objects, from coins to combs, brooches to belts, tobacco boxes to sirih *(betel leaf) sets. A malleable material, it can withstand high-pressure rolling and hammering without cracking or breaking. Although silver does not occur naturally in Malaysia, its use has become widespread. The Malays and the Straits Chinese wore silver jewellery as a symbol of wealth and status, and it is an important part of Iban traditional dress. Kelantan and Melaka are Peninsular states most often associated with silverwork.*

Round silver *sirih* box with implements for preparing the betel quid: (**1**) *gobek* for crushing ingredients; (**2**) container for betel leaves; (**3**) ornamental *kacip* cutter for slicing areca nuts; (**4**) small condiment containers for chalk lime, cloves, and gambier condiment (Muzium Negara Collection).

Early silver objects

The earliest silver objects to be found in Malaysia are religious artefacts and figurines that date back to the Hindu-Buddhist era. These artefacts were discovered in a casket between the foundation stones of a temple in the Bujang Valley, Kedah, and are dated from the 3rd to 12th centuries CE. Silver coins were used from the 16th century.

Silver coins

The earliest silver coins in common usage were Spanish silver dollars or eight-real pieces (**1**), which were adopted as the standard unit of currency in the Malay Peninsula in the mid-1580s. Initially, Portuguese merchants brought these coins from Europe to Melaka, but later supplies came from mints in Central and South America. These minted silver pesos were merely pieces of bar silver that had been roughly hammered into shape and imprinted with the Crowned Arm of Spain on one side and the Cross of Christ on the other. Each coin was of a specific weight and purity—known as 'cob reals' by the Europeans, and '*real batu*' by the Malays because they resembled flat pieces of stone.

In the 1730s, hand-minted cobs were replaced by machine-made ones, called 'pillar' dollars due to the depiction of the Pillars of Hercules (**2**). This design changed in the 1770s to the bust of the King of Spain. Coins of this type were issued until 1821, when Spain lost the majority of their Central and South American colonies. In 1825, silver dollars from the Mexican Republic replaced the Spanish cobs in the Malay Peninsula. Other silver dollars, especially those from the United States and Japan, were also distributed in Malaya in the 19th century.

Islamic silver coins were also produced in Johor, including the Sultan Abdul Jalil Shah III *penjuru* (**3**) from 1623–77 CE. In Kedah, the Sultan Muhammad Jiwa Khalifatur Rahman one rial (**4**), among other coins, was used from 1710–73 CE.

Jewellery

In the Malay Peninsula, jewellery served as heirlooms and status symbols of a family's position and wealth. Noblewomen would adorn themselves with hairpins, earrings, necklaces, bracelets, pendants, anklets, rings, combs, brooches, *pending* (belt buckles) and belts. Most of the jewellery was made from silver, although it was sometimes gilded. For Malays, it was, and still is, customary for jewellery to be exchanged at weddings between the bride's and groom's families. The Straits Chinese, Portuguese and many of the ethnic groups in Sarawak and Sabah also wore jewellery during special ceremonies and community festivities, at which women displayed their jewellery to its fullest.

Silver jewellery, including headdresses, necklaces, anklets, bracelets, belts and girdles, was predominant in the traditional ensemble of a Sarawakian Iban woman. In Sabah, silver coin belts were also favoured by the Kadazandusun, and the Bajau and Dusun Tindal wore decorative embossed silver boxes, often used as part of the *sirih* set,

For ceremonial and festive occasions, Iban women wear traditional finery like this featuring silver jewellery in various forms.

as an adornment. (See 'Jewellery and ornaments of Sabah and Sarawak').

For many centuries, the Malays, Straits Chinese and Melaka Portuguese have worn *baju kebaya labuh*, a long loose-fitting open blouse that reaches below the knee and is worn with a sarong. The blouse was secured by a set of *kerongsang* (three identical circular brooches) or, in the case of the Straits Chinese, *kerongsang toh* (two identical brooches and a large heart-shaped one). The *kerongsang* was usually held together by ornamental chains.

In the Peninsula, bracelets and anklets in silver or gold were customarily worn in pairs. Each bracelet and anklet was made up of two separate parts that were joined by a hinge and a screw. Rings were also very popular. Often, they were decorated with a series of raised pyramids and bands. Techniques used included granulation, repoussé, appliqué or simple engraving.

Set of silver *kerongsang* in the Peranakan style.

Pair of anklets with an Islamic foliate pattern (courtesy of the National Museum of Singapore, National Heritage Board).

Nielloware

A form of enamelled silver which has the appearance of silver designs drawn on a black surface is called nielloware. This technique was learned by Malay silversmiths from Thai craftsmen in Patani, southern Thailand, where it was first established during the 12th century. It involves applying black enamel, composed of metal sulphides, to the recessed parts of the silver object's surface. The item is then fired to fuse the enamel to the silver before being filed to a smooth finish. Common items made from niello were bowls, kettles, *sirih* sets and *pending*.

Receptacles and amulets

Apart from exquisite jewellery, Malay silversmiths fashioned receptacles in the form of tobacco boxes or jewellery boxes and *sirih* sets. The boxes were either octagonal or round and made of three pieces of silver: the bottom, sides and lid. A *sirih* set comprised a *sirih* box, usually a rich ornamented spherical vessel, five small condiment bowls, a *gobek* (crusher) and a *kacip* (cutter) for slicing areca nuts. The practice of chewing betel leaves was traditionally an important social and ceremonial activity, spanning all classes among the Malays, Straits Chinese, and in Sarawak and Sabah. Although now seldom used, *sirih* sets are still valued as heirlooms and antiques, and continue to be used as part of royal regalia of the Malay rulers, and on such occasions as rites of passage, betrothals and weddings.

In Malay society, amulets were worn for protection to ward off evil spirits. It is believed that an amulet reinforces the human strength of the wearer. Amulets were usually in the shape of a cylinder with a few small loops on one side, through which a chain or string is inserted. The amulet was worn around the neck, waist or upper arm. Sacred items, such as a written prayer or scent, were sometimes placed in the hollow cylinder.

A unique item was the *caping*, a heart-shaped modesty disc mainly worn by Malay and Iban children. It was worn by girls, and sometimes boys, and was hung from the waist by a chain or thread.

Niello inlaid *pending* with petal and floral motifs (Perak Museum Collection).

LEFT: The cross design on this *caping* was often used for males.

BELOW: Boy wearing *caping*, late 1800s.

Evolution of the industry

Silverware has always been particularly important to the Peranakan or Straits Chinese of all types of metalware, and out of their combined Chinese and Malay ancestry, a unique style evolved (see 'The Straits Chinese Heritage'). Their silversmiths also reproduced objects in traditional Malay styles, thus competing strongly in the early 20th century with Malay silversmiths who no longer enjoyed royal patronage. Thus, in the 1920s, the industry suffered a decline among the Malays.

A revival of silverworking occurred in Kelantan during the 1930s when a group of Malay and British civil servants and their wives imported raw silver and privately commissioned Malaysian silversmiths to reproduce European-style tableware and brooches, decorated with Malay designs, for local and foreign clientele. Today, the production of Malay silver is largely carried on by a few family-run businesses in the states of Kelantan and Terengganu, some also with branches in Kuala Lumpur. Many of the items produced are specially commissioned one-of-a-kind pieces. The methods and techniques of manufacturing Malay silver have remained basically the same.

Sources and standard of silver

Pre-20th century silver was imported from China, in the form of bars and ingots, and was also obtained by melting down silver trade dollars and antique silver. For this reason, there was no industry standard for the grade of silver used, and it varied from 80 to 90 per cent in purity, sometimes falling as low as 60 per cent.

There are now industry standards of fineness for precious metal content, expressed in parts per thousand, which are 958.4, 925, 830 and 800 for silver objects. Since 1994, the law required that the standard of fineness be marked on articles made of precious metal. However, hallmarking, whereby articles are tested by an independent office and hallmarked with the standard of fineness, the maker's mark, and the tester's mark, is not compulsory, nor widely practised.

Ornate and intricately crafted silver bag.

Kelantan silverwork

'Vessels and ornaments and jewellery as beautiful in form, as original in design and almost as perfect in workmanship as anything of a similar kind to be found in the East' was how Sir Frank Swettenham described the silverware of Kelantan when he visited the state in the 1930s. Kelantan silverware is renowned for its intricate design and superior quality. Items produced range from the functional to the purely ornamental, and includes fruit bowls, tea sets, ashtrays and jewellery in the form of earrings, bracelets, chains and pendants.

Silversmithing techniques in Kelantan have local characteristics. For instance, Kelantan silversmiths use coconut oil to clean silver. Uniquely, moulds are made from the body of cuttlefish gathered from the beach. These are cleaned and left in running water for ten days to get rid of the salt, then left to dry in the sun. After drying, the body is sawn in half and the inner surfaces rubbed down. The two halves of the body are then tied together with metal wire, to form the mould into which molten silver is poured. After a few minutes, when the silver solidifies, the mould is broken and discarded, and any excess silver is trimmed. This technique is particularly good for producing small, flat and round objects.

Craftsman finishing an ornate filigree piece in the form of a Malay kite, symbolic of Kelantan (above) and brooches (right).

A silversmith may take several days to engrave a pattern like this, requiring concentration and precision.

Frequently filigree is used for decoration. Much of Kelantan filigree work is executed with either circular or twisted wires. To make the latter, wires are first flattened between rollers and then cut into short pieces. Using pliers to hold one end, a sliding board then rolls over the rest of the wire to create a torque that rapidly twists the wire. At the optimum rotation, the bends on the wire are not perceptible and the wire looks like a row of fine silver beads. Filigree work is used mostly to adorn fine jewellery and is sometimes enhanced by the addition of intricate little bells and disks.

Another method of decorating silverware is pattern transfer. The design is first drawn on paper and then transferred onto the silver object. A skilled craftsman will use carbon paper to obtain a rough imprint, filling in the details with Chinese ink with his own hand. Using a small hammer and a punch, the craftsman gently carves the design. Less able craftsmen might simply stick the paper on to the object. A master craftsman, however, will engrave the design directly onto the object.

Designs include geometric patterns and stylized floral and leaf motifs, which are interconnected in an expansive design using curves in the form of creepers.

Ancient Malay floral motifs include the *bunga jawa* (tamarind flower) (above) and the *bunga sirih* (betel leaf flower) (left).

RIGHT: This jug has been decorated using the pattern transfer method and features a form of floral design popular in Kelantan.

Pewterware

After platinum, gold and silver, pewter is the fourth most precious metal. It is an alloy of tin strengthened by the addition of small amounts of other metals, and has long been used for domestic ware. Malaysian pewterware is world-renowned. Tin has been mined in the Peninsula for over 600 years, and has been an important source of revenue for Malaysia in modern times. In the early days it was used in different forms as currency.

Tin money

Tin animals and coins
The oldest examples of cast tin objects in Malaysia are roughly fashioned tin animal forms, such as crocodiles, elephants, cockerels, grasshoppers and fish (above). Believed to have first been used in the 15th century as gifts to royalty, and for magical rites related to newly opened tin mines; later they were used as currency, mainly in Perak, Selangor and Negeri Sembilan.

Tin ingots
Traders used tin ingots as trade money as far back as the 9th to the 15th centuries. When Chinese Admiral Cheng Ho visited Melaka in 1413, solid tin ingots were being cast in several states, and used as a form of currency. At the beginning of the 19th century, tin ingots in the shape of pagodas, called *tampang* (right)—also known as 'tin hat money' due to their shape—were widely used in Selangor, Perak and Pahang.

Tin coins
In Melaka, currency in the form of tin ingots became obsolete with the introduction of the first tin coin that was minted instead of cast. This was the *casha* or *pitis* (left)—a highly stylized coin with Jawi and Arabic script, issued during the reign of Sultan Muzaffar Shah of Melaka (1446–59). After 1511, all other existing coinage was melted down and replaced by a more comprehensive coinage, three of which—the bastardos, soldos and dineros—were made of pewter.

Tin money trees
Many states had different styles of tin money trees that were used as currency.

Kelantan
In Kelantan, money trees were used in the 19th century and known as *pohon pitis* (**1**). Two rows of coins were cast in brass moulds with 15 or more recesses along a central duct, branching out on both sides. Molten metal was poured into the mould running along each recess and filling up each branch to form a money tree. When the metal cooled, the coins were broken off and the trunk and branches re-smelted.

Terengganu
Terengganu had more than one type of tin coin tree, all with Arabic inscriptions on the coins. One was in the shape of sunrays (**2**) which was cast using the 'lost wax' method (see 'Brassware'). Others were cast direct from the mould, including a tree with 13 coin pieces (**3**) and another with 12 angular shaped branches (**4**).

Kedah
In Kedah, trees shaped as a fighting cockerel perched on a series of joined rings (**5**) were issued between 1710–73. The cockerel and each attached ring had an accepted value—the cockerel was worth 5 cents of the Spanish dollar, and each ring, 1 cent.

Initial development of the tin and pewter industry in Malaysia
Due to the value of tin, the Portuguese, and later the Dutch, attempted to monopolize it after their respective conquests of Melaka in 1511 and 1641. During the 17th and 18th centuries, the Dutch successfully obtained a monopoly through treaties with Malay chiefs.

In the 19th century, tin became important to the development of the nation due to the discovery of great lodes of the metal. This resulted in the migration of workers from China in the 1840s–60s to work the tin fields of Larut and later Kinta in Perak and parts of Selangor that later become Kuala Lumpur.

Historically, the use of pure tin in the manufacture of household objects was not widespread, as tin was considered too soft to be practical for such applications. To strengthen it, an alloy such as lead, antimony or copper was added to form pewter. By the late Middle Ages, the use of pewter items such as plates, bowls and tankards was well established in Europe. In Asia, China was the first nation to manufacture pewter and Chinese pewter craftsmen introduced pewter to the rest of Southeast Asia. By the late 1800s, a number of Chinese tinsmiths in Malaya started to manufacture pewterware such as tea caddies, teapots, wine ewers and opium boxes for domestic use. Pewterware items were popularly used as wedding gifts, and ceremonial items for use on the altar table such as candleholders, incense and oil burners, were also made from pewter.

Seven-branch antique oil lamp of the kind used as an altar piece for Chinese ancestor worship and in temples.

Pewter touchmarks
Touchmarks, like the hallmark of a goldsmith, were stamped on the bottom of each piece of pewter to identify the maker. These are examples of pewter company touchmarks which may be found on antique pieces:

| Kuala Lumpur Pewter Co. | Gomes & Dustagir Co., Melaka | YSC Pewter, Kuala Lumpur |

Evolution of the modern pewter industry

During the Great Depression of the early 1930s, the tin industry slumped, affecting pewter craftsmen of the Malay Peninsula. Realizing that traditional items such as altarpieces took up too much production time, many experimented with new technology and more modern articles were designed, including beer tankards, ashtrays and flower vases, which were favoured by the British residing in the Peninsula.

Subsequently, during World War II (1941–45), when the Japanese rationed tin, there was no demand for pewter and many companies closed down. One company that survived was Selangor Pewter, whose founder, pewtersmith Yong Koon, had originally sailed from the Guangdong province in China to the Malay Peninsula in 1885 with his simple handmade tools and other implements related to his craft. From these humble beginnings, the family-run business prospered. By the 1970s, Selangor Pewter began branching out of Malaysia and made inroads into Singapore and Australia, followed by the American, European and Japanese markets. In 1979, Sultan Salahuddin Abdul Aziz Shah of Selangor (r. 1960–2001) conferred a royal mandate on the company, which later changed its name to Royal Selangor in 1992.

The first touchmark, *Ngeok Foh* (top) and the present-day design (above) of Royal Selangor.

Malaysia is recognized as a world leader in the manufacture of high-quality pewterware. The revival of interest in pewter is largely due to Royal Selangor's influence on the world market as one of the world's largest manufacturers and retailers of pewter. A number of other pewter manufacturers, including Tumasek, established in 1981, and Kedah Pewter, have entered the market using similar methods of manufacture and products.

Techniques and materials

Initially, all pewter objects were handcrafted. Only the handles or decorative ornamentation were cast in greenstone moulds. Until the 1940s, an object would be manufactured totally by an individual craftsman who would undertake his own casting, shaping, soldering and polishing. The craftsman's ability, dexterity, judgment and accurate timing were all important. In earlier days, the pewter craftsman would first cast sheets of pewter about 46 centimetres square by melting together the correct ratio of tin and lead in an open cauldron over a charcoal flame. Later, the sheet would be cut to the requisite size or pattern with hand shears and hammered into shape with a wooden mallet. The item would then be filed and soldered

The two halves of a greenstone mould were dusted with talcum powder and clamped together before the molten tin was poured into the channels.

together. Today, molten metal is poured into steel moulds, where it is cooled and solidified and then removed. As in the past, more complicated items are cast in several parts and soldered together. The finished article is then polished.

Previously, the content of the lead mixture would differ from one object to another, for example, 20 per cent for making ceremonial containers, 10 per cent for drinking cups and food containers. For others, it could be as much as 50 per cent lead. Articles were sold by weight and, since lead was cheaper than tin, the greater the lead level, the higher the profit margin.

By the mid–1940s, lead alloy in pewter was gradually replaced with antimony and copper, which, besides having the added value of being nontoxic (unlike lead), rendered the pewter more malleable under high temperatures and made way for the introduction of spun pewter.

Antique hand tools of a pewtersmith.

Examples of pewterware produced by Royal Selangor: **(1)** miniature desktop clock; **(2)** ornamental bowl with four seasons motifs; and **(3)** award winning tea-set design with mirror silver-like finish.

Making a pewter object

1. Molten metal is poured into a mould.
2. The mould is cooled with water.
3. After the metal has cooled and hardened the mould is opened.
4. The mould is separated into two halves so that the object can be removed.
5. The pattern is engraved by hand onto the object.
6. Polishing completes the manufacturing process.

87

Gold jewellery and regalia

A material originally only used by the royalty and nobility of Malaysia, gold has an illustrious history in the country. Although Malaysia's gold mines fell into disuse in the 1800s, goldsmiths have continued working, with imported gold, to produce fine royal jewellery and court regalia. From the time of the Melaka Sultanate to the present day, gold items have been specially crafted for royalty, notably the gold kris and pending *(belt buckle).*

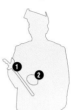

Royal regalia
The gold objects in the Malaysian royal regalia are (1) *Keris Panjang Diraja* (royal long kris) which has a gold hilt and sheath and is the most important symbol of authority during installation ceremonies, and (2) *Pending Diraja* (royal waist buckle) made from 24 karat gold decorated with 11 rubies and embossed with the crest of the Federal Government.

Roots of gold
Gold mining in Peninsular Malaysia began about 2000 years ago, although very little is known about gold production from that period. What is known, however, is that gold was excavated and mined near Sungai Jelai in Pahang, on Gunung Ledang in Johor, at Johol and Gemencheh in Negeri Sembilan and at Ulu Tomok near the border of Kelantan and Patani in southern Thailand. Mining ceased at the end of the 1800s.

Gold foil figures from Santubong (Sarawak Museum).

The earliest gold objects—gold leaf, crockery, rings and beads, and a belt of pure gold weighing about 13.2 kilograms—were found in Kedah, primarily at a Bujang Valley temple site, and date from the Srivijaya period (7th–11th centuries CE). Indian travellers called the Malay Peninsula 'Suvarnaumi' (the Golden Land), while Ptolemy, the 2nd century CE Greek geographer, referred to it as the 'Golden Khersonese' or Golden Peninsula.

Ancient gold disc and crockery artefacts found in Kedah in the Bujang Valley. Some of these were circular in shape, while others were in the shape of Hindu deities.

Jewellery and regalia

The royalty of Malaysia required gold jewellery for personal use and for official functions. Exquisite items, such as state crowns and tiaras, were worn only during palace ceremonies. Royalty also carried kris with hilts and sheaths decorated with gold. In fact, only royalty were allowed to have gold on their kris or any other weapon of state regalia. Kris were prominent during royal weddings, before which they were decorated with personalized designs.

Most of the finest jewellery owned by Malay royalty today was crafted between the 18th and the early 19th centuries. Gold was in plentiful supply then, and goldsmiths enjoyed royal patronage, giving them the opportunity to produce works of incomparable brilliance.

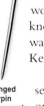

Melaka two-pronged gold Nonya hairpin with rose-cut diamonds in the *parure* style, 1930s (Henry Bong Permanent Collection).

Perhaps the most striking gold object worn by royalty as part of ceremonial dress is the *pending* (belt buckle). It was generally worn just above the navel to secure the man's sarong or *samping*.

The Golden Age

The greatest period for Malay goldsmithing and gold production lasted from the 15th to the 19th centuries. During the Melaka Sultanate (1400–1511 CE), gold dust was used as payment for goods, especially tin and spices. Not just originating from the Malay Peninsula, gold dust was also brought in from Sumatra, Goa and other parts of India, the Middle East and China.

Islamic gold coins were issued in Peninsular Malaysia by sultans in Kelantan, Kedah, Johor and Terengganu. Usually, these coins would be inscribed with the name and rank of the leader(s) of the time, a religious statement, and the place and date of minting. The earliest, from Kelantan, believed to have been issued from 1400, featured a *kijang* (barking deer) and floral motifs. Coins from Kedah and Johor followed later from the 16th century. The courts of Kedah and Kelantan used these early coins to make gold sheets from which the *bunga mas* (golden flower) tribute gift was fashioned and sent to the King of Siam.

Royal patronage ensured a high standard of craftsmanship as well as a continuous demand for gold objects. The need for ceremonial regalia, personal ornaments and luxury items kept

BELOW: Kupang coin, unique to Kelantan, depicting a *kijang* (barking deer), which was the earliest gold coin to be issued in the Peninsula.

RIGHT: Reverse of octagonal gold *kupang* coin minted in Johor and issued during the reign of Sultan Alauddin Riayat Shah II (1527/8–64).

Although they were in a variety of sizes, the *pending* was always oval in shape, with tapered ends, a slightly embossed surface and protruding, graduated or scalloped borders. It could be made from gold or silver. Surface decoration usually consisted of a finely chased central floral medallion surrounded by traditional floral motifs. The *pending* was also worn by Malay women and Straits Chinese women as part of their traditional dress. The best known Malay woman reputed to wear *pending* was Che Siti Wan Kembang, the first ruler of Kelantan, who reigned during the 17th century.

Hairpins (*cucuk sanggul*) in gold or silver and set with stones were used to secure smoothly rolled or plaited hair. The majority of hairpins made by Chinese gold- and silver-smiths were in the shape of large ear picks. Although the hairpins were bulky and top heavy, they were actually hollow. Those decorated with a star and crescent moon were worn by Malay women. For everyday wear, only one or two hairpins would be used, but on festive

the goldsmiths well occupied. No palace was without its resident goldsmiths. In important political centres such as Kota Bharu, Kuala Terengganu and Kuala Kangsar, where goldsmiths gathered, distinct local styles of jewellery developed. This was partly cultivated by requests from the noble families of each area for jewellery to suit their individual tastes. Groups of craftsmen were installed in village communities to cater to their needs. These various groups could be called on to work together for grand palace ceremonies, so there was never any shortage of skills or expertise.

Miniature replica of a *bunga mas*. The actual ones were over 1.6 meter tall and were presented every three years by the courts of Kedah and Kelantan as a tribute to the King of Siam from the late 18th to the early 19th centuries. Two examples from Kedah—one in gold, the other in silver—are in the Royal Palace in Bangkok, while one thought to be from Kelantan is in the National Museum in Bangkok. A miniature gold version is kept at the palace of the Sultan of Kelantan. The leaves of equal size were made using iron moulds.

Dokoh breast ornament with attached amulets in a breadfruit leaf design, decorated with filigree and appliqué work and gemstones (Muzium Negara Collection).

occasions pins were worn in graduated sets of three, five or seven. A bride's formal wedding attire included an elaborate headdress comprising a number of hairpins, the crowns of which were designed to quiver as the bride moved.

The Malays wore a broad necklace, of which the oldest type is the *dokoh*. The main pendant in the centre of the necklace is in the shape of a stylized *daun sukun* (breadfruit leaf). It was common for the pendant to be made three dimensionally, with the centre filled with a resinous substance to add weight to the necklace. It would often be decorated using the granulation method and stained red. Today, replicas are used as wedding jewellery.

Gold jewellery today

Although gold jewellery is no longer reserved exclusively for royalty and the aristocracy, as in the past, for some it is still a reflection of status and position. Many in Malaysia value gold jewellery not only as an item of adornment, but also as a prudent form of financial investment. For the Malays and Indians, it is an essential part of wedding bridal finery, and for Malaysians generally, jewellery to be worn for special occasions.

Malay women often buy gold jewellery for weddings and other festive occasions, for example, Hari Raya or to mark the birth of a child.

For these reasons, the production and sale of gold jewellery has become a large industry in Malaysia. Even small towns generally have at least one local goldsmith. Larger businesses also operate in Malaysia, both foreign and locally owned, some exporting jewellery overseas. Jewellery is also imported from places such as Europe, India and Hong Kong.

Tools and techniques of goldsmithing

Pure gold is preferred for working as it is soft and malleable. However, most jewellery manufacturing houses use a gold alloy because it is harder and cheaper. The purity of gold is measured in carats—24-carat gold is 100 per cent pure, while 14-carat gold contains 14 parts gold to 10 parts metal.

Tools

The most personal of a goldsmith's tools are a series of punches—short metal studs—with a variety of points and edges. They are used for executing the design and, hence, become a goldsmith's signature by which other goldsmiths can identify his work. Other important tools include chisels, tweezers, files, pliers and scribers, which are needle-sharp engraving implements with mushroom-shaped handles. Drawplates are used when gold wire is required. These are thick metal sheets with holes of different sizes through which gold wire is pulled by a steel rod mandrel (spindle) to reduce its diameter.

Goldsmiths would often fashion tools for their own personal use.

Techniques: repoussé and granulation

When making a gold object, the goldsmith first melts gold in a small crucible that is kept hot by a charcoal fire. Bellows ensure that a constant temperature is maintained so that the gold will melt evenly. Most gold objects are wrought by hand. The goldsmith hammers and chisels the object into shape before filing it down and embossing it with its design. A common hammering device is a conical pestle made of buffalo horn with a layer of soft metal on the outside used for forming curves. This is done by positioning its round blunt point on the gold and using a light hammer to apply pressure.

After the object is formed, it is decorated using the repoussé or granulation technique. Repoussé work involves embossing a relief pattern onto a gold sheet by hammering through from the underside; a bed of resin supports the sheet of metal.

Granulation is a technique where tiny granules of molten gold are applied to a surface by soldering. This technique is used to join separate small pieces of gold as well as to decorate the object. Sometimes, to add lustre to the object, each granule was pounded with a flat-tipped punch until it became faceted. To the same end, small flat circular discs or spangles, perhaps punched with a linear design, were also applied. The granules and spangles, together with gold wires of various diameters, were most effectively used in the creation of the traditional Malay necklace (*dokoh*).

Caping (modesty disc) probably worn by a girl due to the embossed flowers at the top and the bamboo shoot motif below.

ABOVE: The granulation technique is time-consuming as the maximum size of each granule is only 1.5 mm in diameter.

TOP: Spherical fluted scent bottle decorated with flower, leaf and bamboo shoot designs and spangles attached to five ornamental chains. Made using the granulation technique and believed to be 200 years old (Muzium Negara Collection).

LEFT: A half-hoop earring decorated with gold granules and fine gold wire. In the centre is a multi-petalled appliquéd flower.

Techniques: Staining

Gold does not fade or corrode. Therefore, if a variation in the natural colour is desired, the gold has to be stained. For example, to stain a small gold object, it is first immersed in four cups of water in which have been mixed, using a wooden spatula, two spoonfuls of salt and one spoonful of alum. The object and the mixture are held in a *periuk tanah* (clay pot). Copper or iron implements should not be used as they will spoil the process.

After one or two days of soaking, the object is removed from the mixture and cleaned thoroughly. It is then placed among hot embers of wood, usually *kemuning* (Chinese myrtle), but any type of hardwood that does not produce ash when it burns can be used. The object rests in the embers for about five minutes, after which it is immersed in another mixture, this time of three cups of water, three slices of *asam gelugur* (a dried acidic fruit) and a teaspoon of sulphur. Used *asam* is preferred as it is less acidic than unused *asam*. Again, the mixture is held in a clay pot, and boiled for about 10 minutes with the lid of the pot tightly closed to keep the steam in. After boiling, the object is cleaned and heated in embers until it changes colour. If the desired colour is not achieved, the object can be boiled again in the second mixture. This method stains the gold red or orange, and works best with pure gold.

Tobacco box in the shape of a 10-pointed star, stained red and decorated with gold wire, granules and spangles, rubies and clear cut stones. Believed to be approximately 200 years old and to have belonged to Sultan Zainal Abidin III (1725–33) of Terengganu (Muzium Negara Collection).

Jewellery and ornaments of Sabah and Sarawak

The story of gold and silver and other types of jewellery in Sabah and Sarawak is a narrative of their history and links with sultanates in the region and the China trade. Apart from these two preferred metals, copper, brass and less expensive imitations were also used for jewellery and ornaments. Weddings and other ceremonial occasions still provide an excuse to display such objects of traditional finery forming part of a family's wealth and heirlooms.

Collection of highly valued Iban silver heirloom jewellery.

Significance of jewellery and ornaments

Objects of adornment usually have a dual function—they serve as jewellery and ornaments for specific purposes and also items of wealth, particularly those made of gold and silver—though the two functions may coincide. Those that have special significance to the owners are treasured as heirloom property to be handed down. These usually constitute an item of family wealth and symbolic status to be fully displayed during special occasions such as weddings and ceremonial events, with lesser importance given to their use as body ornaments. The quantity, type and number owned also may determine social standing.

Silver and gold ornaments

In Sabah and Sarawak, silver and gold ornaments are worn on many parts of the body, including the earlobes, neck, arms, wrists, ankles, waist, hips, and also in the hair. Ornaments include earrings, necklaces, bracelets, anklets, belts, buckles, pins and headdresses (see 'Costumes and ornaments of Sabah' and 'Costumes and ornaments of 'Sarawak'). Depending on the tribe and purpose, several pieces may be worn at the same time.

Silver coin belts are worn by many of the indigenous people of Sabah and Sarawak, both

Neckpiece of glass, shell, claws and brass bells used by a Bidayuh warrior.

Headdresses

The form and style of head ornaments worn by women along the west coast of Borneo exhibit distinct Chinese influences that can be traced to old Chinese trade with Brunei and the region. These headdresses are indigenous adaptations that resemble the traditional Chinese ceremonial bridal crown of pins and combs. *Sugu tinggi*, the silver headdress of the Iban, is a close descendant, as is the bridal headdress worn by Brunei royalty and some members of the aristocracy.

Bajau and Iranun women wear on their heads the distinct boat-shaped *sarimpak* with dangling attachments known as *garigai*, which also resembles the Chinese bridal headdress. *Sarimpak* were originally made of two pieces of embossed and engraved silver plates on wood and were secured to the wearer's topknot with ribbons.

Older women still adorn their hair with gold and silver pins made from coins and other designs. The use of tortoiseshell and wooden combs capped with gold and silver engraved plates has declined. Their occasional appearance is also hidden by other more eye-catching hair adornments worn by older women and stage performers presenting traditional dances, such as glittery, sequinned and faux gold hairpins.

Iban women wearing silver ornaments and *sugu tinggi* headdresses.

women and men. These may be worn around the waist as belts, often several at a time, or across the chest and shoulders. When worn about the waist, they would sometimes be joined by a silver embossed decorative buckle. Another waist adornment is the unusual girdle made of silver rings threaded onto narrow rattan strings (*rawai*) worn by the Iban women of Sarawak.

Detail on a Iban *rawai* corset.

The Dusun Tindal bride and groom of Kota Belud, as do their shamans, wear around their necks several engraved silver tobacco pouches called *tiupu*

Innovation

In Borneo, gold was greatly valued by most groups, but silver jewellery was more abundant, being less expensive and thus more accessible. The west coastal peoples of Borneo generally had better access to gold and silver jewellery, as they inhabited areas within the traditional trading circuits and distribution networks. They also used and wore many similar items of jewellery with minor variations in form and design adapted to suit the wearer's needs.

Where precious metals such as gold and silver were scarce, the people of Borneo have shown an innate talent to innovate and create substitutes to satisfy needs and demands for jewellery and ornaments—gilded silver and copper objects, brass, alloys and other base-metal imitations are popular substitutes. Generally, any substance or object which catches the eye of the beholder is a potential resource for creating these items.

Indigenous people, particularly those living in the rural hinterland, used a variety of materials to make their traditional jewellery and ornaments. Apart from metals, most of the components were gathered from their immediate environment while others were acquired elsewhere through trade or barter. Items ranged from shells, animal bones and teeth to dried plant material and man-made materials such as discarded bits of metal, wire and tubing. Function also determined their construction and composition. For example, religious values based on animistic beliefs and traditions may decide their form and structure. Amulets or talismans endowed and empowered by some ritual performance are worn for luck and protection. Special necklaces or ornaments containing plant and animal remains such as boar tusks, and even human remains, may become insignias of shamans' ritual authority.

Realistic, more cost effective, imitations are now made of *sugu tinggi* Iban headdresses like this antique silver piece.

Modern substitutes

Many antique jewellery and costume pieces have become scarce or are locked away for safe-keeping. A revival in their use has created a demand, so that replicas, now made from brass and aluminium, have become acceptable substitutes and are widely used. Imitations using paper and paste have become an expedient alternative to create inexpensive costume accessories. Cultural dance troupes and the like commission such imitations from Indonesia. In Sarawak, the descendants of the Maloh are still in the business, fashioning very creditable 'silver ornaments' from heavy tin foil, which can be bought in the Sunday Market at Lubok Antu, across the border from the Ulu Kapuas lakes, any week.

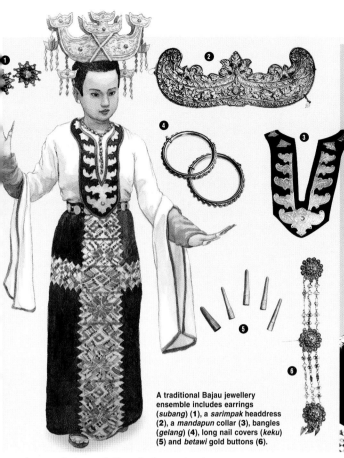

A traditional Bajau jewellery ensemble includes earrings (*subang*) (1), a *sarimpak* headdress (2), a *mandapun* collar (3), bangles (*gelang*) (4), long nail covers (*keku*) (5) and *betawi* gold buttons (6).

Neck ornaments

The Lotud people of Sabah wear several tiers of necklaces, which include the *kokoro'on*, made of small beads, and two to three longer strands (*karo* or *kamuggi*) consisting of silver cones and barrel-shaped beads. A pair of large *karo* strands (*lontugion*) is worn diagonally across the chest. The silver cones are embossed with motifs and are identified by the name of their maker (see also 'Costumes and ornaments of Sabah'). Worn with these necklaces is an ornamental collar, *mandapun*, which reflects the extensive material acculturation among the contiguous coastal groups in the Tuaran and Kota Belud districts of Sabah. Other than the Lotud, the Bajau and the Iranun also wear the *mandapun* as part of their ceremonial costumes. The Lotud prefer red fabric backing for the appliquéd pieces of variously shaped embossed plates of silver and gilt, while the other tribes prefer black. Recent replications contain imitations made from brass and other substitutes, including bits of shiny gold paper, reproduced for stage purposes.

Silver necklaces are worn by Iban women as part of their ceremonial dress. Usually more than one of varying lengths will be worn and they will be of filigree design made up of flower-shaped pieces joined by links or alternating with oval spiral pieces.

BELOW AND LEFT : *Kokoro'on* necklace with large silver cones and beads worn by a Lotud priestess. Such necklaces are highly treasured heirlooms with values calculated according to their worth in buffaloes—one buffalo costs approximately RM1500.

ABOVE: Silver engraved tobacco pouches are worn by various groups as an ornament, for example, around the neck in a cluster by the Dusun Tindal.

and several tiers of silver belts. Bajau horsemen also use these tobacco pouches for the purpose for which they were designed, wearing them hanging from the waist as part of their ceremonial costume. These are usually of Brunei manufacture.

Silver and gold coins were often recycled and constructed into belts, *betawi*, single and three-tier breast pins (treasured by Muslim women on the west coast of Borneo), and gold pins such as breast pins, brooches and hairpins. Gold coin brooches are called *paun* by some groups, taking their name from *emas paun*, the local reference for 22-carat gold coins.

Generally, in Sabah, articles of silver and gilt jewellery decorated with floral motifs were associated with Brunei craftsmanship and origin, but Chinese silversmiths also made those depicting floral motifs and animal forms for the largely non-Muslim market in Sabah and Sarawak. However, traditionally, silverware used by the native peoples in Sarawak, particularly the Iban, was made by itinerant Maloh silversmiths from the middle Kapuas region.

Tangkong brass belt.

Other metal ornaments

Old brass cannons were melted down to produce *tangkong* belts of knobbly brass rings on rattan strings, worn around the hips by Kadazandusun women of the Tambunan and Penampang districts of Sabah. Over time, coiled springs of brass wire made into belts by some tribes became heirlooms.

In Sabah, the Rungus people have a preference for coiled brassware. This is worn about the neck,

Coin belts

The indigenous people of Sabah and Sarawak extensively use belts made from coins of silver and nickel as jewellery. In Sabah, several tiers of coin belts are worn as part of their costume, and the Iban women of Sarawak wear a coin belt (*lampit* or *engkiling*); some of these have several coins or beads dangling from the main strand around the waist (*entelo* or *entelu*).

The most common coin belts are those made from Straits silver dollars or *tongkat* dollars. These and other silver coins were taken out of circulation and transformed into this other type of currency. Their popularity as jewellery induced silversmiths to make silver and gold imitations and replicas to meet demand. Dutch guilders and Mexican silver dollars are two quite common imitations in Sarawak.

RIGHT: Silver *himpogot* coin belt of the Kadazandusun of Penampang, Sabah.

wrists and lower arms, waist and legs below the knees to the ankles. The Biatah women of Sarawak also wear such items, mainly on their arms and legs.

Brass bracelets, arm-rings and leg-rings are also worn by men and women among groups throughout Borneo. Heavy brass and iron ankle rings, that have become museum pieces, had a more practical use. Kadazandusun women in the interior once wore them to keep from falling over while fording fast-flowing streams.

The Kayan, Kenyah, Kelabit and Penan peoples of Sarawak wear heavy solid brass drop earrings, stretching their earlobes to shoulder length. They may wear a single pair or a cluster of earrings. The earrings are usually quite plain in design—simple long citron or fruit shapes— however, some incorporate stylized hornbill or dragon designs.

Heavy brass Sarawak Orang Ulu earrings of various designs—thick and thin solid rings, long fruit drops and the powerful dragon-dog motif. These were traditionally worn by men and women, whose ears would be pierced at a young age.

The Straits Chinese heritage

The Straits Chinese or Peranakan, the descendants of intermarriages between immigrant Chinese males and local females from the 1400s, resided mainly in Melaka, Penang and Singapore. Over the centuries, a unique blend of the two cultures emerged which was reflected in their dress, language, customs and traditions. Elaborate jewellery and metalware items commonly worn and used by the Straits Chinese were best seen during a wedding when these were traditionally displayed on large trays for all to see. Many of the metals, however, were plated. Besides jewellery, the most important characteristic item was the betel leaf or sirih *set.*

ABOVE: Wedding picture of Mr and Mrs Khoo Eng Huat in traditional bridal wear taken at Khoo Kongsi, Penang, on 27 February 1923.

LEFT: An example of a Nonya bridal crown, *tik koay.* Traditionally the crown could only be worn by the first wife.

Craftsmen

Although the Straits Chinese used silver for much the same purposes as the Malays, their silversmiths developed a distinctive style of their own, although they also reproduced objects in traditional Malay styles. They were known for their fine workmanship, and demand for their services was high.

The silversmiths used predominantly the repoussé technique (a form of embossing where the metal is beaten from the underside: see 'Gold jewellery and regalia'). There are, however, numerous family heirloom pieces manufactured in China illustrative of the tracing or chasing technique.

While Chinese goldsmiths were organized into guilds and had hallmarks (see 'Silverware') on their pieces, Straits Chinese silver did not have assay marks; at most, some of the pieces manufactured in China had shop marks. Silver jewellery was also obtained from itinerant haberdashers.

The goldsmiths most favoured by the Straits Chinese were the Singhalese from Jaffna, who would often work in the homes of Peranakan families. They used 20- or 21-carat gold, preferred by the Straits Chinese as it was hard yet malleable for intricate decorations. Wedding sets were usually commissioned in this manner.

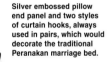

Silver embossed pillow end panel and two styles of curtain hooks, always used in pairs, which would decorate the traditional Peranakan marriage bed.

Common heritage items

Chinese trade with Europe meant that occasionally pieces of European-style silver, including beer tankards, butter and soap dishes, ended up in old Straits Chinese homes. Besides jewellery, other types of Straits Chinese silver were usually connected with ceremonies of rites of passage, especially weddings—for example, heirloom teapots with matching cups (or tea bowls) were often used in the ritual of serving tea to elders as a gesture of respect. A less common object was a wine pot used for pouring wine for the father of the groom upon departure to fetch the bride. Some items, usually made of ceramics, were translated into metal, the most common being the covered potiche (*kam cheng*) used variously for rice, pickles or simply boiled water or sweets.

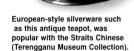

European-style silverware such as this antique teapot, was popular with the Straits Chinese (Terengganu Museum Collection).

Wedding crowns

Elaborate crowns (*tik koay*) were traditionally worn by Nyonya brides. The crown was placed on the bride's head and tied tightly at the back. Her hair was tied into a high chignon (*sanggul*) to support the crown.

Common decorations for such crowns include gilded copper, red velvet pompoms of various sizes, glass baubles, fake pearl beads, images of the auspicious Chinese characters, birds, butterflies, phoenixes, dragons, lotus and peony flowers, and blue iridescent kingfisher feathers. All of these ornaments were suspended on springy wire so that when the bride moved, the crown would quiver and shimmer to bedazzle onlookers.

A shaped black velvet band with red ties is also worn on the bride's forehead just below the crown and is decorated with silver figures of the Eight Immortals (*pak sian*), a female acolyte bearing peaches, a male acolyte bearing gold ingots, and in the centre, a *shou shing* figure sitting astride a stork and a tiny fish.

Sirih sets

The ubiquitous *sirih* sets of Malay and Straits Chinese homes came in a wide variety of styles and materials, the most precious ones being made of metal. As betel chewing was also practised in southern China, such sets were also brought to Southeast Asia by the Chinese trade. While the northern Straits Chinese in Penang were likely to have sets of Thai or Burmese manufacture, those in Melaka often possessed Indonesian sets. Many Straits Chinese families possessed brass *sirih* sets, as this metal was more readily available for local manufacture.

The ornateness and fineness of a *sirih* set reflected the wealth and status of the host, and the rejection or acceptance of the betel quid, signified acceptance or rejection of the hospitality (Terengganu Museum Collection).

Jewellery

Even for daily wear, a Nonya (Straits Chinese woman) would adorn herself from head to toe with jewellery. She might wear hairpins, earrings or ear-studs, necklaces, brooches, belt, bangles and bracelets, rings and anklets all at the same time. Jewellery was a form of financial security.

Some hairpins were large enough to be weapons and have been known to have been used as such. While a single hairpin would suffice, a Nonya used between three and seven to decorate her coiffure—generally, Melaka ladies wore three to five hairpins, while Penang Nonya used five to seven. The hairpins came in sets of graded lengths so that, when placed strategically in the circular hair bun, they protruded at even lengths.

Nonyas had their ears pierced so that on special occasions they could wear dangling earrings which were too heavy to be supported by clips alone. The older generation of Nonya ladies needed the stems of the ear-studs to be quite thick due to the fact that wearing heavy earrings throughout their lives had distended the pierced hole.

A wide variety of *kerongsang* (brooches) were used to fasten the *baju kebaya* (blouse) (see 'Silverware'). A common style was the heart or paisley for the main brooch in a set of three. Some of these were so big and heavy that they were actually sewn onto the blouse because the pins behind the brooch were not strong enough to hold it upright. Apart from brooches for the *kebaya*, cotton blouses carried metal stud buttons, some of which were set with diamonds.

The most common type of belt was made of a flexible network of interlocking rings very much in the style of Victorian metal mesh purses. Some earlier belt types were in fact composed of twisted ropes of metal wires. Connected to belts were purses which looped through and key hooks carrying keychains not dissimilar to the chatelaine. Bracelets, bangles and rings were traditionally worn in pairs. The Nonya did not wear ankle chains, but wore bangle-type anklets which were decorative hollow tubes; a hinge half-way or two-thirds along the tube allowed the anklet to be opened.

Diamonds of various types were set, from brilliant to rose diamonds, with two usual types of stone setting, namely box setting and open-backed setting. Rose diamonds, which are irregularly shaped, must be box-set without claws, compared to high quality diamonds whose refractory nature is best highlighted when set without a base or backing and held in place by claws. Apart from jade (Burmese jade was preferred) and pearls, which were used only during periods of mourning and were set in silver, the Nonya did not indulge in coloured stones.

The Malay-style stained gold (*suasa*), which is a reddish gold alloy, was also popular with the Nonya, as was granulation work (see 'Gold jewellery and regalia'). The Straits Chinese used silver for forging amulets and talismans as it was believed to have protective properties against evil and bad spirits.

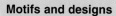

Ear studs with nine pearls called *kerabu* (flower). Traditionally these were worn during mourning as pearls represented tears. A silver setting was used because of its protective qualities.

Motifs and designs

The designs of Peranakan jewellery are a collection of southern Chinese, Malay and European styles, with symbolism prevailing over aesthetics. As a result of this, and the somewhat baroque style of their jewellery, there is often no unity of theme. For example, Taoist immortals may mingle with flowers of the four seasons.

The Malay arabesque of swirling lines also featured in Peranakan jewellery. European influences were Victorian in type, with the paisley motif being popular; this shape lent itself to ear-clips.

A favourite design motif was the auspicious pair of male dragon and female phoenix. Another, the butterfly, signified wedded bliss, while the peony with its abundance of petals symbolized prosperity. Buckles often featured animal motifs, sometimes with a small geometric or floral pattern around the border or on the sides.

Early 19th century repoussé silver gilt belt buckle from Melaka. The auspicious phoenix in the centre circle is surrounded by the eight Buddhist symbols: the bell, wheel of law, conch shell, lotus, endless knot, vase, pair of fish and umbrella. Peonies and mythical *qilin* adorn the outer circle (Henry Bong Permanent Collection).

Beaded wedding belts, this one with a silver buckle, were worn by both brides and grooms.

Mesh purse and keyring set, both of which would be hooked onto a silver belt. This keyring shape represents the Beggar Saint, one of the Eight Immortals and the silver jointed fish symbolizes abundance of wealth, which the two keys can unlock.

Nonya accessories

1. Set of six elaborate silver hairpins (*cucuk sanggul*) from Penang.

2. Gold and rose-cut diamond earrings with floral *parure* work in the shape of a phoenix tail from Penang (1950s).

3. Gold *kerongsang* chained set embellished with rose-cut diamonds in the *parure* style. Such sets were popular in the 1940–70s.

4. Silver chain-linked belts with buckles (*pending*).

5. Gold ring with rose-cut diamonds (Melaka, 1930s).

6. Twisted rope design hollow anklets.

7. Early 20th century beaded slippers from Melaka.

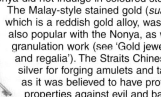
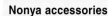

Straits Chinese children dressed in their best finery and jewellery (c. 1910). Courtesy of the National Museum of Singapore, National Heritage Board.

1. The making of ornate and beautiful kites (*wau*) is a skilled Malay craft tradition that is passed down from one generation to the next.

2. Large ornamental lanterns are used to decorate the frontage of Chinese association buildings, temples and, sometimes, houses.

3. This Indian wedding dais is decorated with flowers in auspicious and sacred Hindu designs. Flower garlands adorn the objects used during the wedding and elaborate garlands are worn by the couple around their necks, to be ceremonially exchanged during the marriage ritual, and decorate the bride's hair.

4. The international conference *The Shadow Play as an element in the Development of Civilization*, held at Universiti Malaya in 2004, is an example of the continuing importance of the art of puppetry. Modern and traditional puppet figures are featured on the conference brochure.

5. The interior and exterior areas of temple premises are adorned with elaborate and colourful sculptures of Hindu gods, goddesses and other mythological figures associated with the presiding deity. The statues pictured are located at the Batu Caves Subramaniam Temple in Kuala Lumpur.

6. Dried and cured hide is stretched over local wood to make the *kompang*, a shallow-framed hand-held drum. *Kompang* groups produce special rhythms and sometimes sing religious verses. They play a significant role in Malay ceremonies such as wedding processions and circumcisions as well as other important occasions.

7. Colourful giant joss sticks carved with dragons are lined up in rows, particularly in front of temples, during Chinese festive occasions. Here the joss sticks have been lit at the stroke of midnight by Hokkien in Penang celebrating the Jade Emperor God's birthday.

RECREATIONAL AND CEREMONIAL CRAFTS

The complexity of Malaysian life and heritage is well reflected in its diverse and timeless artistic manifestations, seen in virtually every part of the country in architecture and the various art forms, whether they are ceremonial in function or represent the art of play. The Malay traditional arts of making shadow play (Wayang Kulit) figures, kites (*wau*) and tops (*gasing*) require skill and are significant, even if not religious in character and not as complex as Hindu and Chinese religious arts.

In the Malaysian context, the art of crafting Wayang Kulit figures represents an amalgam of several traditions—Indian, Javanese, Thai and Malay. In traditional puppetry, particularly, the most important form of Wayang Kulit Kelantan, these influences are manifested in the stories and the puppet characters, their physical features, attire and colours, although the overall configuration and expressions of the puppets conform to Malay aesthetic principles. Departing from these traditional styles, modern puppets for newer forms of shadow play developed in Kelantan and Perlis from the 1990s adopt more realistic designs, and are not altogether embedded in the original tradition.

Malay *rebab* with intricate woodcarving, beadwork and painted aspects. Diamond-shaped silver insets have been cut into its stem. A textile pouch at the back held incense which would be burned before a performance.

A similar artistic integrity characterizes traditional kites (*wau*), which continue to be made in the age-old manner from the same materials and conforming to long-used shapes named after birds, animals or the moon. Kite designs are shared with other traditional Malay art forms including batik and woodcarving. The wealth of tradition that lies behind the art of the kite is also evident in the deeper symbolism linking the kite to myth and legend.

Numerous musical instruments are found in Malaysia across all ethnic groups, crafted from a variety of materials including metal, wood, bamboo, plants and animal skin. The music created by them may serve a cultural function or may simply be for pleasure.

Religious art makes itself felt most vibrantly among the Malaysian Hindu and Chinese populations. The Chinese arts are represented in lantern designs, paper effigies, icons and drawings as well as in the decorations found on joss sticks. These art forms, in almost all instances, have been introduced into Malaysia as a result of direct transplantation. Minimal attempts at localization may be observed in some of the objects used in the Chinese *kong teik* effigy ceremony: for example in the occasional use of a Proton car effigy. Direct borrowing, mostly from South India, is also apparent in the ceremonial crafts of the Tamil community in Malaysia. This is best represented in the art of creating *kolam* floor patterns on auspicious occasions, that of *thoranam* (weaving of coconut leaves), the making of flower garlands and, at its most outstanding, the art of temple decoration. Temple sculpture, both within and outside a temple premises, is clearly done in imitation of South Indian styles and connects the Malaysian Hindu community with traditions in India which go back hundreds of years.

Puppetry

There is one major form of puppet theatre, the shadow play (Wayang Kulit), active among Malay communities in the Peninsula, but no puppetry of any kind in Sabah or Sarawak. Different styles of Wayang Kulit share commonalities and each has been influenced by other significant cultures. The appearance and colours of traditional puppet characters are symbolic and depict ancient epics. Today, more modern styles and story lines are evolving to reflect new trends in Malay society.

The puppeteer (*dalang*) manipulates the puppets, and together with narration, music and dialogue, presents the story. The puppets are lit from behind to reflect onto the screen, creating the shadow play.

Wayang Kulit Gedek

Different both in concept and design from Wayang Kulit Siam figures are those used in Wayang Kulit Gedek. These come directly from the southern Thai Nang Talung style of shadow play of which Wayang Kulit Gedek is a derivative. The figures, made of goat skin, are always translucent, and many of the characters actually face the front rather than presenting a side profile. The style of carving is also distinctly Thai.

An interesting feature of Nang Talung is the attempt to introduce Western or even Chinese costumes. This reflects the fact that there is a certain measure of Chinese influence in the overall concept of Nang Talung and, through it, in Wayang Kulit Gedek.

Wayang Kulit in Malaysia

Three styles of shadow play are active in Malaysia—Wayang Kulit Siam (also known as Wayang Kulit Kelantan) in Kelantan, Wayang Kulit Purwa in Johor and Wayang Kulit Gedek in Kedah and Perlis. All three styles share many elements—repertoire, performance techniques and details of design—with shadow play styles in neighbouring countries, particularly India, Thailand, and Indonesia, with lesser influences from China and the Middle East. These influences came about due to historical factors such as colonization and trade, and the spread of Hinduism, Buddhism and Islam in Southeast Asia, including the Malay Peninsula. As a result of the fusion of these various cultural elements, the Malay shadow play forms, in particular Wayang Kulit Siam, developed their own identity, with some remaining resemblances to their counterparts, or parent forms, elsewhere.

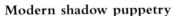

Puppet from Wayang Kulit Purwa, a style of shadow play originating from Java and believed to be the oldest form in Southeast Asia and influencing Wayang Kulit Siam in its early stages.

Demam Bollywood, featuring the well-known Hindustani actor figure Shah Rukh Khan. Other styles are Wayang Kulit Dewan Bahasa and Wayang Kulit Semangat Baru, developed in 2004, introducing a story based on the Japanese Occupation and set in Kelantan. All of these have combined traditional puppet design, that is, two-dimensional figures carved in near-realistic appearance, incorporating some traditional designs in their costumes. Overall, however, such figures tend to be less intricate than traditional designs. The figures are created within short periods of time, for the purpose of developing the new story, and have only tenuous connections with the time-tested designs of traditional puppetry.

VCD cover of *Demam Bollywood* Wayang Kulit. Pictured are Dalang Saufi (centre) and the actor upon whom the story is based.

In addition to hide figures, puppets made of large leaves existed at one time, and currently there have also been attempts to make use of plastic and exposed x-ray film to make shadow play figures. This last-mentioned trend, however, has not caught on in Malaysia, unlike in Thailand.

Modern shadow puppetry

New styles of Wayang Kulit, different from traditional style puppetry, are being developed, particularly in Kelantan. The best known of these is that of Dalang (puppeteer) Saufi, who has introduced modern characters represented by naturalistic figures, such as in his Wayang Kulit story

Wayang Kulit Dewan Bahasa features a modern story line and puppets; for instance, it introduces Malay female characters dressed in *sarung kebaya* with Muslim head scarves (*tudung*) and other characters wearing Malaysian and Western-style costumes.

Traditional style village puppet theatre made of wood and thatched palm leaves, 1974. Shadow play theatre remains a popular form of village entertainment in certain states.

The panggung

The shadow play theatre (*panggung* or *bangsal*) is usually a wooden structure built in the form of a traditional Malay house. A measure of traditional craftsmanship goes into the theatre building and wherever wood is used, as in the making of the lamp holder, a certain amount of carving is apparent. Another important element of the theatre is the white muslin screen (*kelir*).

The Puppets

Making the puppets

Most of an artist's effort naturally goes into the making of the puppets, which, as the name Wayang Kulit implies, are made of hide. In the case of Wayang Kulit Purwa, the figures are imported from Java and thus represent Javanese rather than indigenous Malay aesthetic principles. The figures of the Kelantanese Wayang Kulit Siam, the most important of the Malaysian shadow play forms, are made out of cow hide, while those in the Wayang Kulit Gedek are made from goat hide. Specific processes are involved in preparing the hide for the making of the figures. These include cleaning the hide, soaking it and drying it (**1**). Once the hide is dry the characters to be carved are first drawn onto tracing paper and these are then gummed to the hide before being cut out (**2**). A spine is attached to the puppet (**3**), it is coloured, and the mobile arm is attached (**4**).

Refinement and coarseness

Puppet figures are traditionally seen as being refined (*halus*) or coarse (*kasar*), their first important characteristic. The body size and shape are the first indicators of this. As a general rule, the ogre figures are larger than the gods or human characters, subject to exceptions—the monkey king Hanuman, while being refined, is also physically massive. Nobility and refinement are best seen in the figures of Seri Rama, the hero of the *Ramayana* tale, and his family members, as compared to the demon king Rawana and his companions. However, Pak Dogol, while in essence a manifestation of a god, does not have the appearance of one. He is black and misshapen, a deliberate guise adopted for practical and dramatic reasons. Following size, the next elements determining refinement or coarseness are the shape of the limbs and the stance adopted by a character, the facial expression, the shape of the mouth, nose, the eyes and so on. The details of the various characters, whether they are refined or coarse, are also manifested in their manner of speaking and moving. The success of developing the characters in this way is dependent on the skills of the puppeteer, the real protagonist of the performance.

Refined characters have almost realistic figures, heightened to indicate beauty. The hero and his family members are slim with thin waists (**1**) and a dancer-like posture, their arms, legs and fingers are almost pointed backwards (**2**). Their mouths are usually closed or nearly so, the lips tight (**3**) and the eyes are slit-shaped (**4**).

Coarse characters, particularly the evil ones, have features in violent contrast to the refined characters. They stand feet apart (**5**), with stumpy legs (**6**), heavy arms ending in clawed fingers (**7**), rounded eyes (**8**), and mouths open with their tongues sticking out (**9**).

Seri Rama.

Rawana.

Laksmana.

Sita Dewi.

Hanuman.

Characters

The figures in a Wayang Kulit set, about 65 to 120 figures depending upon the kind of Wayang Kulit involved, are classifiable into divine, semi-divine or human characters, plus those depicting ogres, animals or mixed creatures. The basic characteristics of the figures are determined by the story source.

Wayang Kulit Siam derives its repertoire principally from the *Hikayat Maharaja Wana*, a version of the epic *Ramayana* story, while Wayang Kulit Gedek uses the Thai version of the epic, known as *Ramakien*. Local adaptations have been made and new characters have been created, particularly for the locally developed branch (*ranting*) stories of the *Ramayana* epic. Traditionally, in both of these forms of Wayang Kulit, not all the limbs of the figures are movable. Usually only a single arm is movable while the other is carved in a fixed position holding a weapon or flower, depending upon the character depicted.

Costumes

Costume details are usually very intricately painted in Wayang Kulit figures, with designs often derived from natural phenomena. The costumes of the principal male characters, both good and evil, come clearly from the Indian tradition—the principal male characters are dressed in the Indian *dhoti* rather than in *sarong* or trousers. The female characters, however, are often dressed in the Malay *sarung kebaya*, *baju kurung* or other Malay costumes.

Colour symbolism

To some extent there is a system of colour symbolism operating within the figures of the Wayang Kulit. In Wayang Kulit Siam, specific colours are applied to certain characters— Seri Rama is always green or greenish blue; Laksmana is reddish orange; Sirat Maharaja is yellow; Hanuman is usually white and the other monkey characters red; Rawana is black or green with a red face; Pak Dogol is black, while his partner clown, Wak Long, is usually red; Sita Dewi is gold. This symbolism is reflective of influences from Hinduism as well as Islam. Rama, 'the god with the green face', traces his colour to both Hindu and Islamic sources, as do some ogre characters. Pak Dogol's black universally presents a link with unmanifested divinity, while Sirat Maharaja's yellow connects his figure with the colour of royalty in India and China. Less care is taken with regard to the colouring of the other figures in the Wayang Kulit Siam set. Today the tradition of character colour symbolism appears somewhat forgotten in Kelantan.

Puppet design traditions

Unlike in the Javanese tradition of puppet carving, most of the design details of the Malay shadow play do not possess fixed names. This is essentially because the tradition of puppet designing, unlike the shadow play performance itself, has not been handed down with the keeping of proper records. As a result, much of the information regarding the puppets and their designs, and even some of the technical details regarding puppet making, have already been lost and may never be recovered.

Background setting

The most important figure in a Wayang Kulit Siam set is the tree- or leaf-shaped *pohon beringin*, a banyan or *waringin* tree. The actual shape and size of the figure and its details of design vary. At times it is drawn simply as a tree, but usually the tree contains within it figures of reptiles, animals and birds in addition to foliage. The puppeteers and puppet designers interpret the *pohon beringin* and what it contains in terms of cosmology. Perennial principles, including those coming from Hinduism and Islam, coalesce in some of these interpretations. A common theme is a mountain or forest. Apart from the *pohon beringin*, there may be other stage properties such as palaces, trees and weapons.

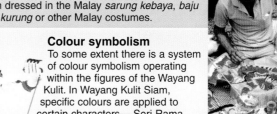

Translucent paint is now used so that coloured shadows, rather than grey, will be cast.

Pak Dogol.

Wak Long.

Malay kites and tops

Kite-flying and top spinning are traditional pastimes. Kites are made and flown in several parts of Malaysia, but with particular enthusiasm along the east coast. The huge and highly decorative kites of Kelantan are particularly famous. That state is also well known for top spinning, although the game is popular throughout Malaysia.

Watercolour painting by Ismail Bukhary depicting two types of *gasing* competition in Kelantan—spinning and striking tops. Top spinning is a seasonal activity, and is popular during the dry season after the rice harvest, particularly in rural areas.

Malay tops (gasing)

A serious and entertaining activity

The origins of the Malay top (*gasing*) and its use in competition, remain unknown. The game is taken seriously in various states of the Malay Peninsula as well as in Sabah and Sarawak. However, Kelantan, with its impressive top spinning competitions, is justifiably the locality most strongly associated with top spinning—it is home to the most famous tops in Malaysia, and the country's most enthusiastic top spinners.

Top spinning is not just associated with the young; the more serious activities, including top making and top spinning contests, involve adults. The significance of making and spinning tops is that they are symbolic of traditional Malay values, customs (*adat*) and discipline. In traditional Malay society, top spinning, whether competitive or not, serves as a form of cooperation (*gotong royong*), social cohesion and brotherhood.

Top shapes

A variety of top shapes and sizes may be encountered in different states of the Malay Peninsula, which have developed over time. Names are given to the tops according to shape or certain specific features. Some of the most common include:

gasing leper (flat top)

gasing jantung (heart-shaped top) **gasing piring** (saucer-shaped top)

gasing berembang (*berembang* fruit-shaped top)

gasing telur (egg-shaped top)

gasing uri (fast spinning top)

A Kelantanese top known as *gasing leper* (above right) framed at the girth in metal, usually tin or iron, with a diameter of 60 centimetres or more, can weigh up to six kilograms. It is famous for the length of time that it can spin. A skilful top spinner (right) can balance a spinning top for up to two hours.

Making tops

Great care is devoted to the choice of wood when making tops to be used in competitions. A variety of hardwoods are used, the best being *bakau* (mangrove). For tops used for pleasure, readily available lighter wood may be obtained from common fruit trees, such as the *ciku* (sapodilla) tree. Tops are usually made with simple carving and shaping tools, although more sophisticated equipment is now used to get the overall shape of the top. In Kelantan and Johor, metal borders or frames (*simpai*) are added to the large tops, and metal pieces may be attached to the top to prevent damage. It is important that the top is not unevenly balanced by even a fraction of a gram. Completed tops are checked for balance by immersing them in water.

1. The wood is dried for about three weeks and then roughly shaped.
2. The outside surface is shaped and then smoothened.
3. A core axis is inserted into the middle of the top. Tin or iron is melted and poured in a mould according to the width and depth required and the top is dipped inside.
4. The sharp edges are trimmed.
5. The top is smoothened and polished.

Kites (wau)

Bamboo for the kite frame is first skinned and pared into thin strips, (left) then joined together to form the basic shape (below). Special care is taken to ensure that the vertical backbone piece is both strong and flexible.

Making a kite

The kite frame (*rangka*) is fashioned out of light, flexible bamboo. The best bamboo is *buluh duri* (thorny bamboo), which is soaked in water for three to four days then dried out in the sun. Perfect symmetry and balance are important to ensure that the kite flies well, and the frame is reinforced with string lines to keep its form when subjected to the stresses of flight, and to support the paper cover.

The completed frame is covered with two or more layers of paper, sometimes up to five depending on the craftsman. The first layer is transparent white or light-coloured, while the others are coloured, providing the elaborate decorations, with special emphasis devoted to the wings. Care is taken over the combination of colours used and their combined effect.

The coloured craft paper to be used in making the decorative designs is measured for size against that of the kite frame. This piece of paper is folded in two, and the selected design is drawn in pencil on its non-glossy surface, before being cut out with a knife. The unfolded piece of paper manifests the symmetry of the pattern. The coloured paper cutout is then pasted over the plain paper base using homemade rice paste. A basic two-colour pattern thus emerges.

Parts of a kite

The connection between kites and birds remains strong, particularly for Kelantanese kite makers, such that different parts of the kite have been designated as the 'head' (*kepala*), 'waist' (*pinggang*), 'wings' (*sayap*) and 'base' (*punggung*).

The kite is often completed with the addition of a bow (*busur*), which yields a pleasant humming sound as the kite is suspended in the air. Folk belief maintains that so long as the humming continues, no evil spirit will venture aboard.

Symbolism and role today

The kite holds an important place in Kelantanese legend and symbolism, and has been connected both to the operation of magic as well as to shamanism—at one time it was believed that beautiful kites would placate and please the spirits above the clouds. This is also reflected in *Dewa Muda* (right) the most important story in the ancient Mak Yong dance theatre, which tells of a golden kite that carries the prince to his love, Puteri Ratna Mas, in her palace in the sky.

Kite flying continues to be popular in Kelantan and other states such as Kedah and Terengganu as a competition event and also as a feature in arts and cultural festivals. It is also a popular recreational activity. Some kites are not for flying, but are created solely for decorative purposes.

Further elaborations to the design may be achieved using the same technique of pasting new cutouts, in diverse colours, over previous ones. Trimmings in the form, for instance, of a bird's head with a long neck, a fringe (*belalai*) and tail decorations may be added even if the final kite is not necessarily a *wau burung*.

1. After the bamboo frame is completed, it is ready for the decorative paper cover to be attached. The design is drawn on the first white paper layer and then cut out.

2. After cutting, the paper is unfolded and opened out in full.

3. The steps described in 1 and 2 above are repeated for the other coloured layers.

4. The layers of cut-out coloured paper are pasted over each other, creating the overall kite design, after which the decorative tassels are attached.

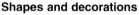

Shapes and decorations

Malay decorative kites, meticulously crafted from paper, appear in many shapes. The best known is the moon kite (*wau bulan*). Others include the bird kite (*wau burung*), the peacock kite (*wau merak*) and the cat kite (*wau kucing*). The largest of these reach up to approximately 2.13 metres from head to tail and perhaps 1.82 metres across the wings. Smaller ones, made both of paper and batik material, and serving as decorative pieces, have become increasingly visible in tourist outlets all over the country.

Designs are dominated by traditional nature-derived patterns, including cloud formations (*awan larat*), young bamboo shoots (*pucuk rebung*) or floral designs. However, modern images, for example of cartoon characters and animals, jarring in contrast to the traditional, are now being included in kite designs.

wau kucing

wau bulan

wau burung

wau merak

Traditionally, before conventional timepieces, coconut husks with holes at the base and filled with water were used to keep time in a kite flying competition. The *wau* had to be kept flying until the water in the coconut husk had drained out, which usually took about 15 to 20 minutes.

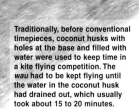

Competitions

There are two categories of kite competition involving the beauty of the *wau* or its flying capability. Competitors in the kite-flying category are judged on their ability to fly the *wau* at a constant height for the longest time. In the beauty category, judging is based on the uniqueness of its decorations. The frame has to be strong and the finishing neat. The *wau* must be made using traditional methods, and use of bamboo is compulsory. The pattern of the *wau* must be symmetrical. The more intricate the pattern, the higher the chances of winning. Traditionally, such events usually take place at agricultural and other festivals, but national and international kite competitions (right) have also become a regular feature in Malaysia.

Traditional musical instruments

While Malaysian traditional music is more frequently heard in rural areas throughout the country, when performed in urban cultural centres, it draws large and enthusiastic crowds—a testament to its continuing vitality. Played for leisure and entertainment, special occasions and ceremonies, a plethora of musical instruments are used in virtually every ethnic group in every state in the country. Often made from readily available local materials, many traditional instruments share common ancestries.

Assembly of traditional Malay musical instruments in Kelantan, used for Mak Yong and other types of performance, including: (**1**) *rebana anak*, (**2**) *serunai*, (**3**) *gedombak*, (**4**) *gendang ibu*, (**5**) *rebab*, (**6**) *canang* Wayang Kulit gongs, (**7**) dance *canang* gongs, (**8**) *mong*, (**9**) *gendang anak*, (**10**) *kertuk kayu*, (**11**) *geduk*, (**12**) large hanging gongs and (**13**) *kesi*.

Making a sompoton

A mature *korubu* gourd is plucked, deseeded and dried. It functions as a wind chamber when blown into.

A hole is made in the narrow end of the gourd.

After it has been dried, a bamboo stalk (*sumbiling*) is pushed into the hole, the length depending on the sound required. The dried, peeled bark of a palm tree (*polod*) is made into *sodi* which is attached to one end of the bamboo stalk to produce the sound.

Bamboo pipes are tied together in a double raft with string made from dried fern stalks.

A special beeswax (*sopinit*) is used to glue *lamellae* onto the bamboo pipes, to fill any gaps between the pipes, and to join the pipes to the gourd chamber. The finished instrument is ready to be played.

Wind instruments

The mouth organ known as a *sompoton* (two reeds), found among the Kadazandusun of Sabah, is a fascinating indigenous instrument. It is constructed of a dried gourd wind chamber from which extend eight bamboo pipes, attached with beeswax and bound with rattan, arranged in a double layer. One pipe has no sound and merely balances the bundle. Played by both blowing and sucking, the instrument produces a harmonious sound because of a small lamella of palm bark in the side of each pipe near its base. The instrument is played in groups to accompany dancing. The corresponding instrument in Sarawak is a circular bundle of six or seven pipes, also embedded in a gourd windchamber, called *engkerurai*, *keluri* or *keledi*.

A likely ancestor of the *sompoton* is the Chinese *sheng* which has a bundle of between 17 and 36 bamboo pipes seated on a small wind chamber into which the player blows and sucks air through a specially designed mouthpiece. Each pipe has a freely vibrating reed above which a finger hole is placed which must be covered to produce a note.

The jaw's harp, also known as 'Jew's harp' or 'mouth harp', is found in Sarawak, Sabah (where it is called a *bungkau*) and among the Orang Asli of the Peninsula (who call it *ginggong*, *genggon* or *ranggon* depending on the material from which it is made). This instrument is usually made from a single short piece of bamboo or wood (although the Penan of Sarawak use the mature stem of the frond of a type of sago palm) and is placed between the lips, while one end is plucked, causing the central lamella to vibrate. The sound resonates in the mouth to produce a wide range of sounds.

An indigenous nose flute is found in Sabah and Sarawak and among the Orang Asli (*turali* in Sabah, *selengut* in Sarawak and *pensol* or *suling* in the Peninsula) where the air which activates the sound comes from air blown gently through the nostril, producing a soft, silky and plaintive sound. A short bamboo flute blown by air from the mouth is also used by these same groups and is called a *suling* by all, but also a *siloy* or *begut* by the Orang Asli.

The Malay *serunai* is a quadruple reed wind instrument, with seven front finger holes and one at the back. The instrument forms part of the orchestras for Wayang Kulit, Mak Yong and the Nobat. Resembling the *serunai* is the Indian *nagasvaram*, which is a longer and less elaborate double-reed pipe and the Chinese *suona*, also a double-reeded wind instrument.

In rural areas, after the rice harvest, groups compete against each other playing the *rebana besar*—two men play each drum with padded sticks.

Drums

Two notable Malay drums originate from Kelantan: the *rebana besar* and the *rebana ubi*. The first, which weighs as much as 110 kilograms with a drumhead diameter of nearly one metre, is hung vertically or placed horizontally on the floor and can be heard two kilometres away. The second is a smaller version of the giant drum.

Drums feature in various traditional Malay performing arts such as Wayang Kulit, during which vertical *geduk* or war drum, a pair of deep-voiced vase shaped drums known as *gedombak*, and double-faced drums *gendang ibu* and *anak* (mother and child)—held horizontally and beaten with curved wooden sticks at one end, and by hand at the other—are played. *Gendang* are also used in Mak Yong dance drama performances, and also by the Nobat orchestra. No Malay wedding is complete without the ubiquitous *kompang* group to accompany the bride or groom as each arrives at the other's house. The group will later be invited to share the wedding meal and the leader will be paid for their services. They may also be used to welcome important visitors to state functions and to provide entertainment at festivals.

The *thavil*, a double-headed barrel-shaped drum which is slightly larger at one end is an indispensable instrument in south Indian weddings, while the *mridanga* drum is an important Indian classical music instrument. The Hindustani *tabla* has a hard central circle in its face. The drummer may wear ceramic rings on his drumming hand to enhance the sound while alternately striking the edge or the hard central portion of the drum.

LEFT: One of the main instruments in a south Indian wedding ceremony is the *nagasvaram* which always accompanies the *thavil* drum.

The Nobat orchestra

Nobat is the name given to the royal ceremonial orchestra that is unique to Kedah, Terengganu, Perak and Selangor. Its instruments form a treasured part of the royal regalia of these states. The full Nobat is infrequently played; aside from a ruler's installation ceremony, it is heard at a ruler's wedding and funeral, or that of his consort or children. In some states it is played outside the palace at the time of the breaking of the fast during the month of Ramadhan. The Nobat instruments are usually only played by hereditary musicians.

The Selangor Nobat orchestra consists of three drums covered in royal yellow cloth, and two wind instruments. One small kettledrum stands upright with a single face, the other two double-headed barrel drums, one large and the other smaller, are laid horizontally. The wind instruments are the silver trumpet (*nafiri*) and an oboe (*serunai*).

Gongs, cymbals and xylophones

Gongs are used by almost every ethnic group in Malaysia and are usually played at festive occasions, weddings and harvest festivals. Although the majority are made in China, the Philippines, Brunei and Indonesia, some gongs are made locally in Sarawak, Sabah and Terengganu.

The Malay *taklempong* is a set of between six and eight bronze gongs in a row on a wooden stand. They are struck with cloth-covered round mallets at the end of a handle. Played as part of an orchestra, they are originally from Sumatra but are found in the Kuala Pilah district of the state of Negeri Sembilan.

In a Wayang Kulit performance, a pair of small shallow gongs (*canang*) lying low on a low wooden stand, two pairs of very small copper cymbals (*kesi*) and a pair of deep-rimmed hanging gongs (*tetawak*) are part of the orchestral ensemble. *Tetawak* are also used in Mak Yong.

The Malay *saron* is a metal xylophone consisting of six keys resting on a rectangular, sometimes compartmented, wooden resonator. Similar to this are the *salun* and a wooden xylophone called a *gabang*, both from Sabah. Another Sabah instrument, variously called a *togunggak*, *tagunggak* or *togunggu*, is played in groups to accompany dancing or processions at festive occasions in lieu of a gong ensemble. It comprises a series of hollowed out bamboo tubes, from six to 30 pieces, depending on the ethnic group. The music is a hollow rhythmic sound of different pitches according to the different sizes.

The Chinese use a set of brass tuned gongs known as *yunlo* as an orchestral instrument.

String instruments

The Sarawak *sapeh* has an elongated body which is hollowed out and functions as a resonator. It is over one metre long and about 40 centimetres wide. It produces a haunting sound and is played for pleasure and for the dance called the *ngajat*. A long-necked strummed lute from Sabah is the *sundatang*.

In Sabah, the *tongkungon*, a plucked zither that imitates gong music, is made from a large bamboo tube with thin strips cut into the surface to form the strings. The names and number of the strings correspond to the main gongs.

The Sarawak version is the *satong* and is made similarly, although its music often imitates work sounds, clucking insects and small forest animals. A *rebab* or spike fiddle is a two- or three-stringed lute with an almost heart-shaped body made from jackfruit tree wood and covered with a thin layer of skin taken from a cow's stomach.

Belonging to the Indian stringed instruments are the sitar, a long necked lute with a gourd sound box at one end, and the vina, a plucked lute which has seven strings of silver or brass.

A decorated *gabang* wooden xylophone used in some parts of Sabah.

The Chinese *erhu* has a small body and a long neck and has two strings with the bow inserted between them. It has a small resonating chamber and sounds similar to, but thinner than, a violin.

The *pipa* has four gut strings and is a short-necked lute with a pear-shaped body, and the four-stringed *ruan* is known also as a moon guitar, probably due to its round shape. An elegant and now rare seven-stringed instrument is the *guqin*.

LEFT: Chinese musicians playing traditional instruments.

BELOW LEFT: The *sapeh* is usually made from a single bole of *tebuloh* (a *Diterocarp* wood). The frets are carved from palm stalk and attached with a gum made by the *kelulut* bee. Traditional Orang Ulu designs and a carved headpiece may adorn it.

BELOW: Woman making a *tongkungon*, a solo instrument of the Sabah Dusunic communities.

Chinese and Indian religious arts and crafts

Many ceremonial and religious objects are the result of arts and crafts. In Chinese temples, as well as clan houses (kongsi), such objects include icons, lanterns and other articles of offering. Indian religious arts are diverse and include symbolic rice flour floor patterns (kolam), temple decorations, flower garlands and woven coconut leaf designs.

ABOVE: Elaborate ornamentation on the Tua Pek Kong temple on Armenian Street in Penang.

RIGHT: Colourful statues decorate the *gopuram* tower of the Sri Markendeswarar Temple in Penang, built directly over the inner sanctum.

Chinese

Lanterns

Chinese lanterns are made of bamboo, cloth or paper, and are sometimes waterproofed. Bamboo frames may be imported from China or locally manufactured. Usually lanterns are spherical or conical and open at both ends. Before the advent of electric bulbs, candles were placed within the lanterns, giving rise to the risk of the lanterns catching fire.

Procession of lanterns on a festive occasion.

Joyful and sorrowful occasions are commemorated with the use of lanterns. The former include deities' birthdays, anniversaries, weddings and festivals. Generally, present-day lanterns lack the colour symbolism that once made them significant. For example, where formerly white lanterns with red characters were featured, today red or yellow lanterns with gold trimmings are popular, especially on Chinese New Year. During funerals, traditionally a pair of black and white lanterns is carried in the procession; such lanterns may be sent by associations to which the deceased belonged.

Big lanterns are always displayed in pairs. The ones hung in an association building, a temple or a house are constructed with substantial frames and are heavier than the longer ones carried in processions. In the past, the front of every house, especially the home of a prominent family, would have a pair of lanterns bearing the family surname. When a pair of lanterns is hung in a temple, the one on the left bears the name of the temple and the other the name of the deity. Lanterns hung in association premises would bear the name of the clan and the name of the clan temple.

Thin strips of bamboo are formed to make the lantern frame which is covered with plain cloth or paper and then decorated according to purpose.

Paper effigies

Kong teik is an elaborate ceremony performed to raise credit for a newly deceased person and to safeguard the soul's passage into the underworld. Paper decorations involving intricate craft work are used. The most elaborate object may be a mountain constructed of paper and bamboo with gold and silver mines presided over by the deities. Other offering examples include paper representations of a house, car, money, personal belongings, clothes and accessories, and servants. When these are burnt, they are believed to be converted into wealth or property in the next world for the arriving soul so that the soul may begin a comfortable life without delay. On the whole, such objects display little artistry, but are instead an important manifestation of the belief in a connection between the world of living humans and that of this community's gods, spirits and ancestors.

Paper effigies used in the *kong teik* ceremony are made by professionals as an adjunct to the undertakers' trade and usually as part of a family business. The frames of the common paper houses and boxes are constructed out of lengths of bamboo strips fastened together with strips of kite paper (rice paper) and starch. The materials used for the walls, baroque decorations, clothes and objects are all made out of paper, gift-wrappings or metallic paper. Very often, though, the small effigies representing the deceased, gods and servants are made with ceramic heads imported from China.

ABOVE: Offerings for the *kong teik* ceremony involve various artefacts including paper imitations of animate and inanimate objects in addition to food and fruit offerings.

RIGHT: Kong teik paper effigies and other funeral items being burnt.

Enshrined icons and wall paintings

Wall fresco and deity statues in the main prayer chamber of the Perak cave temple.

Decoration within and without Chinese temples is basically symbolic. Icons are enshrined, either in halls of varying sizes according to the importance of the deity in a particular pantheon, or in intimate alcoves. Many of the wall decorations are frescoes, while ink drawings are also employed. The subject matter tends to be narrative and didactic although sometimes legends with no religious overtones are included.

Joss sticks

Making joss sticks.

Joss sticks are much used ritual objects which also decorate the temple. Each devotee visiting the temple will generally place joss sticks or batches of them at different altars.

Joss sticks come in different sizes. Smaller ones are hand-held and big ones are burnt upright, like candles. Generally, the small ones are made by dipping a length of bamboo in a wet paste of sandalwood powder and a cohesive agent which is then dried in the sun for two days. Dragon joss sticks, which can be more than 1.8 m in height, are made with hardy sticks as thick as mop handles and decorated with dragons moulded by hand. They are usually dipped in joss stick mixture several times to obtain the desired thickness and dried in the sun over a period of six days. They may be purplish red. Finishing touches include balls for the eyes and pipe-cleaner whiskers. On big festival occasions rows upon rows of dragon joss sticks line the temple fronts.

Man finishing a giant dragon joss stick. The colour is obtained by the addition of red pigment.

Indian

Kolam/rangoli

The creation of floor patterns using rice flour, known in Tamil as *kolam* (*rangoli* in Hindustani), is one of the oldest of India's numerous cultural expressions. It traces its origins to the mythic era of the epic *Ramayana*. Although decorative in character, *kolam* has spread into other areas of human activity, in the process developing a dual character as a sacred as well as secular art. This art was traditionally learnt by girls from an early age as a means of enhancing an appreciation for beauty and the arts, developing discipline, confidence and memory-power, as well as an act of charity since the flour used in creating the patterns was eventually eaten by insects.

White was the traditionally popular colour for the creation of *kolam*, while *rangoli* featured the use of a variety of colours. Today these distinctions have become blurred. *Kolam* designs may, additionally, feature flowers.

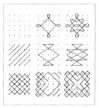

LEFT: To create *kolam*, rice flour is mixed with water to make a paste. Using a piece of clean white cloth soaked in the mixture, the pattern is traced in a dotted outline. These dots are eventually joined into continuous lines forming the desired patterns.

RIGHT: *Kolam* competitions are popular events where colourful and creative designs are created on a grand scale.

In Malaysia, white *kolam* patterns with simple lines are usually drawn in the porches of private residences on auspicious occasions by female members of a family following ablutions and dawn prayers. Most of the patterns featured in Malaysia come from South India, as do the majority of Malaysian Indians. The art of *rangoli*, is, also, however, practised by a small number of North Indian families in Malaysia. A comparatively modern feature in Malaysia is the organisation of *kolam* competitions—their designs tend to be more colourful.

While *kolam* or *rangoli* designs painted in private homes or temples continue to serve as a means of decoration, particularly during festivals or on auspicious occasions such as weddings, they are also believed to be efficacious in warding off evil or malicious influences, including the 'evil eye'. Many varieties of design exist. Specific ones are associated with particular days of the week, with particular deities or particular occasions. In the variety known as *mantra kolam*, charms or religious texts (mantra) are incorporated into the designs to bring good luck, prosperity, success in education, the conception of a child, and as a means of avoiding ill fortune, disease or harm from evil spirits.

Thoranam

The weaving of young coconut leaves into patterns to be hung across house and temple entrances, and sometimes streets, is known as *thoranam* (right). Either single or multiple leaves may be used for each pattern. The woven leaves are decorative as well as symbolic of health, happiness and prosperity, thus the reason for their presence at the celebration of weddings or festivals. For the same reason, mango leaves may also be tied between the woven strands of coconut leaves, or tied at the entrance of Hindu homes to ward off evil spirits.

Thoranam is made (right) and hung as an important symbolic decoration for both temples (above) and homes on important occasions and festivals.

Temple decoration and art

Hindu temples are structured and adorned according to the precise rules of *Sirpa Sastra*, the Hindu manual of architecture and sculpture. As a depository of holiness and divinity, each temple manifests the exquisiteness of Hindu art and the marvel of its architecture. Colours are significant, and traditionally paintings or sculpture represent aspects of, or mythological themes connected with, the presiding deity (from the Hindu pantheon of gods and goddesses) of a particular temple as well as other figures connected with that deity through mythology.

LEFT: The temple exterior and interior areas—walls, pillars, ceilings, walkways and other sections—are decorated with elaborate, colourful and religiously significant sculptures.

RIGHT: Craftsmen from India usually create and paint the temple decorations and sculptures.

Flower garlands

Beautiful and colourful flower garlands (*malai*) are an important part of an Indian Hindu wedding ceremony. The most elaborate and auspicious of these are the wedding garlands (*kalyanam malai*) which are ceremonially exchanged and then worn by the bride and groom. Traditionally, the bride will also wear a thick braid of jasmine flowers (*rakudi*) over her own hair plait which reaches to her hips. Wedding garlands are usually strung with roses and jasmine.

Garlands are also one of the fundamental offerings made to Hindu gods. Temple and home deities are traditionally adorned with garlands, especially on religiously auspicious days and for festivals. Funeral wreaths are usually made from chrysanthemums, frangipani and roses affixed to a laurel. The spine of the wreath is made from twined bamboo and vines.

Generally, married Indian women and girls reaching adulthood wear strung flowers, usually jasmine buds and yellow, red or orange flowers strung together into a chain with white thread, as a form of hair adornment. However, by custom, widows do not adorn themselves.

Garland offerings from devotees adorning a Hindu temple deity.

1. Twine made of screwpine fibre is bunched together to the appropriate thickness to form the garland base.

2. String is twisted around the stem of jasmine flowers separately to tie each one to the length of screwpine.

3. The garland is formed into a loop by tying the ends of the twine.

4. Decorative flowers at the base of the garland (*kunjum*) are tied to the bottom. These are usually flowers such as roses, orchids or chrysanthemums.

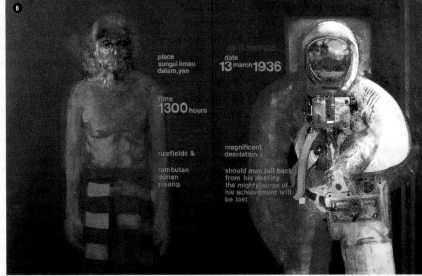

MODERN ART

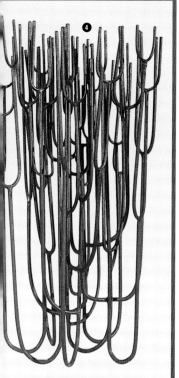

1. The naturalistic, Western influences in early local paintings are displayed in this oil painting *Portrait of My Wife in Her Wedding Dress* (1933) (ht 74 cm) by O. Don Peris, who studied art in Paris from 1912–15.

2. Batik painting *Fruit Season* (1968) (ht 88 cm) by Chuah Thean Teng. The use of the batik technique by artists, beginning in the 1950s, was an attempt to borrow from the region's past traditions.

3. *Woman Pounding Paddy* (1959) (ht 58.7 cm) by Mohd Hoessein Enas, an Indonesian-born artist who founded the Angkatan Pelukis Semenanjung art group in 1956, and introduced Indonesian-derived influences, linked to the idealized 'beautiful Indies' approach of painting.

4. Open-form modern sculpture by Anthony Lau entitled *Forest* (1960).

5. *Pago-Pago* (1964) (ht 98 cm) by Abdul Latiff Mohidin is a composite expressionist oil painting of tropical organic forms and shapes.

6. In this acrylic on canvas painting, *My Father and the Astronaut* (1970), Ibrahim Hussein contrasts his provincial Malay father with an American astronaut.

7. Syed Ahmad Jamal's acrylic on canvas painting *Sirih Pinang* (1986) (ht 199 cm) is one of a series based on Malay cultural elements. This artist is well known for his Abstract-Expressionist style.

8. Ismail Hashim's interest in depicting common objects, everyday life and the vanishing scene is evident in his hand-tinted photograph, *The Barber Shop* (1986).

9. Sculpture constructed from welded metal and plaster of paris by Bayu Utomo Radjikin, called *Bujang Berani (Bujang the Brave)* (1991) (ht 100 cm). The old Dayak warrior chief is engaged in a primordial scream. The sculpture highlights issues related to the displacement of tribal peoples, the encroachment of modernization and destruction of the rain forests.

A modern Malaysian art tradition emerged from modernization processes set in motion at the beginning of the 19th century. Colonialism, under the British, introduced secularization which fostered new individualized, self-expressive art making approaches, different from the earlier traditional symbolic artistic endeavours. The emergence of new multi-racial, urbanized towns during the 19th and 20th centuries accelerated socio-cultural transformations that subsequently introduced modern ideas in the visual arts.

Western-style paintings were introduced during the 19th century, but this type of artistic activity among the locals only began during the early 20th century. Reasons for this included Malay-Islamic fears and suspicions of Western education and cultural forms, the lack of exposure of non-Malay immigrants to Western artistic ideas and non-encouragement of artistic development by the British. By the early 1920s, watercolour and oil painting techniques were adopted in the larger towns. Beginning with naturalistic, idyllic modes of representation, Malaysian artists later became exposed to the modernist tendencies of the School of Paris introduced by the Nanyang Academy of Fine Arts—its émigré Chinese teachers provided exposure to Impressionism, Post-Impressionism, Fauvism and Cubism. Other locally trained figurative artists who featured during the pre-independence period included those from the Wednesday Art Group and Angkatan Pelukis Semenanjung in Kuala Lumpur and the Penang art groups. Batik painting was introduced during the 1950s.

By the late 1950s and 1960s, Malaysian artists pursued artistic studies in art colleges abroad and were exposed to Western international avant-garde art impulses. The emotive-expressive Abstract Expressionist idiom was introduced during the late 1950s. Yet other artists linked to abstractionist influences included the 'New Scene' group (late 1960s) who introduced non-emotive 'hard-edged' Constructivist ideas and, later, Conceptual Art tendencies.

Complex questions pertaining to cultural and nationalistic identity had surfaced by the mid-1970s, in the wake of the 13 May 1969 inter-racial riots and then the National Cultural Congress of 1971. A re-questioning of the dependence on Western humanistic ideas and self-expressive values was initiated by the exhibition *Towards A Mystical Reality* (1974). The emergence of regional-centred sentiments and the need to define ideas pertaining to a 'national identity' witnessed attempts by some Malay artists to project Malay-Islamic values during the 1980s.

The introduction of post-modernist elements from the late 1980s up to the present time by a younger generation of figurative artists has marked new creative approaches. They have dealt with sociological issues, politics, race, ethnic marginalization, environmental problems and gender issues. They have projected a new interest in discourse.

The Kampung Boy cartoon series is one of the most famous creations of cartoonist Lat, known for his humorous portrayal of Malaysian life and politics.

The beginning of landscape painting

British involvement in Malaya had various influences on the local culture, including its art and architecture. The emergence of a modern art tradition has been attributed to Westernization, the British educational system and immigration. The British contribution to Malaysian art can be traced to the presence of British traveller-artists and their naturalistic documentations of the beauty of the local landscape, rendered through their scenic topographical views of the place.

View of the Cascade, Prince of Wales's Island, 1818 by William Daniell is an example of an early oil painting from Penang (c. 1800s) where the British landscape tradition prevailed.

Artist Lee Cheng Yong studied at the Shanghai Academy of Fine Art in the 1930s. His oil painting *Rock Forms, Penang* (c. 1941) reveals his analytically structured approach to painting landscapes, influenced by the ideas of Paul Cézanne.

Influence of the British education system and the emergence of naturalism

The introduction of Western-style education to Malaya allowed for a new approach to the understanding of nature and the environment. Based on an essentially rational and investigative depiction of reality, artistic interpretations differed from earlier symbolic and religio-centred views, founded on mystical and magical considerations.

Derived from the European Renaissance, this new artistic paradigm allowed for an analytical study of the real world and led to the emergence of Naturalism in Western art. This naturalistic approach to depicting nature and the environment was initially brought to the country by the British military traveller-artists who were assigned to make topographical views of the place during the 18th and 19th centuries. Influenced by ideas pertaining to the Cult of the Picturesque, the watercolours and oil paintings of local landscapes produced by these British artists featured a foreground, a middle ground and a distant background. Further, their approach was influenced by romantic notions of nature, highlighting the idyllic, the tranquil and the scenic. When Malayan artists began initially to produce landscapes in the early 20th century, they utilized these pictorial conventions.

LEFT: Yong Mun Sen, a significant pioneer local artist, studied at the Shanghai Academy of Fine Art and started painting around 1922.

BELOW: Yong Mun Sen's watercolour painting, *Fishing Nets* (1941).

Watercolour paintings

Stylistically, colonial watercolour and oil paintings influenced the beginnings of modern Malaysian painting. Traceable to the early 1930s, the initial interest was in watercolour painting, perhaps due to the easy availability of the medium during the pre-war years. The nature of watercolour, which can be used in wash and gouache techniques, also allowed for a variety of artistic styles—it could be applied either spontaneously or in a more controlled manner.

Among the early practitioners of the watercolour landscape commitment were Yong Mun Sen, Abdullah Ariff, Khaw Sia and Tay Hooi Keat. They had been exposed to the reproductions of local landscapes produced by British artists which were exhibited in government offices, hotels and schools. Apart from British military artists, there were also a number of British colonial civil servants who depicted aspects of the Malayan landscape and its exotic peoples in the watercolour medium during the 19th century.

Coconut Plantation-Dawn (1948) by Abdullah Ariff is composed of three pictorial spatial divisions—the foreground, the middle ground and the misty background. Apart from the arrangement of the coconut trees according to size, the spatial depth of the picture is also defined by a combination of bright and dark tonalities, as well as various colour hues.

LEFT: The works of Abdullah Ariff were shown in watercolour exhibitions in Charlotte, North Carolina in 1955, the same year that he was made a Fellow of the Royal Society of Art (FRSA), London. In 1956, one of his works earned a place in the prestigious Le Salon Gallery in Paris and he later participated in a world tour in 1959.

The Penang Impressionists

In 1930, a group called The Penang Impressionists was formed, which comprised the wives of British expatriates. The group's annual exhibitions, held in Penang, were visited by budding local artists and allowed for a stylistic transfer.

One of two Asian members of the group and the only Malay was Abdullah Ariff, an art teacher at the Penang Methodist Boys' School and mainly

Colonial paintings of Malaya

Since the late 18th century, colonial artists have captured the beauty of local flora, fauna and tropical landscapes, particularly of places such as Melaka and Penang. These paintings were mainly created in watercolour, a suitable medium for outdoor sketching and capturing quick impressions of a place. These artists presented nature somewhat romantically. The choice of colours and brushstrokes, as well as the organized composition of the picture, were reminiscent of the great tradition of British landscape paintings pioneered by Constable, Turner, Reynolds, Gainsborough and other Victorian painters. Colonial government buildings such as Suffolk House, the Kelso Bungalow and British officials' residences were also depicted.

The enthusiasm of colonial painters in capturing the beauty of local landscapes coincided with the discovery of the aquatint printing technique and the prosperous era of the British East India Company. This helped to proliferate the art form and encouraged the conversion of such paintings into prints. Later, in the 19th century, picturesque landscapes were used to illustrate travel books and posters and became commercially valuable.

ABOVE: View of Suffolk House, Prince of Wales's Island, 1818 by William Daniell, an aquatint of the mansion known as Suffolk House sited on the estate originally owned by Captain Francis Light. Aquatints like this were used to illustrate travel books with pictures of landscapes, government buildings and British residences.

LEFT: One of a number of 1937 posters utilizing watercolour art of local scenes produced by painter Abdullah Ariff for the Federated Malay States Railway company advertising travel to Malaysia.

a watercolour exponent. He was included because of his skills; the amateur British housewives needed an instructor to teach them the watercolour technique. Also, his style of landscape painting was influenced by ideas relating to the picturesque and the idyllic, an approach that accorded with the aims of the group, who aspired to impressionistic renderings of the local landscape. Abdullah Ariff's work was marked by an eye for minute details and the depiction of light and shade effects.

The watercolourists of the Penang Chinese Art Club

The formation of the Penang Chinese Art Club in 1936 by a group of Chinese artists based in Penang was marked by the membership of Yong Mun Sen, Khaw Sia and Tay Hooi Keat who also produced watercolour landscapes during the pre-war era. If the approach of Abdullah Ariff was more European in its orientations, the works of these watercolour artists were more syncretic, revealing both Western and Chinese influences. If Abdullah's works were abundant with naturalistic details, the works of these artists were stylistically linked to Chinese sensibilities. Stylistic characteristics such as opaque transparency, fluid washes and the rendering of warm and cool colours to define spatial depth, however, certainly owed something to the English watercolour tradition.

On the other hand, Yong Mun Sen, Tay Hooi Keat and Khaw Sia were influenced more by the Chinese tradition of landscape painting that emphasized the spontaneity of vigorous brush-strokes and a sense of immediacy rather than an interest in details as witnessed in the work of the Penang Impressionists. This can be appreciated in Yong Mun Sen's *Fishing Nets* (1941). This approach of spontaneously capturing the romantic qualities of nature was part of a Chinese cultural tradition as demonstrated during the Southern Sung Dynasty (1128–1279) landscape paintings by Ma Yuan, Hsia

Kuie and others. In this respect, it may be suggested that these Chinese artists in Penang were already trying to fuse artistic styles and techniques. Possibly they were aware of developments taking place in mainland China, where pre-war Chinese modern artists were attempting to marry Western and Far-Eastern artistic influences in their search for pertinent modern art forms.

Early landscape paintings in oils

While the interest in the watercolour technique was especially popular during the pre-war period, there were a number of artists who depicted the local landscape in the oil medium. Included among these pre-war artists are Tsai Horng Chung, Lee Cheng Yong, Yong Mun Sen and Kuo Ju Ping. Tsai Horng Chung who lived and practised in Sarawak was trained at the Shanghai Academy of Fine Art in China and produced many impressive Sarawakian landscapes. His oil painting *Pepper Farm* (1941) utilizes the Western picturesque convention of a foreground, a middle ground and a background with distant mountains. The work is notable for its thick, expressionistic painterly treatment. Lee Cheng Yong's tightly structured oil painting *Rock Forms, Penang* (c. 1941) is a more analytical work influenced by Paul Cézanne.

An early oil painting by Abdullah Ariff of a Penang scene, entitled *Counter Hall* (1932).

ABOVE: Pre-war oil painting *Sampan* (c. 1940) (ht 48 cm) by Kuo Ju Pin. The landscape interest included scenic and idealized renderings of riverine and seashore views.

LEFT: Pepper Farm, an oil painting by Tsai Horng Chung (1941) (ht 34 cm), is set in Sarawak which is known for its pepper farms. Two Iban men are shown walking in the foreground.

Artists of the Nanyang school

Apart from colonization, education and socio-political developments, immigration was an important factor that influenced the development of art in the country. The arrival of artists from mainland China during the 1930s and 1950s enriched the stylistic experimentations. The Chinese immigrant community was proud of its cultural traditions and promoted art education and Chinese artistic developments in this country. An example was the formation of the influential Nanyang Academy of Fine Arts in 1938, the first art academy in what was then British Malaya.

ABOVE: From the 1950s, for about 30 years the Nanyang Academy of Fine Arts occupied this campus at 49 Saint Thomas Walk, Singapore.

RIGHT: The first logo of the Nanyang Academy of Fine Arts designed by artist Cheong Soo Pieng.

An oil on canvas portrait by Xu Beihong (1939) (ht 49 cm) of Lim Hak Tai, a leading figure in the establishment of the Nanyang Academy of Fine Arts. Collection of the Singapore Art Museum.

BELOW RIGHT: Georgette Chen's oil on canvas *East Coast Vendor* (1965) (ht 92 cm) depicts a Malay woman and daughters in Terengganu. Collection of the Singapore Art Museum.

BELOW: *Tropical Life* (1959) (ht 43.6 cm), a Chinese ink and gouache painting on rice paper by Cheong Soo Pieng which illustrates the Nanyang style. The work depicts a rural Malay scene with stylized figures.

Early efforts to preserve and promote Chinese art

As early as the 1920s, there was an ongoing effort to preserve and promote Chinese art—calligraphy, painting and poetry—in Malaya by groups of Chinese artists with significant support from the merchant class. They supported the formation of the earliest known Chinese art society, the United Artists, Malaysia, F.M.S. Formed in 1929, the society's constitution indicated its aim of preserving and promoting Chinese arts. Similarly, the formation of the Penang Chinese Art Club (see 'The beginning of landscape painting') in 1936 by Chinese artists in Penang was another example of local Chinese artists supported by the merchant class. The existence of such art societies attests to attempts to promote artistic activities in Malaya, developments no doubt influenced by the modernization processes taking place in pre-war mainland China. Chinese calligraphy and painting were also taught in Malayan Chinese medium schools.

The Nanyang Academy of Fine Arts based in Singapore

Singapore, which was at one time part of British Malaya and, later, Malaysia until it became an independent republic in 1965, was an important art centre in the early development of modern Malaysian art. Factors such as its geographical location and multi-cultural entrepôt status made it a meeting point between Eastern and Western business worlds. Affording job and economic opportunities, it attracted immigrants from the region, including China and Indonesia. Apart from its attractive cosmopolitan ambience, other factors contributed to the Chinese influx of intellectuals and artists into Malaya during the 1930s and in the immediate post-war years. The Japanese invasion of China in 1936 was one reason. Another was the ideological conflict between the nationalist forces of Chiang Kai Shek and the communists under Mao Tse Tung which had made conditions difficult in China.

Wealthy Chinese merchants, proud of Chinese art and culture, and a group of Chinese émigré artists led by Lim Hak Tai started the Nanyang Academy of Fine Arts in 1938. It was the first art college in British Malaya and was staffed by émigré artists who had studied modernist art in Paris or in the port cities of China. Lim Hak Tai, a trained art educationist and painter, was the Principal of the Academy and also a member of the Society of Chinese Artists, Singapore. Modelled on the Beaux Art-type art academies of Europe, the Academy offered a three-year course in painting and sculpture. It was closed during the World War II years.

Roadside Stalls (1962) (ht 89.7 cm), Chinese ink and gouache on rice paper by Jehan Chan.

Reopened in 1946, the émigré teaching staff included Lim Hak Tai, Cheong Soo Pieng, Chen Wen Hsi, Chen Cheong Swee and Georgette Chen, artists who had been directly exposed to School of Paris modernist idioms during the pre-war years. Having been trained in both Western and Far Eastern painting techniques, their main interest was in fusing both Western and Chinese art influences. Their experimental syncretic approach to creativity was influenced by traditional Chinese painting influences and Post-Impressionism, Fauvism and Cubism. They introduced the ideas of Cézanne, van Gogh, Gauguin, Matisse and Picasso to their Malayan Chinese students.

There was a new sophistication within the local Malayan art scene, especially among the younger Chinese artists associated with the Academy. Among the significant Malaysian-born post-war graduates of

the Nanyang Academy may be included Lim Yew Kwan, Lai Foong Moi, See Cheen Tee, Chung Chen Sun, Chia Yu Chian, Tew Naitong, Khoo Sui Hoe, Cheah Yew Saik, Lu Chon Min, Seah Kim Joo, Jehan Chan and Wong Nai Chin.

The 'Nanyang School' approaches

Given their Western and Eastern artistic orientations, it was to be expected that the Nanyang artists would paint in the Chinese and Western styles as well as produce experimental works that attempted a synthesis of both artistic traditions. Their Western approach was derived from the various idioms of the School of Paris as is reflected in the still life executed in oils on canvas by Chia Yu Chian entitled *Still Life With Wine Jugs* (1967). The empty white background on which the still life forms exist is clearly derived from Chinese painting. Lai Foong Moi's *Dayak Longhouse* (1959) is another oil painting that reveals both Chinese linearisms and the expressive influence of van Gogh. The distinctive Chinese approach is also discernible in Jehan Chan's *Roadside Stalls* (1962), which uses the vertical format of the traditional Chinese hanging scroll and the admixture of traditional Chinese inks and gouache colours, rendered on rice paper. It allows for a top-to-bottom or bottom-to-top reading of the composition, recalling the spatial construct of the Chinese hanging scroll.

The Nanyang artists' attempt to produce syncretic art works was marked by the clever invention of Southeast Asian figure types as well as the use of pictorial formats derived from traditional Chinese paintings. An excellent example is Cheong Soo Pieng's *Tropical Life* (1959) which displays his inventive figure types and spatial cells demarcated by the tree trunks. The painting allows for a left-to-right or right-to-left reading, reiterating peripheral vision common in the traditional Chinese scroll paintings.

Referred to today by local art writers as the 'Nanyang School' these experimental Chinese modernist artists not only introduced a new sophistication in the search for artistic directions but they also preserved and appropriated their own Chinese artistic traditions at the same time in ways that were innovative.

Still Life With Wine Jugs (1967) (ht 76 cm), an oil on canvas painting by Chia Yu Chian.

BELOW LEFT: Oil painting *The Dayak Longhouse* (1959) (ht 58 cm) by Lai Foong Moi.

BELOW: Wong Nai Chin's *Serene Village* (1994) utilizes the Chinese hanging scroll format and the Chinese ink technique for a Malaysian scene.

Art groups

The growth of a modern art tradition in this country, during the pre-Independence era, is marked by the emergence of local art groups which provided the impetus for artists to work and exhibit together. Influenced by the multi-racial social contexts, this development was initially determined by particularized ethnic groupings, influenced by linguistic orientations. In recent years, such formally structured groupings have decreased, but artists have continued to come together in important group exhibitions to project commonly shared ideatic preferences and artistic approaches.

ABOVE: Some members of the Wednesday Art Group in the mid-1950s including Peter Harris (centre in coat), the founder of the group, and well-known members Cheong Laitong (seated in front) and Patrick Ng Kah Onn (front third from right). The group met on Wednesday afternoons, hence the name Wednesday Art Group.

BELOW: Patrick Ng Kah Onn of the Wednesday Art Group was inspired by Balinese painting and culture in this 1959 painting *Spirit of Earth, Water and Air* (ht 137 cm). The painting is divided into three zones—upper (sky), middle (earth) and lower (water)—and utilizes regional symbolism.

Yati (1964) (ht 62 cm), a pastel on paper artwork by Mazli Matsom of the Angkatan Pelukis Semenanjung group.

Early art movements

The emergence of local art groups, either formally or informally structured, since the pre-war era, was an important development. In the earlier absence of proper art colleges (see 'Art education'), the existence of these groups allowed local artists to come together and participate in artistic activities and to exhibit together. Bearing in mind the multi-ethnic make-up of the modern Malayan context, these art groups were often formed along linguistic lines and orientations.

The first art group to be formed in the country was the United Artists, Malaysia, F.M.S., founded in Kuala Lumpur in 1929. It was made up of Chinese artists whose aims included the preservation of Chinese culture and art, the study of foreign art and the publication of materials related to the fine arts. Activities included classes in Chinese calligraphy, ink brush painting and Western oil painting techniques.

The formation of two pre-war art groups in Penang, namely The Penang Impressionists (founded in 1930) and the Penang Chinese Art Club (1936) (see 'The beginning of landscape painting') was responsible for artistic activity on the island. The Penang Impressionists, composed of colonial housewives, was a watercolour society. Abdullah Ariff was one of only two non-European artists in the group. The Penang Chinese Art Club was made up of Chinese members and included Yong Mun Sen, Tay Hooi Keat, Lee Cheng Yong, Quah Khuan Sim and Kuo Ju Ping.

Keeping Nets (1962) (ht 59 cm), an oil painting depicting an East Coast fishing boat by Ho Khay Beng, who was a graduate of the Nanyang Academy of Fine Arts.

Pre-Independence era

The founding of the Nanyang Academy of Fine Arts in 1938, and its subsequent emergence as a strong artistic movement in the post-war years in Malaya, was especially significant (see 'Artists of the Nanyang school'). The teaching staff, émigré artists from mainland China, introduced School of

Nanyang Academy of Fine Arts graduating class of 1957 with their teachers (seated from left): See Cheen Tee, Cheong Soo Pieng, Lim Hak Tai (Principal), Georgette Chen, Chen Wen Hsi and Lim Yew Kwan. Students from the Chinese language high schools in Singapore, the Malay Peninsula, Sarawak and British North Borneo (now Sabah) came to study fine art at the Nanyang Academy.

Paris influences and also the tenets of traditional Chinese painting. Modernist art proper emerged in Malaya with these Nanyang artists, who introduced Post-Impressionist, Fauvist and Cubist approaches.

The formation of the Wednesday Art Group ('WAG') in Kuala Lumpur in 1952 by Peter Harris, an expatriate English art educationist (see 'Art education') was notable for its multi-racial membership. Its members were encouraged to find individual approaches to creativity. Among the important members of the group were Patrick Ng Kah Onn, Cheong Laitong, Dzulkifli Buyong, Ismail Mustam, Syed Ahmad Jamal, Nik Zainal Abidin, Ho Kai Peng and Sivam Ponnampalan. The WAG was an influential art group before and after Independence, affording various degrees of modernist experimentations. Patrick Ng's *Spirit of Sky, Earth and Water* (1959) is a good example of a search for Southeast Asian roots and sensibilities.

The formation of the Angkatan Pelukis Semenanjung ('APS') art group in 1956, composed mostly of Malay artists, was initiated by Mohamad Hoessein Enas, an émigré artist from Java. Influenced by the 'Beautiful Indies' art movement in Indonesia, Hoessein Enas served as the teacher of the group

ABOVE: APS painting class, Kuala Lumpur, 1964.

LEFT: Self-portrait of Mohamad Hoessein Enas (1958) (ht 44 cm).

and introduced an academic naturalistic style. Artists produced idealized portraits and landscapes that celebrated, for the most part, the rural Malay world and its inhabitants. Among the well-known pioneer APS artists may be included Mohamad Hoessein Enas, Mazli Matsom, Hamidah Suhaimi, Idris Salam, Mohd Sallehuddin, Zakaria Noor and Yusof Abdullah.

Post-Independence era

The tendency for Malayan artists to go to England, Europe and the United States for formal artistic studies in the post-Independence era has witnessed more individualized approaches in the search for artistic directions—hence, the smaller number of formally structured art groups. In some instances, artists sharing common stylistic preoccupations have come together to exhibit as a viable group for a number of exhibitions, before going their separate ways.

The *GRUP* exhibition held in 1967 may be cited as an example. Newly returned artists sharing the Abstract Expressionist idiom (see 'From modernism to post-modernism') came together to exhibit works. These artists included Syed Ahmad Jamal, Abdul Latiff Mohidin, Cheong Laitong, Jolly Koh, Anthony Lau and Ibrahim Hussein. The exhibition is important in

that it introduced emotive abstraction as a new artistic force within the Malaysian art scene during the 1960s.

Similarly, the coming together of Constructivist artists calling themselves the 'New Scene' artists in various exhibitions—*New Scene* (1969), *Experimentasi '70* (1970) and *Dokumentasi '72* (1972)—witnessed a grouping of artists that included Redza Piyadasa, Sulaiman Esa, Tang Tuck Kang, Tan Teong Kooi, Tan Teong Eng and Choong Kam Kow, who shared Neo-Constructivist and Minimalist art orientations. A manifesto called *The New Scene* was published for the 1969 show. After 1972, the group disbanded (see 'From modernism to post-modernism').

The formation of the Anak Alam (Children of Nature) art group in 1974 witnessed the emergence of the first artistic commune, made up of a breakaway group of younger members of

Angkatan Pelukis Malaysia. This more experimental group of Malay artists had as their spiritual mentor and leader, Abdul Latiff Mohidin. Inspired by Latiff's romantic approach towards nature, and a more expressionistic approach, the group included Mustaffa Haji Ibrahim, Siti Zainon Ismail, Mad Annuar Ismail, Dzulkifli Dahalan and Lat, among others. The group disbanded during the early 1980s.

The formation of the Artists' Association of Malaysia in 1978, under the leadership of Syed Ahmad Jamal as President, was a bold attempt to bring together all artists under one umbrella so that they could have a collective voice and assert artists' opinions in the formulation of cultural policies undertaken by the government. The demise of the association by the late 1980s was regrettable.

The new proliferation of art colleges in Malaysia since the 1990s (see 'Art education') has witnessed the decline of art groups as such. Now, artistic activity is often centred around art colleges such as the MARA School of Art and Design, the Malaysian Institute of Art, the Kuala Lumpur College of Art and the Pusat Seni (art centre) of Universiti Sains Malaysia. Younger artists have nevertheless attempted to form art groups, including the Matahati art group led by Bayu Utomo Radjikin and the Air Panas art commune, led by Liew Kungyu and Yap Sau Bin. Both groups are located in Kuala Lumpur; the former was founded in the mid-1990s and the latter in 2002.

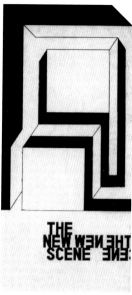

ABOVE: Cover of the New Scene exhibition catalogue (1969).

LEFT: *My Love ... Have You Ever Suffered?* (1973) by Mustaffa Haji Ibrahim, who was a member of the Anak Alam art group.

Original committee members of the Artists' Association of Malaysia (Persatuan Pelukis Malaysia) in early 1980. Seated front from left to right: Sulaiman Othman, Syed Ahmad Jamal, Yeoh Jin Leng, Ham Rabeah Kamarun. Standing from left to right: Mazli Matsom, Syed Hood Alhabshi, Ahmad Khalid Yusuf, Ruzaika Omar Basaree, Hashim Hassan and Redza Piyadasa.

RIGHT: Logo of the Artists' Association of Malaysia.

ABOVE: From left to right: Cheong Laitong, Anthony Lau, Jolly Koh, Abdul Latiff Mohidin, Syed Ahmad Jamal and Ibrahim Hussein, members of the *GRUP* exhibition at its opening in March 1967.

LEFT: Invitation to the opening of the 1967 *GRUP* exhibition.

From Modernism to Post-modernism

Whereas some Malaysian artists had turned to traditional influences and techniques in their attempts to define artistic identity, other artists were exposed to the international avant-garde art contexts. During the 1960s, newly returned, Western-trained artists introduced abstractionist approaches in creativity. Since the 1980s, local artists have become involved with figurative art, socio-political critiques and globalization issues, motivated by the new influences of post-modernist thinking. They project more reflexive and critical attitudes in their artistic endeavours.

Tradition and continuity

ABOVE: *Feeding Time* (c. 1951) batik painting by Chuah Thean Teng.

RIGHT: Nik Zainal Abidin's *Wayang Kulit Kelantan* oil painting (1961) (ht 56 cm).

Modern Malaysian artists have borrowed from Southeast Asia's past artistic traditions in their need to project a sense of regional identity and cultural continuity. This was first manifested in the efforts of Chuah Thean Teng to employ the batik technique on cloth to produce easel-type paintings. During the early 1950s, he began producing paintings that incorporated this region's traditional batik technique with modern expressionistic figurative influences and bright colour schemes derived from the West. His stylized *Feeding Time* (1951) is an early example of his portrayals of everyday rural scenes and pastoral events (see 'Modern art').

Chuah Thean Teng spawned a number of Malaysian figurative batik painters such as Tay Mo Leong, Khalil Ibrahim, Yan Shook Leong and Seah Kim Joo who emerged during the 1960s. More recently, Fatimah Chik has, since the late 1970s, used a more abstract symbolic approach, employing actual printing blocks, complex printing and dyeing processes and decorative textured effects in her batik paintings (see 'Contemporary Islamic art').

The painter Nik Zainal Abidin drew his influences from the *Ramayana* mythical stories of the Wayang Kulit or shadow puppet tradition of Kelantan. He transferred the puppets onto canvas or paper surfaces, reiterating the two-dimensional quality of the original forms. If, in the Wayang performances, the puppets are projected as black shapes onto a flat, white cloth surface, in Nik Zainal's highly detailed paintings, initially begun during the late 1950s, the original colour schemes of the puppets, juxtaposed against each other, result in decorative narrative works reflecting an authentic sense of cultural continuity. His *Wayang Kulit Kelantan* (1961) is an example.

Syed Thajudeen's similar borrowings from the *Ramayana* repertoire of mythical stories, rendered in the oil medium on canvas, have resulted in different visual effects from those of Nik Zainal. Relying on stylizations and subtle colour hues and dense textures, his *Hanuman visits Sita* (1972) exemplifies his unique narrative approach.

Syed Thajudeen's *Hanuman Visits Sita*, oil on canvas (1972) (ht 151 cm).

Introduction of abstract art

The Malaysian involvement with abstract art can be dated to the late 1950s when a generation of local artists left to study in art colleges in the West. Exposed to international avant-garde trends, they initially accepted the emotive tenets of Expressionism and, later, the American-derived Abstract Expressionism aesthetic.

Syed Ahmad Jamal's *The Bait* (1959) was, arguably, one of the first completely abstract art works produced in Southeast Asia. By the 1960s, other newly returned artists such as Ibrahim Hussein, Abdul Latiff Mohidin, Yeoh Jin Leng, Jolly Koh, Anthony Lau, Cheong Laitong and Lee Joo For had begun producing abstract works influenced by Abstract Expressionism.

This emotive idiom has its younger adherents even today, nearly 50 years after its initial appearance here. They include Sharifah Fatimah Zubir, Awang Damit, Tajuddin Ismail, A. Yusof Ghanie, Jailani Abu Hassan, Rafie Ghanie and Azman Hilmi, among others. The idiom's romantic underpinnings highlighting ideas of artistic uniqueness, a creative sub-consciousness, plus its emphasis on gestural brushstrokes and thick use of paints has proved appealing. For the most part, the thematic interest has been in organic forms and shapes derived from the tropical landscape.

Abdul Latiff Mohidin's *Pago-Pago* series of paintings are examples (see 'Modern art'). Yeoh Jin.

1. *The Bait* by Syed Ahmad Jamal, oil on board (1959) (ht 122 cm).

2. *Human Rot* by Yeoh Jin Leng, oil on canvas (1968).

3. *Sri Jingga Indera Kayangan* by Sharifah Fatimah Zubir, oil on canvas (1998)

4. *Collection* by Jailani Abu Hassan, acrylic on canvas (1988) (ht 122 cm).

Leng's *Human Rot* (1968) reflects the earlier emotionally-charged gestural treatment while Sharifah Fatimah Zubir's emotive *Sri Jingga Indera Kayangan* (1998) reflects interests in complementary colour contrasts and textural effects. More recently, younger Neo-Expressionists artists, while alluding to recognizable forms, employ stylistic mannerisms derived from the original idiom. Jailani Abu Hassan's *Collection* (1988) is an example.

The introduction of abstract Neo-Constructivist tendencies here is traceable to the 1969 *New Scene* exhibition. The exhibition manifesto challenged the emotive-expressionist approach of Abstract Expressionists, advocating an 'alternative aesthetic' founded on investigative and non-emotive orientations. The idea that art making can be scientifically programmed and mathematically structured allowed for new perceptual attitudes to emerge. The subsequent emergence of Minimalist Art and Conceptual Art developments in this country, during the 1970s, may be attributed to some members of the New Scene group (see 'Installation art').

The New Scene artists included Redza Piyadasa, Sulaiman Esa, Choong Kam Kow, Tang Tuck Kang, Tan Teong Eng and Tan Teong Kooi. The group disbanded in 1972 (see 'Art groups'). Tang Tuck Kang's *49 Squares* (1969) and Choong Kam Kow's *SEA Thru-flow 3* (1974) are examples of this approach. The precise, geometric approach in these works reflect affinities with modern architecture and modern packaging design.

In more recent years, the abstractionist approach has been largely adopted by Malay-Islamic artists in their attempts to produce contemporary Islamic works. The assumption, among these Islamist artists is that Muslim artists cannot produce art works that are figurative in character (see 'Contemporary Islamic art').

ABOVE: **SEA Thru-flow 3 (1974) (ht 30 cm) by Choong Kam Kow is a Minimalist object based on mathematical serialization. It is non-emotive.**

BELOW: **49 Squares (1969) (ht 203 cm) by Tang Tuck Kang relies on mathematics, optical illusions and is also non-emotive.**

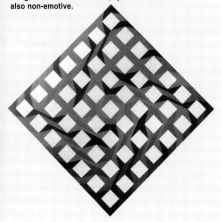

Social narratives and critiques

The move away from abstractionist and formalist concerns towards socio-cultural contexts, initially undertaken by a small number of older artists during the early 1980s marked a search for pertinent sociological content and social critique. Much had changed in the country since independence and new tensions had emerged, namely, the official division of the multi-racial population into indigenous and non-indigenous segments. The rise of the new Islamist tendencies (see 'Contemporary Islamic art') was another factor. Rapid industrialization and urbanization processes had further transformed traditional society. Ideatically, the rise of 'the new art history' and art theory studies, calling for post-formalist attitudes in art making, was a vital factor. Figurative art and realism returned to the art scene.

DOT: The De-Tribulization of Tam Binti Che Lat (1983) (ht 121 cm) by Ismail Zain was one of the earliest Malaysian works to depict the displacement of traditional communities in the face of rapid social change and consumerism.

Ismail Zain's *DOT: The De-Tribulization of Tam Binti Che Lat* (1983) was an anthropological commentary and critique on the displacement of traditional communities and cultural values in the face of mass-culture influences. An old Malay woman in the foreground mutely surveys the new urbanized settings surrounding her. From 1982 onwards, Redza Piyadasa began addressing the issues of growing ethnic marginalization. He turned to period photographs of Malaysian families, highlighting the social histories of the different ethnic groups. His recent *Malaysian Story No. 2* (1999) postulates a more composite modern history and a pluralistic Malaysian identity in the face of politicized divisions.

The 1990s and after have witnessed the emergence of significant younger artists who employ reflexive, post-modernist and post-formalist approaches to re-question the narrative discourses of history, politics, ethnicity, identity, class and gender. They also highlight environmental degradation, social injustice, globalization and Euro-American cultural hegemony. These provocative artists include Wong Hoy Cheong, Hasnul Jamal Saidon, Liew Kungyu, Bayu Utomo Radjikin, Nadiah Bamadhaj, Jegadeva Anurendra, Eng Hooi Chu, Tan Chin Kuan, Shia Yih Yiing, Hayati Moktar, Yee I-Lann, Simryn Gill, Niranjan Rajah, among others (see 'Issues based art' and 'Installation art').

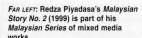

FAR LEFT: **Redza Piyadasa's Malaysian Story No. 2 (1999) is part of his Malaysian Series of mixed media works.**

LEFT: **Eng Hooi Chu's feminist work The Great Supper (1999) (ht 166 cm) celebrates her sense of womanhood and motherhood and asserts her distinctive individualism in the midst of a festive family reunion and dinner.**

Electronic art

Recent artistic explorations in electronic media by Malaysian artists complement this country's rapid industrialization process. Malaysia, one of the leading micro-chip makers in the world today, is geared toward achieving fully industrialized nation status by 2020.

The exploratory work of the painter Ismail Zain, from the early 1980s, was significant in drawing attention to the possibilities of electronic art expression. His exhibition and manifesto entitled *Digital Collage*, held in 1988, was ground-breaking. Embracing post-modernist ideas of globalization, cultural pluralism and post-formalist thinking, he produced computer-generated print-outs that were highly eclectic in their scope. He made witty commentaries on history, the mass media, on tourism and the transfer of cultural values, on censorship and the impending impact of the borderless world.

Other younger, socially committed, post-modernist artists who have been associated with electronic media explorations include Hasnul Jamal Saidon, Niranjan Rajah, Wong Hoy Cheong, Liew Kungyu, Ting Ting Hock and John Hii.

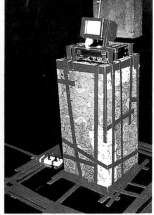

RIGHT: **Al-Kesah (1988) by Ismail Zain depicts the popular Ewing family, of 1980s TV soap opera Dallas fame, visiting a Malaysian kampung house as happy American tourists.**

FAR RIGHT: **Hasnul Jamal Saidon's Kdek, Kdek Ong! (1994) is an electronic installation that uses witty animation techniques and a traditional Malay proverb to make a biting statement about closed, parochial minds.**

Sculpture

Sculpture, three-dimensional visual art that is typically displayed on a pedestal, always exists as an object, rather than primarily as a concept or an experience. Although it can be based on both, sculpture always focuses on its form and materials. Unlike installation art, sculpture does not usually bring the viewer into it. Instead, sculpture invites contemplation and scrutiny.

Gerak Tempur (1996) (ht 61.5 cm) by Raja Shahriman is a welded metal sculpture of a warrior that suggests the dehumanizing effects of violence.

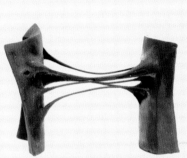

The Link (1963) (ht 39 cm) by Syed Ahmad Jamal, a welded metal sculpture, is a metaphor about delicate relationships between two entities or persons.

Anthony Lau's *Spirit of Fire* (1960) (ht 95 cm) is a mythological representation of fire. The elongated shape of the work and its details evoke a flickering flame.

Emergence of modern sculpture

The history of modern sculpture in Malaysia began in a meaningful way just after Independence. Before the 1950s, there were sporadic sculptural works made, but the bulk of three-dimensional objects created were to express the indigenous beliefs of the peoples of Sabah and Sarawak and the Peninsula Orang Asli tribes. (See 'Wood and other carvings' and 'Carvings and sculptures: From cradle to grave').

Sculpture devoted to the expression of an idea, a specific aesthetic or for formal concerns, without specific spiritual or religious meanings, is largely a product of the second half of the 20th century. The reasons for this can be found in dominant religious practices and cultural beliefs. Amongst Muslims, the prohibition against possessing graven images could preclude three-dimensional figures, and has led to the avoidance of creating lifelike figurative sculptures. Large representational figures were found in both Indian and Chinese temples (see 'Chinese and Indian religious arts and crafts') but were not usually found in homes or public spaces. Within other indigenous groups, three-dimensional forms related to protection and commemoration, and were not for purely aesthetic purposes.

Much of this changed in the 1950s, and certainly the 1960s, when Malaysia embraced modern art (see 'Modern art'). Yet, at the same time, there has never been a large movement to produce life-like figurative nudes as there has been in Europe, in emulation of the Classical period. Instead, what emerged was a three-dimensional practice rooted in expressing the natural world and the cultural practices of Malaysian peoples. In the following decades, abstraction and formal concerns have been important dimensions of sculptural practice.

Engagement with Modernism

Anthony Lau was the most significant sculptor of the 1950s and 1960s. After pursuing fine arts and education studies in the United Kingdom, he also received an M.A. in art education from Indiana University. A Fulbright scholar, he returned to Malaysia and taught at the Specialist Teachers' Training Institute (see 'Art education') for over ten years. Lau's sculptural practice followed the modernist principles of revealing the essential nature of his medium. Hence, his works that use concrete, wood and metal fundamentally demonstrated the

unique qualities of his materials. Take, for instance, his elegant and deceptively simple work *Forest* (see 'Modern art'). Representing a wooded thicket, after the leaves have fallen, the individual strands are bent in a U-like shape to form the base of the work. The multiple strands that spread from the main trunks suggest branches. The visual effect simulates a view of tree trunks. The multiple metal strands appear impossibly light and demonstrate the strength possessed by the metal itself. Lau's adherence to the 'truth to material' aesthetic is also discernible in his biomorphic *Spirit of Fire* (1960). Evoking the mystical essence of fire, he personifies the element in this vertical, flame-like wood carving. His interest in this highly polished work lies in the aesthetic quality of the wood medium, emphasising its block-like origins, its tonal gradations and organic wood grain patterns.

In the 1960s and the 1970s, several artists who were primarily known for their two-dimensional work also produced sculpture. Syed Ahmad Jamal, Lee Joo For and Yeoh Jin Leng all produced three-dimensional work as part of their overall art practice. Notably, all three artists, as well as Anthony Lau, had taught at the Specialist Teachers' Training Institute. The abstract painter, Abdul Latiff Mohidin also produced several notable sculptural series, namely the *Pago-Pago* series in the 1960s and the *Langkawi* series in the 1970s.

Globe (1990) by Ham Rabeah Kamarun, an organic ceramic sculpture evoking biomorphic energies.

Developing materials

Although they had been producing work since the 1970s, ceramic works by Ham Rabeah Kamarun and Yeoh Jin Leng started to significantly emerge in the 1990s. Largely concerned with formal concerns, Ham Rabeah's work experiments with texture and materials. Using natural glazes, she produces works that focus on shape relationships. Yeoh Jin Leng's ceramic and bronze works reflect his intense personal research into glazes and surface treatments, revealing his deep engagement with the making process.

The 1980s saw the emergence of a sculptor and teacher who exerted a profound influence on the sculpture of the 1990s. Ramlan Abdullah, a graduate of Institut Teknologi MARA (ITM) (see 'Art education'), went on to study at the Pratt Institute and subsequently spearheaded the sculpture programme at ITM. His wood sculptures and glass and metal sculptures brought together elements of Modernism and Minimalism in a way that was relevant to the Malaysian context. Avoiding direct representation, Ramlan used industrial materials and revealed how his work was constructed. His sculptures introduced an aesthetic that echoed the burgeoning urban development in Kuala Lumpur. In the 1990s, Ramlan received the bulk of public commissions and so his work came to represent the artistic dimension of the thrusting, high-tech vision exemplified by the Kuala Lumpur Twin Towers.

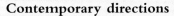

Rebab Player I (1991) by Mad Annuar Ismail is carved from wood. As suggested by the title of the work, it presents an abstracted image of a seated musician playing the traditional Malay instrument, the *rebab*.

Drawing from cultural traditions

One of the most significant sculptors who emerged in the 1970s was Mad Annuar Ismail. Originally a designer, he produced many two-dimensional works in the 1970s but found his signature sculptural style in the 1990s. He drew upon his experiences from the 1970s as a member of the Anak Alam group (see 'Art groups'). The group advocated looking at nature and Malay life and culture as a source of creative ideas. His later sculptures, including *Rebab Player I* (1991) and *Storm Riders*, introduced a muscled and mystical dimension to Malaysian sculpture.

Powerful expression of a deeply rooted aesthetic emerged in the 1990s through the work of Raja Shahriman, Tengku Sabri and Bayu Utomo

Radjikin. Raja Shahriman's anthropomorphic warriors show sophisticated workmanship and a skilled manipulation of the metal medium. Constructed with materials from the junkyard and using the welding approach, the series exudes a powerful tension and dramatic energy.

Tengku Sabri's work combines the refinement of traditional craft with the heft of political commentary. His virtuoso carvings incorporate a Western sense of shape relationship and composition with the all-over patterning and intricacy of traditional Malay woodworking. His wire work, however, demonstrates the same deft delicacy but always comments on social and political issues. Tackling such diverse topics as revolutionary thought and Western warmongering, Tengku Sabri articulates his political views with elegant forcefulness.

While Bayu Utomo Radjikin's work has largely been two-dimensional, his sculptures also demonstrate a unique expressiveness. His *Bujang Berani* (1991) (see 'Modern art') and related work from the same series speaks of frustrated manhood. Using the aesthetics of Sarawakian warriors, the dynamic diagonals and arched back of his truncated warrior embodies the rage and energy of thwarted young men.

Contemporary directions

Industrial materials such as wire mesh, wire and brass feature significantly in the work of Sharmiza Abu Hassan. Rather than focusing on the materials, she uses them to express narrative and thought. Her *Puteri Gunung Ledang* series addresses allegories chiding the arrogance of powerful men, while other series, such as *Coaches*, speak of yearning and nostalgia.

An interesting counterpoint to the glossy optimism of shiny surfaces comes through the controlled rusting of many of Abdul Multhalib Musa's works. His large works use stainless steel and mild-steel, often treated to rust until a designated point. They incorporate precision cutting made possible by the great push towards industrialization Malaysia has undergone in recent decades. These materials are harnessed to express Multhalib's thoughts on mathematics, music, the environment and serial progression.

Perhaps the only other artist to engage with materials with the same degree of intensity as Anthony Lau is Terry Law, a sculptor who started exhibiting in the 1990s. Law takes on steel filings, video projection, aluminium and plastic to express their essential qualities as materials. She engages with form and space in challenging and unexpected ways.

ABOVE: Tengku Sabri's *Siri Warga Terakhir–II Anak Dagang* (1991) (ht 78 cm) wood sculpture.

LEFT: Freedom Monument (1995) (ht 141 cm) by Ramlan Abdullah is a metal and glass sculpture.

ABOVE: Norazizan Rahman Paiman's *Peristiwa Tanjung Antu* (1992) is inspired by Malay fishing traps and uses local materials.

BELOW: Faltered Wings (2003) (ht 100 cm) by Abdul Multhalib Musa is constructed of mild steel with a clear enamel coat. It has been exhibited overseas.

Metal wall reliefs featuring railway coaches by Sharmiza Abu Hassan, entitled *Coaches* (1995) (ht 22.8 cm).

Installation art

Installation art in Malaysia emerged in the 1970s and has subsequently played a major role in the nation's art history. The origins of this form of art-making can be traced to European avant-garde movements of the early 20th century and to American art movements of the 1960s. Fundamentally, installation art is shaped by ideas and expressed through objects in space. Distinct from sculpture, installations seek to bridge the gap between art and the viewer through the use of unconventional materials, scale and space, thus bringing viewers closer to the work.

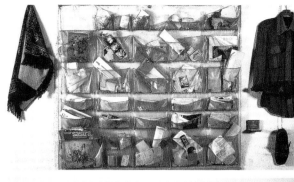

ABOVE: Zulkifli Yusoff's installation *Immunity I* (1993), comprising ink on canvas, plastic, metal, wood and canvas constructions.

TOP: Sulaiman Esa's original 1973 mixed media installation *Man and His World*, part of the National Art Gallery collection, was subsequently partially restored as shown in this picture. The use of everyday objects insisted on the specific time and place that the artist lived in.

Emergence of installation art

The 1970s witnessed a fervent debate about the direction of art. Heightened national identity and race relations issues (see 'Issues based art') forced individuals to make choices that changed the direction of the nation. The events of the late 1960s tempered the optimism of Independence and ushered in a spectrum of responses that ranged from urgency to futility.

Artists looked at man's behaviour and sought to confront and examine the human condition. Modernity, urbanization and environmental degradation were addressed in their work. Installation art, with its inclusion of mundane objects and physical spaces, proved an effective means to communicate their ideas (see 'Issues based art').

A key figure in this new artistic spirit was Redza Piyadasa. An articulate, confident man fresh from his studies in London and Honolulu, he set about making his name through confrontational and thought-provoking art events in the early 1970s. Piyadasa made his mark in Kuala Lumpur through a series of exhibitions: *New Scene* (1969), *Experimentasi '70* (1970) and *Dokumentasi '72* (1972) (see 'Art groups'). Piyadasa's work at this time focused on questioning current events and the expectations of conventional art-making practices. His art works marked the emergence of Conceptual Art in Malaysia. In addition to participating in and organizing exhibitions, Piyadasa proved tireless in challenging the ways art is made. Through his writing, art, judging in art competitions and

teaching, he provoked thought and debate in ways that forced his audience to question their points of view. Fundamentally, he helped to provide a favourable context and climate for installation art. Art historian T.K. Sabapathy discusses Piyadasa's artworks in a book published by the National Art Gallery to accompany a retrospective exhibition held in 2002.

Institutional support

Institutions played a major role in encouraging the development of installation art. The director of the National Art Gallery (see 'National and state art organizations'), Ismail Zain, sought to inject fresh thinking into the art scene. To this end, the Gallery organized thematic exhibitions such as *Man and His World* (1973) to urge artists to engage with the world around them rather than solely focusing

TOP: *Curse* (1990), a mixed medium installation by Tan Chin Kuan.

ABOVE: Installation by Chuah Chong Yong *Pre War Building For Sale: Welcome to the era of the biggest, the highest and the the longest......* *Phase I* (1999) (ht 600 cm). The images were printed on fax paper and will fade in time.

RIGHT: *Situational Piece No. 5 for T.K.S.*, a 1978 installation by Redza Piyadasa composed of found objects, a spotlight, wood, carvings and actual artworks.

FAR RIGHT: Multi-media installation-cum-performance space by Liew Kungyu entitled *Who Am I?* (1991).

on aesthetic ideals. The resulting work marked the first time installation work was displayed in the National Art Gallery. The two major winners of this exhibition, Nirmala Dutt Shanmughalingam and Sulaiman Esa, produced work that used everyday objects. Shanmughalingam's untitled work sharply condemned the irresponsible dumping of industrial debris, destroying lovely natural sites. Her point was made with text explaining her social commentary, documentary photographs and a collection of industrial debris placed in the National Art Gallery itself. Sulaiman Esa's work entitled *Man and His World* placed a large plastic sheet with pockets to hold the pieces of papers that define urban life, such as tickets, notebooks and newspaper articles. A shirt on a hanger and shoes flank the sheet, while the other side displays a prayer rug hung on the wall.

From the 1970s onwards, installation art has had a place in both established and alternative art venues. While its introduction provoked outcry, the advocacy provided by Piyadasa in his writing and institutional validation proved a compelling combination.

Throughout the 1980s, the most significant installation art emerged through the Young Contemporaries competition held by the National Art Gallery (see 'National and state art organizations'). Aimed at young artists, the competition encouraged adventurous use of materials and clear conceptual thinking. Zulkifli Yusoff and Tan Chin Kuan garnered critical attention in the early 1990s through their participation in this competition. Zulkifli Yusoff's stunning black and white installations incorporated drawing and structures to create spaces that resembled an abstracted theatrical set. Executed on a human scale, they addressed issues such as the confrontation between village and international life, the use of implied force in maintaining power and corruption in political life. Tan Chin Kuan's work is largely based on painting but also incorporates sculptural objects that intrude into the viewer's space. Urban alienation, racism and fears of religious fundamentalism comprise some of his themes.

Artist-led initiatives

It was only in the 1990s that installation art finally became an accepted and integral form of art making. A unique confluence of strong work, capable artists and regional interest resulted in sustained production of thought-provoking work.

Wong Hoy Cheong and the Matahati group emerged in the early 1990s. Wong returned from his studies in the United States in 1987. From 1990–95 he curated exhibitions at the Galeri MIA, an exhibition space connected with the Malaysian Institute of Art (MIA) (see 'Art education'), where he also taught. Various experimental shows were exhibited there, including Liew Kungyu's *Who am I?* (1991) installation that incorporated performance and multimedia to question identity issues. Other artists that have emerged from MIA include Chuah Chong Yong whose work focused on the destruction of heritage buildings and MIA lecturer Bibi Chew whose installations speak of a universal humanism in the face of growing communal divisions.

In 1995, Wong also curated *Skin Trilogy* at the National Art Gallery, a seminal exhibition of installation works at the Gallery. Including work by Zulkifli Yusoff and Liew Kungyu, the exhibition also featured three performances on the installations, incorporating dance, sound and narrative. In addition to his teaching and curating, Wong is also one of Malaysia's most stimulating artists today. He has made several memorable installations such as *Re:Looking*, displayed in the 50th Venice Biennale of 2003 and comprising an installation work, video and a website.

The artist group Matahati (see 'Art groups') has also proved a key influence on installation art in Malaysia. Comprising several fine arts graduates of the Universiti Teknologi MARA (UiTM) (see 'Art education'), the members banded together to display group exhibitions and to help each other attain solo exhibitions. Matahati consistently engages with current events and regularly produces installation art. They have provided an example to young artists that reputations can be made outside of the commercial sector and have themselves actively assisted young artists through holding discussions and curating young artists' exhibitions.

An exciting artist to emerge in the first decade of the 21st century is Nadiah Bamadhaj. Her exhibition *1965: Rebuilding its Monuments* addresses issues of state-sponsored violence and political will. Her works incessantly question issues of human rights and demand the accountability of political leaders for human tragedies.

In his mixed media installation *Re:Looking* (2003), Wong Hoy Cheong rewrote history, proposing that Malaysia had conquered the Austro-Hungarian empire. To this end, he created a fictitious historical record, doctored archival photographs and enlisted prominent Austrian and Malaysian historians to take part in a fictitious documentary video discussing the conquest and its implications on modern Austria and Malaysia. The complex installation included furniture, photographs and decorative objects to further this alternative history.

ABOVE: An installation work by Nadiah Bamadhaj from her exhibition *1965: Rebuilding its Monuments*, held in 2001. The artist makes a witty statement about political power, its hierarchies and the square-shaped odd-man-out at the bottom left.

LEFT: Insect Diskette II (1997) (ht 200 cm) by Ahmad Shukri Mohamed of the Matahati art group. The installation is made up of computer diskettes arranged in a grid-like configuration. Images of fragmented and dismembered insects are stencilled on the diskettes. In front of the work is a white chair with many computer mouse connected to the diskettes.

Issues based art

Issues based art includes work that directly addresses and re-questions social narratives and contexts, national and international political events. From the late 1960s to the present time, some of the most important art produced has been of this genre. While approaches and mediums differ greatly, such works address contemporaneous problems and comment on sociological issues and values of their era.

Artist Ibrahim Hussein pictured with his acrylic on canvas painting entitled *May 13, 1969* (1969) which represented one artistic response to the tragic May 13 riots. When questioned by Prime Minister Tun Abdul Razak as to the meaning of the painting, the explanation given by Ibrahim Hussein was that painting the Malaysian flag black represented the artist's feelings for his country when he saw news footage of the tragedy while overseas. The red line showed the twilight of the nation in eclipse and the white circle suggested a new beginning.

Installation by Redza Piyadasa, also entitled *May 13, 1969* (ht 182 cm) created in 1970.

Effect of 13 May 1969

13 May 1969 had a significant effect as it shattered the outward appearance of harmony within newly independent Malaysia. From beneath the placid appearance of national unity suddenly emerged previously suppressed disaccord and tension over perceived economic and political inequality, deep-rooted racial insecurities and distrust.

In terms of artistic responses, Ibrahim Hussein, Syed Ahmad Jamal and Redza Piyadasa produced work that addressed the riots that had occurred, marking a new role for local art, that of commenting on socio-political issues.

Ibrahim Hussein's work *May 13, 1969* (1969) featured a Malaysian flag covered with black paint. Beneath a thin horizontal red band in the middle was a full moon and the number '13'. When the work was exhibited at Universiti Malaya, the Prime Minister Tun Abdul Razak called the artist into his office to explain the work, concerned that its appearance might provoke further unrest. The artist pointed out that the riots were tragic for the nation as a whole but that hope remained for the future. Its exhibition was conditional on the work never being sold, except to the government, or taken out of Malaysia.

Syed Ahmad Jamal's *One Fine Day* (1970) presents a stylized representation of a large pointed red shape, resembling a drop of blood, bisecting an abstracted representation of the city and a darkened sky.

Redza Piyadasa's work on this subject was the most direct. His *May 13, 1969* (1970) stemmed from a poem by Usman Awang entitled *Kambing Hitam* (*The Scapegoats*). Produced as part of the exhibition *Manifestation of Two Arts*, the exhibition saw artists producing work inspired by Malaysian poetry. Piyadasa's piece was a life-size coffin painted with an abstracted and fractured Malaysian flag streaked with black and positioned on a square mirror. Viewers close to the work saw themselves reflected in it—in this way, the work suggests collective responsibility for the tragedy.

One Fine Day (1970), an acrylic painting by Syed Ahmad Jamal.

ABOVE: Artists Sulaiman Esa (left) and Redza Piyadasa (right) photographed in 1974.

RIGHT: Cover of the *Towards a Mystical Reality* exhibition manifesto (1974).

TOP: A view of the *Towards a Mystical Reality* installation exhibition (1974) featuring common everyday objects, such as a bird cage, Coca-Cola bottles, a chair and a potted plant.

Pan–Asian inspiration

With debates about the direction of national cultural policy raging throughout the 1970s, two artists staged an event to redirect creative attention away from the West and towards the East. *Towards a Mystical Reality. A documentation of jointly held experiences by Redza Piyadasa and Sulaiman Esa* (1974) argued for a shift in the Euro-American perception of art and creative influences. As an exhibition, it featured many commonplace objects culled from daily life such as the ashes of mosquito coils, empty birdcages, worn shirts. They celebrated the ephemeral debris of daily life and the right of the artist to assert it as art. In so doing, they argued against the precious, handmade and the unique art object. Significantly, the exhibition was accompanied by a 20 page manifesto that declared the importance of turning towards the philosophical approaches and belief systems of Asia, such as Taoism and Zen. The exhibition marked a turning point. Just as the Vietnam War provoked questioning about Asian sovereignty and the Cultural Revolution in China violently rejected emblems of Western culture, artists in Malaysia also questioned the dominance of Western influences.

Nirmala Dutt Shanmughalingam has based her painting practices on highlighting injustice and suffering. From her work in the 1970s that addressed environmental destruction and domestic poverty to paintings that addressed American aggression in Vietnam, the artist has consistently addressed issues that move her. One of her strongest works is *Friends in Need* (1986) which addresses the joint Anglo-American bombing of Libya. She casts United States President Ronald Reagan and British Prime Minister Margaret Thatcher as Wayang Kulit (shadow puppet) figures surrounding images of a dying Asian child. In this way, the artist uses regional symbolism to expose the posturing of Western political leaders who further their hegemonic ambitions; despite causing the death of innocents.

A post-modern generation

The 1990s witnessed the emergence of sustained and provocative art. The most interesting and innovative artist of this era is, arguably, Wong Hoy Cheong, who returned from his studies in the United States in the late 1980s and taught at the Malaysian Institute of Art (see 'Art education'). He championed post-modern ideas in his teaching and has had a profound influence on a significant generation of younger artists. Post-modernism's focus on validating varied points of view, critiquing institutional discourse and ideology provides a different way of looking at issues (see 'From Modernism to Post-modernism'). His own work has challenged narratives dealing with official versions of Malaysian history, issues of ethnicity, identity and also socio-political developments. His early work *Sook Ching* (1990) addressed the Japanese Occupation and the hardship and suffering faced by Malaysians of all ethnic groups. His *Migrant Series* (1994) featured three sections: a series of charcoal drawings juxtaposing aspects of his family history, a series of portraits of various migrants and a collection of objects and texts related to the cultivation of rubber. In this way, Wong used the cultivation and exploitation of the rubber industry to explore issues related to his family, the movement of people and our perceptions of migrants, at a time of strong emotions about ethnicity and nationality.

Other artists who address socio-cultural and political issues include Nadiah Bamadhaj, Yee I-Lann and Anurendra Jegadeva. Nadiah Bamadhaj's exhibition *1965: Rebuilding Its Monuments* (2001) (see 'Installation art') focused on the events of 1965 in Indonesia and Malaysia. Sukarno's fall and Suharto's rise, the Confrontation between the two nations, and personal family tragedies related to Indonesia's violent suppression of East Timor's demonstrations for independence were among the themes addressed. In contrast to the tumultuous events depicted, her charcoal drawings and plaster

ABOVE: Nirmala Dutt Shanmughalingam's *Vietnam* (1981), acrylic on canvas work, deals with the American war against Vietnam. This artist utilizes images from the mass media and magazines which are stencilled onto canvases using silk screens. Her work generally has a severe stark style rendered in black and white and employs techniques such as image repetition and structural composition to heighten emotional impact.

LEFT: Artist Nirmala Dutt Shanmughalingam.

works were cool and controlled. Bamadhaj has also explored issues of political hegemony created through the manipulation of race and the influence of money. In one work, handmade elements such as sections of drawings made in a basket weave and small forms in the shape of hands praying made up of the first Malaysian king's profile from Malaysian ringgit notes, introduced elements that personalized Malaysia's formative historic events.

Yee I-Lann's varied artistic output reflects the broad spectrum of her interests (see also 'Photography'). Works from her *Horizon* (2003) series and the *Sulu Stories* (2005) use digitally manipulated photographs to address issues of land and belonging. *Horizon* explores the limits we seek and impose on the land and people. For example, Yee links the cultivation and numbering of oil palms with the education and socialization of young people in *In the Palm of Putrajaya* (2003)—as each palm is numbered and harvested, so too are young people through identity card numbers and productive professional lives. Both, she suggests, are being nurtured to provide for the nation's future. Her *Sulu Stories* series looks at the regional identity of the peoples who share this key regional sea—Indonesia, the Philippines and the people of Sabah and Sarawak share overlapping mythologies and peoples. Her work on the history and culture of these lands and magical images of the land and water argue for a more complex view of the region than tourist brochures and nationalistic rhetoric can express.

Anurendra Jegadeva's paintings turn towards issues of masculinity, militancy and ethnicity. His *Running Indians and the History of the Malaysian Indian in 25 Cliches* (2001) comprises two parts: six large horizontal panels atop 25 intimate squares of Malaysian Indians going about daily life. The six large works present a series of young men in sarongs, running, twisting, floating from left to right. In the middle are two lovers, swirling about each other. The chiselled torsos of the young men depicted express vitality while their languid yet powerful movements suggest vulnerability as well. The small portraits show jewel-like portraits of everyday life: praying to the gods, barber's chairs, and an old woman standing next to an election poster are amongst the images captured. Anurendra's work also comments on the eruption of racial violence locally as well as the conflict in Sri Lanka. His images confront the hypocrisy of espousing peace while propagating death. Despite the weightiness of his subject matter, his work also consistently advocates a practical humanity expressed through small acts of kindness and the appreciation of nature and people.

RIGHT: Artist Wong Hoy Cheong.

BELOW: This work *She Was Married at 14 and She Had 14 Children* (1994) (ht 190 cm) by Wong Hoy Cheong is a charcoal drawing from his *Migrants Series*. The painting depicts his paternal grandmother and her suffering in raising her family. By contrast, Wong's maternal grandmother enjoyed a highly privileged life and emblems such as the Yardley's Lavender Soap allude to the varied experiences people have, even within an ethnic group.

Images from two large panels (from six pieces) (ht 76 cm) and selected small portraits (from 25 pieces) (ht 13 cm) from Anurendra Jegadeva's *Running Indians and the History of the Malaysian Indian in 25 Cliches* (2001) oil on canvas.

Contemporary Islamic art

Islam arrived in the Malay Peninsula in the 14th century. Malay-Islamic revivalist tendencies developed within the contemporary art scene from the late 1970s, inspired by local socio-political influences and global Islamist developments. They were also prompted by the search for non-secular values and the need to define nationalistic identity within the visual arts context. These factors contributed to recent attempts by some contemporary Malay artists to draw from their Islamic heritage and produce art works that consciously mirror Islamic influences.

ABOVE: Omar Basaree's *Surah Ar-Rahman, Verse 12, Khat Diwani* (c. 1970s) utilizes Arabic calligraphy and geometric designs.

LEFT: This ceramic work, *Tombstone* (1992) (ht 107 cm), by Hamzun Harun, also displays calligraphic influences.

Fatimah Chik's *Keyakinan* (2001) is a prayer mat design executed in the batik medium. It was the First Prize Winner of the 2001 National Prayer Mat Competition, organized by the National Art Gallery.

Islamic influence in the Malay Peninsula

The historic acceptance of the Islamic religion and its cultural influences in this country can be dated back to the 14th century and is a development that is mirrored in traditional art forms (see 'Influences on arts and crafts: A historical perspective'). Islamic ornamental embellishment and an interest in aniconic motifs are detectable in traditional architecture, in the applied arts and in the production of the Qur'an during the pre-colonial period. While the country has embraced modernization processes since the mid-19th century, Islamic religious and cultural values still assert considerable influence among the Malays, up to the present time.

Search for a Malay–Islamic identity

Contemporary visual artists have attempted to re-introduce Islamic influences in their creativity. The emergence of Malay-Islamic revivalist tendencies has been influenced by socio-political developments since the 1970s, following the 13 May 1969 riots and the setting up of the National Cultural Congress of 1971, which witnessed the new introduction of Islamization processes by the government during the 1970s and after.

Also in the 1970s, the Arqam and Tabligh dakwah (missionary movements) created a new socio-cultural ambience that eventually initiated a corpus of modern Islamic art approaches as well. Other factors included the emergence of the Malay

Tulisan (1961) is an oil painting by Syed Ahmad Jamal. The artist has combined flowing Arabic calligraphic script with the emotive-gestural expressiveness of the Abstract Expressionist idiom. This work was one of the first to appropriate Jawi calligraphy in the context of modern Malaysian painting.

middle class in urban environments, the ensuing crisis of moral values and role models, the increased revulsion towards unbridled Western materialism, and the success of the 1979 Islamic Revolution in Iran.

The wider search for Malay-Islamic meaning permeated the thinking about art in two ways. First, there was an upsurge in the appreciation of Malay identity, fostered by the National Cultural Congress of 1971 and exhibitions such as *Rupa dan Jiwa*, curated by Syed Ahmad Jamal and held at Universiti Malaya in 1977. There was an attempt by Malay intellectuals and artists to rediscover their Malay roots, traditional cultural forms and aesthetic sensibilities.

These new developments need to be understood in the light of the growing global Islamist movement and the re-questioning of the materialistic underpinnings of a secularistic, Western-derived modernism. The Malay-Islamic impulses in the arts were also vital to the new idea of 'national culture'.

Contemporary Islamic artworks

Syed Ahmad Jamal adopted a new artistic stance as early as 1959, when he produced *Khairul Anwar* and then later *Tulisan* (1961). Employing the tenets of the emotive-expressive Abstract Expressionist idiom (see 'From modernism to post-modernism') and thick painterly brushstrokes, he relied mainly on swirling sweeps from right to left. These two works, produced in oils, were the first to suggest the possible uses of dramatic calligraphic forms in the context of modern Malaysian painting.

The contemporary Islamic impulses of the late 1970s and after were notably linked to the Malay artists of the MARA School of Art and Design (see 'Art education') and their varied experimentations. Ahmad Khalid Yusuf's *Alif Ba Ta* (1971) backtracks to the roots of his faith by affirming the alphabet's primacy, out of which emerge the Qur'an and the

Hadith, as well as the long tradition of learning, memorizing, comprehending and debating. Ahmad alludes also to the hardship of the life of restraint and conformity that Islam implies. However, he parodies the rules by arranging his letters on, above and below the grid lines. By darkening half of the pouches of *dad*, *zha* and *ya*, he teases the authorities of correct penmanship, insisting that a letter is free to appear as it pleases.

ABOVE: Calligraphy exhibition, Penang, December 1976.

RIGHT: *Alif Ba Ta 71* (1971) by Ahmad Khalid Yusuf.

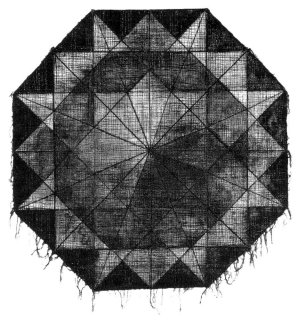

Nurani by Sulaiman Esa (1983) (ht 150 cm), hand-made from paper, yarn, bamboo and acrylic paint, is an octagonal work emphasizing an interest in traditional Islamic geometric design, mystical esoteric mathematic proportions and subtle colouristic effects, with lines leading to a radiating centre.

Sulaiman Esa shifted the emphasis from letter renditions to abstract wall hangings, as in his work *Penghormatan untuk Nakula* (1983). Paying homage to the author Nakula of a pioneering book, Sulaiman takes off from the rectangularity of the prayer mat, extending its size and adding mixed media techniques and tassels along the edges. The idea of *Tawhid*, denoting the concept of unity and convergence— 'a unity in multiplicity and multiplicity in unity'—is a central idea influencing his octagonal work *Nurani* (1983), which has a tightly structured irradiating geometric design.

Upon returning from the San Francisco Art Institute where he studied modern sculpture, Zakaria Awang shifted his attention to incorporate Qur'anic verses on various materials. This was propelled by his profound experience after rearranging his priorities so that serving God came first. The religious verses are carved, chiselled or pasted, and either hung or placed on the floor to demand that the viewer read and contemplate. An example is his *Murakabah* installation (1991).

The photographer Raja Zahabuddin bin Raja Yaacob has produced several photo montages influenced by his interest in

Calligraphy

One manifestation of the Malay-Islamic revival of the 1970s and the ensuing change in focus by Malay artists was an interest in the use and depiction of Arabic calligraphy. The first calligraphy exhibition, in which specimens of the Kufi, Tuluth, Naskh, Farsi, Dewani, Riqa'ah and Tugra scripts were shown, was held at Universiti Malaya and other venues in 1975, under the leadership of Professor Ungku Aziz and with Syed Ahmad Jamal as the curator. A number of books also helped foster an interest in calligraphy, giving the public a perspective that was previously unavailable. For example, in *Pandangan Islam tentang Kesenian* (*Islam Looks at Art*), Sidi Gazalba argued that art incorporating calligraphy was indeed permitted because it conveyed beauty and helped believers to do good and to fight evil. Such liberal views provided the more hesitant Muslim artists a recourse against the prevailing orthodoxy of many *ulama* concerning the making of images. In 1979, the book *Bentuk-Bentuk Bangunan Masjid* (*Shapes in Mosques Forms*) by Abdullah bin Mohamed (Nakula), an ustaz-cum-self-trained art historian, appeared, in which he used the shape of the lotus flower to comprehend the three-tiered roofs of the 17th-century Masjid Kampung Laut in Kelantan (see 'Traditional wooden architecture').

Such forages into the realms of interpretation inspired artists to experiment. Calligraphers such as Syed Abdul Rahman al-Attas, Mohd Yusof Bakar and Omar Basaree were already active in the field. All three were especially adept in writing the Tuluth script. Their works were largely a straightforward transcription of the holy book, whose rules concerning the pronunciation or *tajwid*, aided by diacritical marks, had already been laid down. The transition they made was therefore less than drastic. Now they re-conceptualized each work as a thing by itself, to be exhibited in art galleries and sold. Western-trained artists, on the other hand, were satisfied with rendering a series of letters, or a word, either as a spoof or in homage—it was difficult to tell which. Traditional rules concerning proportions, relationships and syntax were disregarded. Instead, modern artists saw in the Arabic alphabet a whole world of expressive forms, one that was plastic and limitless. They freed these forms from the clutches of the religious people whose ideas on the man–God relationship they re-articulated in larger holistic terms, namely fashioning the script in any number of ways as part of *ibadah*, or worship.

Islamic themes. His work *The Greatness of God* (1991) portrays the centre of the Shah Alam Sultan Salahuddin Abdul Aziz Mosque. The view is one that looks up into the dome. Between the two centralized buttressing columns, on the red grid-like formation of the wall, the artist has pasted squarish shapes in green that spell out the word Allah.

Fatimah Chik's prize-winning prayer mat design entitled *Keyakinan* (2001), rendered in the traditional batik medium, is yet another example. Her technique, dependent on the use of traditional printing blocks, complex waxing and dyeing processes and the inclusion of regional motifs, has resulted in a prayer mat that is distinctly South East Asia in character and flavour.

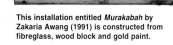

This installation entitled *Murakabah* by Zakaria Awang (1991) is constructed from fibreglass, wood block and gold paint.

Photo montage *The Greatness of God* (1991) (ht 97 cm) by Raja Zahabuddin bin Raja Yaacob, an artistic photographer.

Photography

No longer simply a form of documentation or visual record, photography is also an art—the image is filtered through the eyes of the photographer (artist) and is in turn subject to the intricacies of its creation and production (medium). In the past, photography was a novelty and the process was more complicated, but with the advent of technology it has become a relatively simple task that can be contrived, taken and retaken, now with the aid of digital cameras. Nevertheless, photography remains a medium that offers the instantaneous capture of a moment in history.

Nomadic Penans, Sarawak (1978) by Dennis Lau, who is particularly known for his images of the indigenous peoples of Sabah and Sarawak.

ABOVE: Portrait of Malay noblewomen, Perak, c.1903.

BELOW: Seated Nonya lady taken in a photographic studio, c. 1920s.

This early picture postcard depicts Melaka's old Town Square and its famous river, c. 1906.

Early Malayan photography

The roots of Malaysian photographic culture are invariably tied in with the colonial past, as the first photographic equipment, technology and approaches originated from the West. With colonialism, came the desire to chronicle indigenous scenarios in photography. The earliest evidence of photographs is from 1844 with daguerreotype (an early camera, invented in 1837) pictures taken of the Singaporean landscape by Jules Itier, the head of a visiting French Commercial Mission.

In the 19th century, there was an influx of commercial photographers in Singapore. The style and composition of photographs of this time were reflected by stiff and posed depictions, sometimes with exotic costumes and backdrops. By the 1890s, postcards became immensely popular as a cheaper and more prolific avenue for European colonizers and visitors to reveal the mystery and exotic character of the East. These showed scenes as varied as newly erected administration

Detail of a hand-coloured portrait postcard of a Malaysian Chinese lady, c. 1930s.

buildings to dilapidated slum dwellings, portraits of toiling emaciated labourers to smartly dressed-for-the-tropics colonizers resplendent with their *topi* and bamboo cane. Such postcards became possible when photographic prints, which enabled reproduction, superseded the daguerreotype type process. Once admired for their kitsch and novel properties, these old postcards have today become important pictorial documentations of the past. In the Malayan mainland, a less regular demand did not call for a permanently based photographic studio. However, some photographers, including the renowned John Thompson, famed for his ethnographic and topographic studies, did make photography expeditions to the mainland.

Late 19th-century visual annals of the Malayan mainland are predominately derived from the personal photographs of the ill-fated first British Resident of Perak, James Birch and Leonard Wray of the Perak Public Works Department. It was Wray who founded the beginnings of what is now known as Salon art photography as he founded the Perak Amateur Photographic Society in 1897.

Being a relatively expensive pursuit, it was only when economic and political stability came to the region that photography could be established as a commercial business or hobby.

Salon art photography

By the early 20th century, the increasing number of commercial photographic studios also led to the formation of several salon groups. Examples include the short-lived Perak Amateur Photographic Society and the Singapore Photographic Society (founded in 1887). These amateur photographic societies helped to establish a foundation for the exchange of ideas and modes. The early 1900s saw the emergence of hand-colouring which considerably enhanced black and white photographs. Photography at this time remained a novelty and the work from this period was predominantly of townscapes, landscapes and portraits, including that of Malay royalty. With growing affluence in the 1920s, there emerged a style of portrait postcards and calling cards (*carte de visite*).

The first Malayan Photographic Competition was held in 1953, and thereafter, photography competitions were held locally at least four times a year. The Royal Photographic Society of Great Britain was an international society that was a leading example. The Photographic Society of Malaysia was founded in 1956 and photography clubs and societies were formed in almost every state.

Images that will be ingrained as visual documentation of Malaysia's past are by the photographers HRH Sultan Ismail

ABOVE RIGHT: *Morning Prayers* (1950) by K.F. Wong won awards in salon competitions. He set up the first Sarawak photographic studio.

RIGHT: HRH Sultan Ismail Nasiruddin Shah experimented with colour photography from the mid 1950s. This idyllic photograph, *Perahu Biduk* (1960), is of a small boat in Terengganu.

Nasiruddin Shah of Terengganu (1907–79), Loke Wan Tho (1915–64), K.F. Wong (1916–98) and Koh Eng Tong (1921–). These photographers were proponents of the Salon style of clear illumination and high contrast. Loke Wan Tho's donation to the National Art Gallery Malaysia in 1963 of 539 photographs encapsulating the pictorial movement is, arguably, one of the most comprehensive collections of such photographs in Asia.

An untitled photograph (1970s) taken in a Thai temple in Kangar, Perlis by the artist-photographer Eric Peris. The image appeared in the book *Images of Gitanjali* which contains Peris' illustrations for Rabindranath Tagore's poems. Peris is inspired in his work by Zen Buddhism and nature.

Late 20th-century developments

The breaking down of the earlier academic Salon tradition in Malaysia, beginning around the 1970s, may be attributed to a number of reasons. The new availability of sophisticated cameras and colour film to the wider population and their easy ability to create their own images heralded the slow but growing decline of the earlier role played by commercial photo studios. These studios would now become outlets for the sale of photographic film and for the technical processing of the public's pictures. In addition, time had begun to take its toil on the earlier generation of self-taught Salon photographers. Further, the introduction of the new photographic departments in the newly-established art colleges, from the early 1970s onwards would produce more sophisticated practitioners, better equipped with the latest aesthetic concepts as well as a more meaningful understanding of the history of modern photography. The emergence of serious artist-photographers such as Ismail Hashim, Eric Peris, Md Yusoff Othman, Raja Zahabuddin bin Raja Yaacob, Dennis Lau, Ismail Abdullah and Alex Moh by the early 1980s and after hastened the process of change. Many of them had studied in the United States and Europe.

By the early 1980s, the bi-annual *ASEAN Travelling Art Exhibition* (initially begun in 1970) had included a photographic component within its set-up, thereby encouraging the participation of serious artist-photographers from the ASEAN region. By the 1980s, a number of Malaysian art galleries had begun to market the works of the more serious artist-photographers, thereby lending a new prestige to photography as fine art and collectible art objects. Small numbers of Malaysian art collectors began to invest in the works of the new Malaysian artist-photographers. There is a growing market for serious photographic works today.

What is interesting about the new Malaysian photography is the experimental modes and highly individualized visions that have emerged. On one level, photographers have looked more pragmatically at the reality around them and recorded it without idealizing its subject-matter. The photographer acts as a social commentator and exposes issues that matter to him. The role played by Ismail Hashim in introducing new realist modes of perception and social commentary merits special mention. His interest in the 'vanishing scene' in the face of rapid urbanization processes has resulted in his hand-tinted realist works such as *The Barber Shop* (1986) and *The Bathroom* (1988). His work has been recognized internationally. On another level, Eric Peris' use of Zen Buddhist influences and attitudes in his work has introduced a philosophical dimension into local photography. His works are usually imbued with a quiet spirituality and a notion of transience that is distinctly Buddhist and Asian. His illustrations for the book *Images of Gitanjali* (1984) are fine examples.

Md Yusoff Othman is another significant artist-photographer of the 1980s whose sensitive use of surrealistic effects and overlapping images have resulted in haunting, dream-like worlds. Raja Zahabuddin bin Raja Yaacob has used the photo-collage technique to project Islamic themes (see 'Contemporary Islamic art'). The younger post-modernist artist Yee I-Lann, has used period photographs drawn from the collections of the older photo studios in her installations to highlight modern Malaysia's multi-ethnic histories and realities. The above-mentioned works serve as examples of the new and diverse approaches in Malaysian photography today.

ABOVE: Ismail Hashim's hand-tinted *The Bathroom* (1988) reflects his interest in Malaysia's vanishing environment—here, the bathroom in an old Malay *kampung* house.

BELOW: Surrealistic hand-tinted work (c. 1984) by Md Yusoff Othman.

Yee I-Lann's *Kerana Mu Malaysia* (*Because of You Malaysia*) is part of a larger photographic installation featuring Malaysia's complex multi-ethnic realities, installed at the National Art Gallery in 2002.

Graphic design

Graphic design is a creative form of visual communication that usually combines words and images. Today, it encompasses a wide variety of applications including advertising, signage, product packaging, posters, industrial and internet web design through print and digital media and film. Malaysia's cohesively diverse society, history and rich cultural traditions have infused and influenced all aspects of Malaysian life, including graphic design. Development of this discipline has also parallelled the economic, political and social development of the country.

With the establishment of a postal service came a vibrant form of graphic art, postage stamps. Stamps document Malaysian life, culture and icons. These examples (clockwise from top left) feature Malaysian batik textile, traditional kite flying, the Kuala Lumpur Twin Towers and the performing arts.

ABOVE: This manuscript, *Undang-Undang Pahang*, was written in the 16th century and contains the rules and laws governing the people of the state of Pahang. It is exquisitely illuminated with gold and other colours.

BELOW: Malaysian-produced Qur'an, commissioned by the government and completed in 1999. It features traditional designs from the Malay Islamic world.

An artistic and cultural heritage

Although a young nation, the artistic and cultural heritage of Malaysia is diverse, drawn from the races who make up its society—Malays, Chinese, Indians and indigenous peoples—from visiting traders and also from former European colonial powers. Even today, this cultural diversity and artistic inheritance are apparent everywhere and are woven into the fabric of modern Malaysian society. They are shown by an extraordinary fusion in food, fashion, art and architecture, and in the lifestyle of contemporary Malaysians, many of whom are trilingual.

This diverse legacy has had a tangible impact on graphic design, and to understand the present state of the industry in Malaysia means looking back through history. This presents a real challenge, however, in part because of the numerous cultural strands that must be woven together to create the full picture, and in part because records of Malaysia's early design history are threadbare, mainly comprising the documents of explorers, merchants and colonial administrators.

The earliest forms of graphic design can be said to have appeared during the Melaka sultanate in the 15th century. Melaka's strategic position made it a major port on the international trade routes and a place where merchants from East and West converged. Arab merchants brought illuminated Islamic texts, the Chinese brought the printing press and several types of paper, and Indian traders introduced their own ornamental sensibilities through their textiles.

The 16th century saw a burgeoning of Malaysian design, perhaps in part influenced by these visiting traders and the techniques and materials they brought, which was manifested in royal scriptures and letters, illuminated frontispieces, elegant calligraphy, theological headings and delicate seals.

Emergence of modern graphic design

Under colonial rule, Malaysia's first sight of modern Western graphic design came with the unveiling of flags, crests and badges—the insignia of the colonizing powers, who also brought in political ephemera as propaganda. The establishment of a postal service meant the design of new stamps, while education required books. During this time, colonial advertising also emerged, often featuring watercolour paintings (see 'The beginning of landscape painting').

Malaysia became a nation state in 1957 upon gaining independence from Great Britain. Initially known as Malaya and composed of the Peninsular Malay states, the later joining of the states of Sabah and Sarawak in Borneo and the departure of the island of Singapore, resulted in present-day Malaysia. This brought about a different perspective to the forms of graphic design that had already emerged.

Many early 20th-century posters advertising Malaysia featured watercolour paintings of local scenes.

The gateway of the Portuguese A'Famosa fort in Melaka has a Dutch coat-of-arms carved in relief, added in 1669 after the Dutch conquest. This type of Western colonial graphic design also served to signify authority.

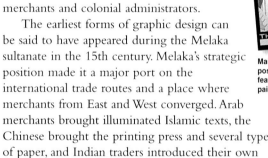

LEFT: The cover designs and internal layout of books and magazines, such as these examples of a heritage publication (far left) and a Malay magazine for women (left), are created by graphic designers.

RIGHT: Electronic publishing and, in particular, website designing, is an area of graphic design that has grown with the development of information technology.

Development of formal education

Formal graphic design education in Malaysia began roughly a decade after Independence, with the introduction of programmes at the Malaysian Institute of Art (MIA) in 1966, the MARA Institute of Technology in 1967 and Universiti Sains Malaysia (Science University of Malaysia) in 1969 (see 'Art education'). The curriculum of the universities was based on the Western model and included courses in typography. The intention was that graduates would go on to play a role in nation building. Although it was accepted that art was needed to enrich the country socially, it was not recognized that art, and more specifically design, could also be a resource for economic development. As a developing nation, Malaysia needed technocrats, and so greater emphasis was placed on science and engineering disciplines.

However, by the 1990s it became fashionable to study graphic design. There was a mushrooming of private graphic design colleges in the country. While many institutions include graphic design courses in their curriculum, some well known private colleges include Limkokwing University College of Creative Technology, Center for Advanced Design (CENFAD) and The One Academy of Communication Design. In 1997, the Faculty of Creative Multimedia was established at the Multimedia University in Cyberjaya, and courses became available at Universiti Tunku Abdul Rahman (UTAR), which was established in 2002. To turn out graduates in the shortest time possible, most design institutions, especially the private ones, resorted to a more vocational approach to graphic design, thus minimizing academic aspects.

The corporate sector

In the professional arena, graphic design companies started to make an impact in the 1970s. But it was the advertising industry that dominated, enhanced during the 1980s by mergers and affiliations with international agencies and media conglomerates from the United States, Britain and Japan. For a long time graphic design was largely perceived as subordinate to advertising, and it has only been in the last decade or so that these giant firms have seen the need to diversify and form sister companies specializing in graphic design. At the same time, independent design firms have now flourished, each creating its own individual style and identity.

Legitimization and development

The fine arts have fared rather better in Malaysia, with some local artists winning awards and international acclaim. However, in order to legitimize the arts in Malaysia, organizations such as the National Art Gallery (see 'National and state art organizations'), the Malaysian Design Council and the National Cultural Centre were established. At one time it was also part of the national agenda to define a Malaysian identity in art and design. In 1999, a voluntary professional organization was established called WREGA.

From the late 1980s, some fine artists, one of the most notable being Ismail Zain, have utilized technology to create computer generated fine art. In recent years, the intermarriage of art and science has taken centre stage, most notably in animation (see 'Cartoons'), cinematic special effects, cyber communication, software development and graphic and industrial design. The establishment of the Multimedia Super Corridor in the mid-1990s created a demand for greater numbers of professionals with specialist skills in information technology, design, content development and entertainment. This has prompted both the government and private corporations to increase their investment in the arts.

Modern tools

Modern technology, particularly the computer and other electronic accessories, obviously play a major role in graphic design today, especially in terms of the commercial disciplines. Many different types of software which are able to deal with graphics are used by designers including for print and online publishing, industrial design, film and animation.

Experimental computer fine artwork *Penyanyi Pujaan* (*Popular Pop Singer*) (1988) by the painter Ismail Zain displays the intermarriage between the fine and graphic arts. This artist created a significant body of work in the electronic medium.

The creation of corporate logos by graphic designers, as in these Malaysian examples, is an important part of the branding process.

Patriotic advertisement for national Independence Day 2002 by PETRONAS, portraying Malaysia's multi-racial population.

These vernacular greeting cards utilize traditional Malaysian and ethnic designs and motifs.

LEFT: Information brochures and pamphlets display design creativity. This example is a brochure for the Museum of Asian Art (Muzium Seni Asia) at Universiti Malaya.

RIGHT: An exhibit at the *National Branding and Packaging Exhibition,* held in 2005, featuring blown-up packaging designs for Malaysian food products.

Cartoons

Cartoons—drawings exaggerating or distorting a subject for satirical or comic effect—started locally in the 1930s in newspapers, and spread in the 1970s to cartoon magazines and animated films. The style of cartoons evolved from the blunt and direct critical humour of pre-Independence cartoons aimed at creating political awareness on issues such as colonialism and immigration, to the more subtle and regulated post-Independence cartoons which commented on society and local and international issues.

Reggie Lee often portrays the multi-cultural nature of Malaysian society, such as these caricature figures drawn from most of the ethnic groups.

This 1936 *Warta Jenaka* cartoon by Abdullah Manan 'The West Must Stay in the West, the East Must Stay in the East' expresses an anti-Western sentiment and criticizes those who were fascinated by the West—the two monkeys symbolize Malays aping Western attitudes.

ABOVE: Cartoon from *Majlis* (1948). The caption in Jawi script reads 'Administration, Defence, Economy. The current needs of the Malays'.

TOP: The cartoons published in *Utusan Zaman* were dominated by those illustrated by Ali Sanat until World War II. These cartoons were mainly based on a character called 'Wak Ketok', as in this example from 1939.

Pre-Independence (1930–1957)

Local cartoons of the pre-Independence era were dominated by editorial cartoons that first appeared in the 1930s in Malay newspapers *Warta Jenaka* and *Utusan Zaman* and another publication called *Majlis*. Many of these cartoons were instruments of criticism and satire to raise Malay consciousness as to their rights and future, and thus covered Malay political, social, cultural and economic issues. For instance, *Warta Jenaka* published cartoons by regular cartoonist S. B. Ally and reader contributions dealing with subjects that included the perceived detrimental influence of Western culture and modernism, British colonialism and Chinese and Indian immigration, Malay poverty and so-called bad attitudes such as indebtedness, carelessness, laziness and shyness, which the paper criticized as factors contributing to the lack of Malay economic advancement. The cartoons of *Utusan Zaman* were also aimed at uplifting the spirit of Malay nationalism, but also covered international political issues such as the rise of Hitler. *Majlis* cartoons were more direct and propagandistic in nature, often supported by poems, proverbs and rhymed or elaborate sentences. Ordinary objects and images were manipulated as secondary symbols, replacing the animal imagery that was widely used in *Warta Jenaka's* cartoons.

Editorial cartoons

Unlike strip cartoons which appeared continuously in newspapers from independence, editorial cartoons only became popular from the 1980s through the works of cartoonists such as Lat, Nan, Zoy, Zunar and Rossem, even though such cartoons had appeared in *Berita Harian* from 1957–1958 (Peng) and in *Utusan Zaman* in 1963 (Rahim). Following Independence, the context in which cartoonists worked changed due to factors such as government policies, newspaper ownership and legal regulation which included printing and publishing laws introduced in 1984. In line with the government's intention to promote racial harmony, sensitive subjects, especially those which might hurt the feelings of any ethnic group, were avoided. Editorial cartoonists concentrated on less controversial socioeconomic issues rather than political ones. However, in the late 1990s, Malay editorial cartoons took a new shape. Cartoonists such as Zunar, Rossem, Brain and Asrie came out with strong aggressive cartoons attacking government leaders and policies in opposition party magazines and newspapers, *Detik* and *Harakah*. In

Post-Independence and contemporary

After Independence in 1957, the prevailing social, economic, and political conditions played an important role in shaping the form and content of cartoons. The nature, ownership, target audience and policies of newspapers, as well as rules and policies implemented by the government, determined what was politically and stylistically acceptable in terms of criticism. Compared to most pre-Independence cartoons which directly criticized their targets, post-Independence cartoons took a milder approach which was within the boundaries of legal regulation

Cartoonist Lat

Mohd Khalid Nor, popularly known as Lat, has had a lengthy career as a cartoonist, dealing with a wide spectrum of issues including politics and Malaysian life and culture. Born in 1951, and drawing from a young age, he published a book in 1964 while in school and went on to publish many more. One of his most famous creations is the cartoon series based on his own life, *The Kampung Boy* (1979), which has also been translated and published overseas and animated.

Lat at the National Art Gallery's drawing demonstration in April 2006.

LEFT: This 1995 cartoon by Lat comments on the government structure.

BELOW: Nan (*Utusan Malaysia*, 1993): 'National athletes must be shaken to shed their 'Village Hero' mentality'.

response, cartoonists such as Juragan, Miki and Zoy, who worked for mainstream newspapers—*New Straits Times*, *Utusan Malaysia* and *Berita Minggu*—published cartoons that criticized the leaders and policies of the opposition parties. This phenomenon was evident in the 1999 General Election campaign and illustrates the role of editorial cartoons as a political weapon.

Overall, contemporary editorial cartoons have a more aggressive and direct style that is similar to, but more restrained than, the style of pre-Independence cartoons.

ReGGie Lee

and the culture of contemporary mass-media. Cartoonists generally avoided socially and politically sensitive subjects, the humour was more subtle, and themes concentrated on the nature of a multi-racial society and international issues rather than focusing on a specific ethnic group.

Two types of cartoons were prevalent in newspapers of the post-Independence era—strip and single-frame cartoons. Strip cartoons appeared regularly in newspapers from Independence and mainly dealt with social themes, especially family life and spousal relationships, as well as social attitudes, modernization and moral crises. However, single-frame cartoons only began to thrive in the 1980s, although the genre had appeared in the 1930s. They sometimes served as editorial cartoons and generally depicted contemporary local and international events.

In the late 1950s, cartoons and comics from the West as well as those of local cartoonist Peng were published in papers such as the *Straits Times* and translated for the Malay newspaper *Berita Harian*. The latter was the first paper to organize a cartoon competition for readers in 1958.

Throughout the 1960s and 1970s, family-based strip cartoons by Raja Hamzah and Lat's celebrated work 'Keluarga Si Mamat' ('Mamat's Family') were popular. Malay cartoonists such as Rahim (*Utusan Melayu*) and Razali MHO, Rejabhad, Mishar, Shukorlin and Rizalman (*Utusan Zaman*) also became known—their works largely depicted humorous, social and political scenes. In 1978, the

Peng, *Berita Harian* (18 October 1958). 'Ubat-Socialism' ('Socialist Medicine').

first Malaysian cartoon magazine *Gila-Gila* was published. Its success led to the continuing publication of other cartoon magazines.

This development, together with the emergence of new cartoonists, animated cartoons, exhibitions and the support given by the public and the government turned the 1980s into the golden age of Malaysian cartoons. A number of animated cartoons were produced from the mid-1980s. In 1983, the first Malaysian cartoon exhibition was held at Universiti Kebangsaan Malaysia. Other important events include the formation of the Malaysian Cartoonists' Association (PEKARTUN) and the first International Cartoonists symposium and exhibition held in Malaysia, both in 1990.

Contemporary cartoonists such as Lat, Rejabhad, Jaafar Taib, Nan, Zoy, Zunar, Zainal Buang Hussein, Rossem, Reggie Lee and C.W. Kee represent the 'old and the new'. They have played an important role in portraying the nature of and issues affecting Malaysian society.

Animated cartoons

In 1978, the first local animated cartoon, *Hikayat Sang Kancil* (The Story of Mousedeer), was produced for television by Filem Negara (the national film agency), which produced four other short animated cartoons in the mid-1980s: *Hikayat Sang Kancil dan Buaya* (The Story of Mousedeer and Crocodile) (1984), *Sang Kancil dan Monyet* (Mousedeer and Monkey) (1984), *Gagak Yang Bijak* (The Clever Crow) (1984) and *Singa Yang Haloba* (The Greedy Lion) (1985). After this, production of animated cartoons recommenced only in the mid-1990s. There are four main themes in animated cartoons—folk tales, scenes from daily life, fantasy, and superhero adventures. Examples include Filem Negara's *Hikayat Sang Kancil* (folk tales); Ujang's *Usop Sontorian* and Lat's *The Kampung Boy* (scenes from daily life); *Keluang Man* (superhero adventures); *Yokies* (right) and *Sang Wira* (fantasy).

The first full-length animated feature 'Silat Lagenda', produced in 1998 and directed by well-known animator Hassan Muthalib, signalled a turning point and a greater confidence in animation as a commercial and communication medium in the local film industry.

This 13-minute animated cartoon for television, 'Hikayat Sang Kancil', is based on a folk story about a mousedeer.

Cartoon magazines

Malaysian cartoon magazines developed rapidly after publication of the first local magazine *Gila-Gila* in 1978. Initially, cartoon magazines were influenced by Western magazines such as *Mad* and *Crazy* until they found their own local identity.

The success of *Gila-Gila* encouraged the publication of other magazines such as *Gelihati*, *Mat Jenin*, *Humor*, *Batu Api*, *Telatah* and *Relek* which portrayed slapstick humour and humorous aspects of daily life. By the late 1990s some of these magazines had not survived due to competition and the economic downturn, leading to the development of magazines for a particular readership with specific themes: *Cabai* for women; *Ujang* for teenagers; *Lanun* had religion as a theme; *Gempak* included animation, illustrations and foreign cartoons; and *Mangga* focused on local entertainment. Other cartoon magazines were directly associated with music groups, such as *Senario*, or with an animated cartoon series, such as *Usop Sontorian* and *Keluang Man*. This period also saw the unification of print and electronic media to promote local cartoons. By 2000, there were more than a dozen magazines on the market, many of which are still published today.

Gila-Gila (top right) contains strip cartoons, editorial cartoons (mainly on international issues), humorous short stories and anecdotes and articles and news on cartoons and cartoonists. Later publications like *Gelihati* (right) were greatly influenced by *Gila-Gila* in terms of format, presentation and content.

KELUARGA MAT JAMBUL

ABOVE: Raja Hamzah's 'Keluarga Mat Jambul' (Mat Jambul's Family) was a popular strip cartoon series from 1960–68.

LEFT: Single-frame editorial cartoon on the Indonesia-Malaysia Confrontation, contributed in 1963 by Rahim, a reader of *Utusan Zaman*. The translated caption is 'A Victory for Tunku'. The Malaysian Prime Minister and Deputy Prime Minister are in *songkok* headwear.

1. Cover of the first Salon Malaysia national art competition catalogue, 1968. It features the logo of the National Art Gallery, which organized the competition. The second Salon Malaysia took place in 1978.

2. Independence day pubiic paint-in event in Kuala Lumpur, 1970.

3. Galeri Adiwarna at Universiti Sains Malaysia (Science University of Malaysia) in Penang. The university's significant art collection was started in 1978.

4. Children in an art class at Sekolah Kebangsaan, Shah Alam in 1977. By this time, academic prejudices against the visual artists and art education had been overcome with art courses being offered at a teritary level.

5. Students participating in an art class at the Universiti Teknologi MARA (UiTM) School of Art and Design. This institution has produced many artists who have made important contributions to modern Malaysian art.

6. Banner for art event *Manifestasi Wawasan 2020 Inspirasi Pelukis* (*Manifestation of Vision 2020 Art Inspiration*), held in 1991.

7. Entrance lobby of the National Art Gallery of Malaysia. The establishment of the Gallery has had a significant impact on the development of modern Malaysian art.

MW20 20iP
MANIFESTASIWAWASAN20 20inspirasiPELUKIS
11 ogos 1991 ... dewan bandaraya k.l.

ART ESTABLISHMENTS

Local manifestations of the Western convention of pictorial art had their beginnings in the 1920s, at first in Penang, and later in other urban centres such as Ipoh, Kuala Lumpur and Johor Bahru. Art infrastructure in the country developed gradually, culminating in a vibrant art scene towards the end of the 20th century.

The Malayan Arts Council, established in 1952, was the first art organization to promote art activities on a national scale by organizing art exhibitions and competitions. It was also the first to initiate the concept of a national art gallery to collect, keep and preserve works by Malaysian artists, thus ensuring the continuity of artistic traditions, preserving cultural heritage and encouraging artistic developments in the nation. While the early patrons of art were mainly Malay royalty, businessmen, professionals and expatriates, the opening of the National Art Gallery in 1958 by then Prime Minister Tunku Abdul Rahman marked the beginning of official government support, which boosted the morale of artists. The government patronizes national and state galleries, which are also sponsored by the public and corporate sectors.

During the post-Independence period, artists who were greatly affected by the spirit of nationalism and the aspiration of freedom of expression sought a national cultural identity in art. Artists and art teachers who had returned from training abroad become the vanguard of art in the country; some of them being prominent artists as well as art educators, contributing greatly to the advancement of art and art education in Malaysia. The Specialist Teachers' Training Institute, established in 1960, provided professional training for teachers, thus greatly improving the standard of art teaching in schools. The School of Art and Design of MARA Institute of Technology, established in 1967, provided professional courses for art and design at diploma level. The Fine Art Department of Universiti Sains Malaysia, established in 1972, offered a three-year degree course for studio art and theory. Its curriculum, which emphasized both theory and practical aspects of the subject, has contributed greatly in the development of the critical mind and intellectual consciousness of aspiring artists and art teachers. Private institutions also helped to produce a number of skilful artists and designers to cater for the demand for art arising from the rapid advancement of the local economy and industries. Computer-aided design and multimedia art soon became a core art and design curriculum.

As Malaysian society has become more affluent, art appreciation has become widespread. Economic progress and the emergence of a new group of collectors contributed to a booming art market in the 1990s. With the increasing number of art activities and exhibitions organized by both the government and private galleries, the artistic atmosphere in Malaysia has further been enhanced.

Cover of the pioneering art history book on modern Malaysian art by T.K. Sabapathy and Redza Piyadasa, published in 1983.

Art education

Historical and political factors influenced the development of art education in Malaysia. Initially treated as unimportant by the British colonialists, it was not systematically promoted. This changed during the 1950s when the seeds of modern art education were planted. During the 1960s, the establishment of local art colleges began to take place. An increased demand for skilled artists and designers occurred with the advent of industrialization processes. The new respectability commanded by visual artists has seen a demand for tertiary level art education.

Syed Ahmad Jamal (wearing tie) conducting an art class at the Specialist Teachers' Training Institute in 1963. The Institute was an important training centre for art teachers in the 1960s.

Left: Pioneering art educationist Tay Hooi Keat (1980).

Above: Tay Hooi Keat's *Plantscape* (1961) is a cerebral work that reveals his significant contribution in the area of modern Malaysian painting as well.

Early art education in Malaysia

Unlike British India, where the systematic introduction of Western art values and the establishment of Western art academies was viewed as an integral and necessary part of the imperial British policy of culturally indoctrinating the minds of the Indian intelligentsia, the British in the Malay Peninsula did not view Western-type art education as vital to their overall plans of governance. There was no formal promotion of Western-type art education in the local schools. There was therefore no formal art academy established in the country, during the 19th and early 20th centuries.

When some kind of art education was eventually introduced in schools, its focus was on craft-oriented rather than fine art approaches. Initially, the emphasis was on the training of crafts such as basketry, pottery, basic carpentry, making bric-a-brac from sea shells, coconut shells and bamboo and the making of paper flowers. As belatedly as 1916, the then assistant director of education in the Straits Settlements, R.O. Winstedt, urged that a Malayan child should learn what is useful for his culture and the school art curriculum was geared toward this objective.

The emphasis on a Victorian 'Art and Crafts' approach, with the emphasis on crafts, seems to have prevailed. In 1924, art was finally included as an examinable subject for the Overseas Cambridge

The Selangor Art Society, a multi-racial art group made up of art teachers, was set up in 1954. Peter Harris is seated front, third from the right.

School Certificate examinations and an initial shift towards fine art orientations took place. However, the pre-war emphasis was on technical skills in the copying of nature and everyday objects and not on individualized creativity, founded on new theories of modern psychology.

The beginnings of modern art education

Modern ideas in art education were introduced only during the 1950s, when the demands of the Cambridge University Overseas Examinations Board, following new changes in post-war Britain, demanded a new, creative approach in the teaching of art in local schools, in fulfilment of the new examination syllabus. The appointment of Peter Harris, an English artist and art educationist, as Superintendent of Art Education in the Ministry of Education in Kuala Lumpur in 1950 was prompted by these new changes. A newly returned Malaysian art graduate from England, Tay Hooi Keat, was also appointed in 1952 as Superintendent of Art Education for the northern region to assist Harris. Tay was based in Penang.

The initial introduction of modernist ideas in art education into Malaysian schools may be attributed to the efforts of these two dedicated educationists in inculcating among local art teachers, all over the

Malaysian Institute of Art at Taman Melawati, Ampang, established in 1966.

The School of Art and Design Annex at the Universiti Teknologi MARA (UiTM) campus in Shah Alam, established in 1967.

The Art Centre (Pusat Seni) of Universiti Sains Malaysia, Penang, was established in 1972.

country, new ideas emphasizing self expression and individual creativity. Harris also founded the Wednesday Art Group in 1951 (see 'Art groups') and the new interest in modern art education was reflected in the formation of the Selangor Art Society in 1954, also by Harris, composed of art teachers. Tay Hooi Keat initially founded the Thursday Art Group in 1957 and, later, the Penang Art Teachers' Circle in Penang in 1965.

The formation of the Specialist Teachers' Training Institute (presently Maktab Perguruan Ilmu Khas) in Kuala Lumpur in 1960 by the government, as a result of the suggestion and planning of Peter Harris, was significant as the institute became, during the better part of the 1960s, the only place for training qualified art teachers in the latest ideas in art education. The one year in-service course of study was taught by a significant generation of newly returned Malaysian artists sent to England, on government scholarships to study in English art colleges. These lecturers included Syed Ahmad Jamal, Anthony Lau, Yeoh Jin Leng, Lee Joo For, Grace Selvanayagam and Tay Hung Ghee. Subjects such as Art History and Art Appreciation, Modern Ideas in Art Education and Creative Design were introduced. Conditions for art education were improving.

Art education at the tertiary level

The Malaysian Institute of Art was privately established in 1966 by Chung Chen Sun, a graduate of the Nanyang Academy of Fine Arts in Singapore. It was the first proper art college established in Peninsular Malaysia, offering a three-year course of study in painting, sculpture and graphic art. Mandarin was the language of instruction, and the institute, for the most part, received students from the local Chinese high schools. The institute has expanded considerably since then. It was followed by the establishment of the Kuala Lumpur College of Art in 1968, privately founded by another alumni of the Nanyang Academy of Fine Arts, Cheah Yew Saik (see 'Artists of the Nanyang school').

The establishment of the MARA School of Art and Design at the MARA Institute of Technology (now Universiti Teknologi MARA (UiTM)) by the government in 1967 was part of a national scheme to provide higher education for the indigenous peoples in an attempt to rectify the economic inequalities among the populace. From the beginning, it was envisaged that the art college would produce art graduates to supply the work force needed for the new industrialization developments being set in motion. Besides painting and sculpture courses, subjects such as graphic design, textile design, industrial design, ceramics, fine metal and jewellery design and photography were introduced. A one year postgraduate Art Teacher's Diploma programme was later instituted. Today, undergraduate and postgraduate degree studies are offered.

The establishment of the Art Department at Universiti Sains Malaysia (Science University Malaysia) in Penang in 1972 was significant as, at long last, a local university had deemed it fit to start an art department within its own premises. Apart from painting and sculpture courses, the teaching of art history, photography, graphic design and textile design was introduced. Undergraduate and postgraduate degrees are offered today. The inclusion of an art department at the Universiti Pendidikan Sultan Idris (UPSI) (Sultan Idris Education University) since early 1997 was another advancement for visual artists, signifying art education's growing acceptance and respectability. Undergraduate and postgraduate courses are offered at UPSI. Universiti Malaysia Sarawak (UNIMAS) also offers Fine and Applied Arts courses.

The emergence of private art colleges

Expanding demand for skilled artists and trained designers in the computer field and mass communications areas has witnessed the proliferation of private art colleges since the early 1990s. Among the many such art institutions that have emerged may be included the Kuala Lumpur Institute of Art, the Saito Academy of Graphic Design, The One Academy of Communication Design, the Limkokwing Institute of Creative Technology (now Limkokwing University College of Creative Technology), the Center For Advanced Design and the New Era College of Art and Design in Kajang (see 'Graphic design'). In 1987, the Conservatory of Fine Arts was established in Penang. Most of these privately funded colleges presently offer twinning programmes with American, British and Australian universities as well. Today, young Malaysians can obtain proper artistic education within the country.

A five year old boy working on an abstract painting at the first anniversary of the Laman Seni Kuala Lumpur arts market, held at the National Art Gallery in August 2005.

A tertiary art student from the Faculty of Applied and Creative Arts of Universiti Malaysia Sarawak campus (UNIMAS) working on an electronic artwork, 1998.

Universiti Pendidikan Sultan Idris at Tanjung Malim, Perak, established an art department in early 1997.

The One Academy of Communication Design in Bandar Sunway, a private art college established in 1991.

Limkokwing University College of Creative Technology campus at Cyberjaya, established in 1992.

National and state art organizations

Art was first promoted in Malaysia through the Malayan Arts Council who recognized the need to protect and encourage Malaysian art, crafts and culture, and was further advanced with the establishment of the first National Art Gallery. Since then, art exhibitions have been held locally and overseas. The establishment of state and other museums and art galleries added a new dimension of public exposure to art.

Malaysia's first Prime Minister, Tunku Abdul Rahman, addressing the first meeting of the Board of Trustees of the National Art Gallery on 11 June 1963. The government gave a donation of $25,000 and promised a plot of land for a more permanent gallery to be built in the future.

The Malayan Arts Council

The British colonial government in Malaya was largely disinterested in the advancement of arts in the country. However, in 1952, a group of expatriate and local advocates that included Mubin Sheppard, a government servant who worked in the Malaya Civil Service, Peter Harris, the Art Superintendent in the Education Department, Zainal Abidin Abas, Nik Ahmad Kamil, P. G. Lim and Kington Loo recognized the need to preserve local arts and crafts and to stimulate and encourage Malayan artists.

This led to the formation of the Malayan Arts Council in 1952, a non-profit organization whose aims were to promote the development of art and culture (including drama, music and visual arts), to protect local art and crafts, as well as to uplift the standard of art and art appreciation in the country. The Government of the day, under General Sir Gerald Templer, was persuaded to provide an annual grant for the running of the Council.

This momentous step represented the promotion of art and culture at a national level for the first time, particularly as for many years the Council was the only sponsor of national-level art exhibitions, such as the first exhibition in 1954, the Malayan Open Art Exhibition. Apart from sponsoring art exhibitions locally and abroad, the Council also organized national art competitions.

The Council initiated the idea of establishing a national art gallery to house the artworks of local artists and an art school for the training of artists and craftsmen (see 'Art education'). Mubin Sheppard and Frank Sullivan, a serious collector of Malaysian art as well as an active art promoter, played a role in persuading the Prime Minister Tunku Abdul Rahman of the importance of a national art gallery, which led to its subsequent establishment in 1958. The Council ceased in 1964.

Islamic Arts Museum Malaysia

Opened on 13 December 1998, the Islamic Arts Museum Malaysia is the result of a collaboration between the Albukhary Foundation, a private non-profit institution which funds and runs the museum, and the government, which contributed the land upon which the museum is located and, through the Islamic Affairs Department (JAKIM or Jabatan Kemajuan Islam Malaysia), a foundation collection of artefacts that included old manuscripts and Qur'ans. The museum has a built-up area of more than 23,000 square metres and occupies four levels, containing 12 galleries—jewellery, arms and armour, textiles, metalwork, woodwork, coins and seals, ceramics and glassware, architecture, Qur'an and manuscripts, India Gallery, China Gallery and the Malay World Gallery—of Islamic art displays, student and workshop facilities, an auditorium and briefing hall and laboratories for preservation and restoration work. Works are added to the museum's collection continually while other artefacts on display are donated, sponsored or on loan from private collections.

The Islamic Arts Museum Malaysia is contemporary but, overall, has an Islamic design flavour which is manifested in many of its decorative features such as ceramic tile work and beautiful domes.

The Ibrahim Hussein Museum and Cultural Foundation's modern building, completed in late 1998, contains galleries and exhibition spaces, workshop and visitors facilities.

Ibrahim Hussein Museum and Cultural Foundation

Established in 1991, the Ibrahim Hussein Museum and Cultural Foundation is a non-profit private organization dedicated to the promotion, development and advancement of art and culture. The land upon which its two-level complex stands was donated by the Kedah State Government, with the full blessing of the Federal Government. The founder Ibrahim Hussein, after whom the Foundation is named, is a significant Malaysian artist.

State and other galleries

There are now a number of state galleries throughout the country. One of the oldest is the Penang State Museum and Art Gallery established in 1965 (see 'Patronage and art'). Penang also has the Penang State Art Gallery. Other state art galleries include Balai Seni Lukis Kedah established in 1983, Balai Seni Lukis Sabah established in 1984, Balai Seni Lukis Kelantan established in 1988, Galeri Shah Alam established in 1991, Galeri Seni Johor established in 1993 and Balai Seni Lukis Melaka established in 2006. In addition, art has been promoted through the inclusion of art galleries at institutions such as Universiti Sains Malaysia (since 1978) (see 'Art establishments' and 'Art patronage') and Muzium Seni Asia at Universiti Malaya (since 1980).

RIGHT: The Penang State Museum and Art Gallery is housed in a heritage building built in 1821.

BELOW: Galeri Shah Alam in Selangor.

BELOW RIGHT: Muzium Seni Asia at Universiti Malaya, Kuala Lumpur.

The National Art Gallery (Balai Seni Lukis Negara)

Report with the first logo of the National Art Gallery.

Inception and establishment of the National Art Gallery

Since Independence, art in Malaysia has developed into an identifiable form of manifestation of culture. The simple watercolours of the pre-war and early post-war years were soon followed by oils which subscribed to modern art trends. The initial development of art in this country from the 1930s was due to the pioneering efforts of individuals without institutional support and evolved from exposure to contemporary conceptions and idioms of art through literature, visual means, formal and informal education. Those involved in this development felt the urgent need for a national art gallery which would be a legitimizing force as well as a guardian of national art treasures. The concept of a national art gallery was approved by Tunku Abdul Rahman in 1957 and passed by the Federal Cabinet. The gallery came under the then Ministry of Culture and Welfare, which provided it with funds. Its setting up was supervised by a working committee which comprised many members of the Malayan Arts Council as well as representatives from some government agencies. In 1963, the committee was replaced by a Board of Trustees appointed by the Ministry of Culture, Youth and Sports. The Directors of the National Gallery from its inception are: Ismail Zain, Sulaiman Othman, Syed Ahmad Jamal, Wairah Marzuki, Rahime Harun and Dr Saharuddin Haji Ismail.

The National Art Gallery was first housed temporarily in Dewan Tunku Abdul Rahman (**1**) at No. 108 Jalan Ampang in Kuala Lumpur and was declared open on 27 August 1958. In 1984, it shifted to a six-storey building provided by the government at No. 1 Jalan Sultan Hishamuddin, Kuala Lumpur, formerly the Hotel Majestic (**2**), another temporary, but larger site, capable of housing the expanded Permanent Collection of just over 1000 works. The gallery took up final residence at its present site at No.1 Jalan Temerloh (**3**) off Jalan Tun Razak, Kuala Lumpur, where it was opened to the general public from 13 November 1998, but was only officially opened on 25 September 2000. It has five spacious galleries used for the display of its Permanent Collection as well as for holding exhibitions.

Today, the National Art Gallery receives an annual grant from the Ministry of Culture, Arts and Heritage as well as support from PETRONAS, Esso, Shell, Philip Morris Group of Companies and other corporate organizations (see 'Patronage and art').

Permanent Collection

The Permanent Collection of the National Art Gallery started in August 1958 with four works: *Self Portrait* (**1**), a pastel by Mohd Hoessein Enas; an oil painting (**2**) by Howard Barron; *Solomon Performing* (**3**), a pastel by Patrick Ng Kah Onn; and *Penang Waterfront* (**4**), a batik artwork by Chuah Thean Teng. Since that time, the National Art Gallery has acquired works through purchases as well as gifts from individuals, artists, public organizations, the commercial sector and foreign governments. Today, the number of works in the Collection, including works of historical value, indigenous art and sculpture, textile art, Malaysian contemporary art and multi-media and electronic art, exceeds 2500. These works represent the diversity and depth of the Malaysian modern art movement (see 'Modern art').

Role and activities of the National Art Gallery

The objectives of the National Art Gallery, besides building and maintaining a Permanent Collection, also include presenting the works of local and foreign artists, sponsoring exhibitions and competitions, and projecting the country's artistic image overseas through the organization of travelling exhibitions and participation in international events.

From its inception, the National Art Gallery has promoted Malaysian art both locally and internationally through numerous events and exhibitions. In the 1960s and 1970s, exhibitions of local art were organized in Europe, Australia and New Zealand. From that time, Malaysian artists have continued to participate in various international art exhibitions, often with either sponsorship or assistance from the Gallery. On the local scene, the Gallery, in addition to becoming a museum of contemporary art open to the general public and art lovers alike, has played a multifaceted role in the development of a national identity, represented in part by the showcasing of Malaysian artists as well as multi-ethnic locally and culturally themed works. A major Malaysian art competition that was organized by the Gallery for many years from 1968 was the 'Salon Malaysia', which had a panel of foreign judges from Australia and Singapore. The Young Contemporaries Art Competition, with the aim of discovering young art talent, was first held in 1981. In addition, many catalogues of exhibitions, historical publications, quarterly bulletins containing current events and art news and books have been published by the Gallery.

Flanked by the National Theatre Complex and the National Library, the National Art Gallery continues to provide the ideal environment for the nurturing and development of Malaysian art. All the galleries are fully accessible to the disabled. It opens daily from 10 am to 6 pm, except for certain public holidays.

ABOVE: Book published by the National Art Gallery in 2002 featuring selected works from the Permanent Collection.

RIGHT: Advertisement for an exhibition on Malaysian Contemporary Art held in Paris, 1966.

Patronage and art

The art market flourished after the setting up of the National Art Gallery, the establishment of private galleries following suit. Although earlier watercolour artworks were bought by foreigners, many locals became collectors as well. Later, during the 1990s, more corporations and private collectors from the middle class began to invest in the local art market. While the art market was depressed during the economic crisis of 1997, a demand for early local works continued. The art market has become lively again in recent years.

Visitor studying photographs by Soraya Yusof Talismail at an exhibition by photographers from Malaysia, Britain and Indonesia called *Common Ground* held at the National Art Gallery in 2004.

Exhibition of modern Malaysian art at Burlington House, London, 1965. The Malaysian artworks from this exhibition were also shown elsewhere in Europe in 1966.

ABOVE: Cover of the book *Seni dan Budaya* (*Art and Culture*), published by the Perak Art Foundation for the Ipoh Arts Festival in 1999.
BELOW: Members of the public looking at an exhibit at the Ipoh Arts Festival 1999.

The collection of art

The history of art collecting in Malaysia is recent, probably starting in the 1930s, concurrently with the development of local art (see 'The beginning of landscape painting'). Art collecting in Penang, the earliest centre of art in Malaysia, was the consequence of historical, social and economic factors. The early collectors were foreigners, mainly British, who were residing in Penang and who bought as souvenirs small watercolour paintings of local themes produced by the first generation of Malaysian artists. Nationwide, with an increasing interest in art collecting, came a change in the trends of collection. Art collectors became predominantly professionals and business people who were not influenced by the artist's status and reputation, but relied more on their own intuition and experience. They focused mainly on the works of contemporary artists who shared with them a common rapport and sensibilities. Similarly, young collectors were clear in their minds what they wanted to buy. While they had knowledgeable friends, among them dealers, they independently chose what to collect and their collections reflected their own tastes and personalities. Some collectors accumulated personal collections exceeding 1000 individual works, ranging from the early pioneer artists to living established local artists. A later trend has been the demand for the works of early Malaysian masters.

The Permanent Collection commenced with the establishment of the National Art Gallery in 1958 (see 'National and state art organizations'). With the government as patron, and the gallery's founding members as initiators, the focus was on the collection of contemporary art. The Permanent Collection acquired its first painting, *Penang Waterfront*, a batik painting by Chuah Thean Teng (see 'National and state art organizations'), through the donation of Donald MacGillivray, the last British High Commissioner in pre-Independence Malaya, in 1957 who offered it at the opening of the first Young Artists exhibition. Currently more than 2500 artworks form the

The book *200 Malaysian artists* published by The Art Gallery, Penang in 2002 showcases local artists and their works.

Collection. Established in 1965, the Penang State Museum and Art Gallery built its permanent collection from artworks of mostly Penang artists. In 1995, the Art Acquisition Fund was launched, and with corporate companies donating money as well as paintings, the Penang State Art Gallery was able to increase the number of artworks to 121, which then included the paintings of prominent Malaysian and Asian artists. Other important state art galleries include the Galeri Shah Alam, Balai Seni Lukis Kedah, Balai Seni Lukis Sabah, Balai Seni Lukis Melaka, Balai Seni Lukis Kelantan and Galeri Seni Johor (see 'National and state art organizations').

In 1978, the museum and gallery of Universiti Sains Malaysia started its collection which included the artworks of Malaysian masters as well as younger artists. Its core collection was purchased from Frank Sullivan a serious collector of local art and art promoter, who contributed to the cultivation of a general interest in collecting original paintings by Malaysian artists. Muzium Seni Asia at Universiti Malaya started a collection in 1980.

Private art galleries

The first art gallery in the country was Mun Sen Art Gallery in Penang, started in 1941 by Yong Mun Sen, a pioneer of Malaysian watercolour paintings (see 'The beginning of landscape painting'). The Galaxy Gallery was the first private art gallery in Kuala Lumpur, open from 1965 to 1973 and managed by Mr Yin Hong. The Samat Gallery, started by Frank Sullivan and several artists in 1966, was run along the lavish lines of an urban gallery. Works by established Malaysian artists were shown, its exhibition openings were always well attended and, at that time, were regarded as important events in Kuala Lumpur's cultural calendar. Galeri 11, situated in Jalan Pinang, Kuala Lumpur, was less lavish. It focused more on the avant-garde works of Malaysian and foreign artists. A short-lived gallery which opened for two years from 1967 was the Angkatan Pelukis Semenanjung (APS) Gallery at Jalan Muda, Kuala Lumpur, representative of the art group of the same name (see 'Art groups'). Sum Art

Gallery was open from 1972 to 1982 at Jalan Ampang and was founded by Anthony Sum, an artist who taught Chinese ink painting and batik on weekends at the gallery. Saujana Fine Arts in Subang Jaya, run by artist Redza Piyadasa, was open from 1983 to 1987.

In Penang, Yahong Gallery founded by Chuah Thean Teng, a pioneer batik artist (see 'From Modernism to Post-modernism'), relocated to Tanjung Bungah in 1975. The earliest Yahong Gallery was established in the late 1950s at Leith Street. In 1976, Galeri Art Point (formerly CFA Gallery) relocated at Sunny Point Complex, Jalan Sultan Azlan Shah. The Art Gallery is situated at Burmah Road. Other privately run galleries can also be found in Ipoh, Melaka, Kota Bharu, Johor Bharu, Kuching and Kota Kinabalu.

In the 1990s, the flourishing art market led to an increasing number of private galleries. In Kuala Lumpur, the Galeri Citra has been in the business of selling contemporary Malaysian art for over 10 years. Another, the Art House gallery promoted contemporary Chinese art. Other galleries established in Kuala Lumpur during this time include the Art Salon, Valentine Willie Fine Art in Bangsar, NN Gallery and Anugerah in Ampang, Art Case Galleries and Art Folio at City Square Complex. These private galleries organized regular exhibitions to feature the works of established Malaysian artists, as well as newcomers. Central Market in Kuala Lumpur contains shops that display artworks and crafts to cater to the tourist market.

The collective efforts of all of these private galleries have mainly focused on the promotion of the market sale of artworks and have contributed to a lively art scene and the gearing towards a common goal: 'To make art a part of our daily life.'

Art patronage

From the 1940s to 1970s, the first local art patrons were prominent businessmen and professionals (such as lawyers and doctors), who patronized both local and visiting artists. They were the preservers of artistic traditions.

Banks have also been important patrons and art supporters. Bank Negara of Malaysia (Central Bank of Malaysia) started its collection in the 1960s. Other bank art patrons include Malayan Banking Berhad (Maybank), Public Bank, Bank Bumiputra (now CIMB), Oriental Bank and Hong Leong Bank. During the 1980s in particular, art patronage

TOP: An art studio at Central Market where portrait paintings can be commissioned from photographs. Caricatures are also done by some studios there.

ABOVE: Art event at Valentine Willie Fine Art, a private art gallery. The gallery also promotes South East Asian artists.

burgeoned. Banks and other corporate entities purchased art from galleries, commissioned artists to create paintings for specific purposes, built collections of Malaysian art to be displayed in their buildings, and some also provided art exhibition spaces and facilities within their buildings. Among the corporations may be included Tenaga Nasional Berhad, Petroliam Nasional Berhad (PETRONAS), Sime Darby Berhad, Esso Malaysia Berhad, Shell Malaysia and the Philip Morris Group of Companies. Several own a permanent collection.

The booming economy of the 1990s boosted the art market. Many private companies, hotels and individuals started to acquire original paintings for hanging on the walls of their offices. Interior decorators and architects played a significant role in selecting suitable paintings and giving aesthetic advice on art decoration. Among other examples of privately funded patronage may be included the artist's residency programme at Rimbun Dahan in Kuang, Selangor and the Mahani Daim Foundation.

Art patronage has thrived in Malaysia largely due to the support of the government, corporations and the emergence of the new middle class in the 1980s. Gallery directors invited artists to exhibit and also catalogued major works, critics explained and defended artworks, art historians curated major exhibitions and published art books and owners of private galleries provided sophisticated facilities for the presentation of artists' works. Their dynamic and positive roles fuelled the machinery of the art market.

The Nanyang Gallery of Art, established in 1992, sponsored some important art publications. It is no longer operating.

ABOVE: Galeri PETRONAS has been located at Kuala Lumpur City Centre (KLCC) since 1998. The gallery has one of the largest corporate art collections in the country.

RIGHT: Petronas Art Collection: Series 1, part of a series of books, was published in 2004.

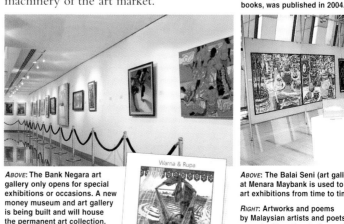

ABOVE: The Bank Negara art gallery only opens for special exhibitions or occasions. A new money museum and art gallery is being built and will house the permanent art collection.

RIGHT: Warna & Rupa, published by Bank Negara in 2002, features 51 artworks by Malaysian artists which form part of the bank's permanent collection.

ABOVE: The Balai Seni (art gallery) at Menara Maybank is used to hold art exhibitions from time to time.

RIGHT: Artworks and poems by Malaysian artists and poets are paired together in Suara Rasa: Voice From Within, published in 1993. The paintings are from the collection of Malayan Banking Berhad (Maybank) and its related companies.

Glossary

A

Abstract art: Art characterized by geometric or other non-representational qualities.

Abstract Expressionism: 1940s New York school of painting combining the spontaneity of expressionism with abstract forms in unpremeditated compositions.

Anyam dua: Two-over-two-under plaiting technique.

Arabesque decoration: Ornate style of decoration using flowers, foliage and, less often, animal and geometric figures to produce a pattern of interlaced lines.

Asam gelugur: A dried acidic fruit.

Atap: Nipah palm-leaf roof thatch.

Avant-garde: Techniques and ideas which are markedly experimental or in advance of those generally accepted.

Awan larat: Arabesque Malay decorative pattern.

B

Backstrap loom: A portable loom still used in Sarawak and Sabah. The tension is created by placing the backstrap behind the weaver's back with the other end attached to a solid support.

Badan kain: Main body area of a traditional sarong.

Bajau: Second largest indigenous ethnic group in Sabah.

Baju Melayu: Traditional attire of Malay men; a shirt (*baju*) worn over trousers (*seluar*) with a short sarong (*samping*).

Bangau: Decorative carved guard on traditional east coast boats.

Bas-relief: Sculptural relief which protrudes only slightly from the background surface.

Batik: Process of hand-drawing or stamping designs on cloth with wax before dyeing.

Beautiful Indies: Indonesian 19th– 20th-century romantic style of painting.

Belanga: Pottery cooking pot.

Belian: Borneo ironwood.

Bidayuh: Sarawak indigenous group formerly known as Land Dayak.

Bobohizan: Kadazandusun ritual specialists or priestesses.

British Malaya: States colonized by the British essentially comprising Peninsular Malaysia and Singapore.

Bunga cengkih: Clove flowers.

Bunga mas: Small tree of silver or gold sent as tribute to Thai rulers by the northern Malay states.

Bunga padi: Rice flowers.

Buyung: Wide-mouthed pottery water jar.

C

Caping: Heart-shaped modesty disc worn by young girls and boys to cover the genitalia.

Cengal: Rainforest hardwood.

Cindai: Local name for imported Indian *patola* textile. See *limar*.

Ciré perdu: 'Lost wax' method of metal casting.

Conceptual Art: Art where the idea behind a work and the means of production are more important than the finished work.

Constructivism: Post-World War I Russian abstract art movement which explored the use of movement and machine-age materials in visual art.

Cubism: Movement in painting and sculpture developed by Picasso, Braque and others (1907–14). Natural forms are depicted as multifaceted surfaces of geometric planes.

Cucuk sanggul: Ornamental gold or silver hairpins.

Cult of the Picturesque: Mid-18th century idea of travelling in search of landscape views.

D

Daun sukun: Breadfruit leaf, used as a motif in Malay designs.

Daun tarum: Indigo plant leaves.

Dongson: Influential Vietnamese cultural style (from c. 500 BCE) characterized by bronze drums.

E

Emotive: Tending or designed to arouse emotion.

Expressionist: Early 20th-century German artistic movement which sought to express emotions rather than represent external reality.

F

Fauvism: Style of French painters including Fauve, Matisse, Derain and Vlaminck prominent from 1905, and characterized by bright colours and simplified forms.

Figurative: Depicting figures or objects in a recognizable way.

Filigree: Silverworking decoration using thin wire.

Formalism: Adherence and emphasis on outward form.

Frame loom: Loom introduced in the 16th century on which many Malay textiles are woven.

Fretwork: Timberwork decorated by cutting with a fretsaw.

G

Gawai: Iban ritual ceremonies or festivals.

Gouache: Painting technique using opaque watercolours in which the pigments are bound with glue and lighter tones contain white.

Granulation: Decoration of jewellery with small granules of gold.

H

Hallmark: Official mark on jewellery made of precious metal guaranteeing standard and maker.

Hikayat: Traditional Malay literary genre; legendary story.

Hilt: Handle or shaft of a sword or dagger.

I

Iban: Largest indigenous group in Sarawak.

Ikat: method of creating patterns by tie-dyeing yarn before weaving.

Impressionism: 1870s French movement originating chiefly with Monet, Renoir, Pissaro and Sisley. Technique of conveying experience by capturing fleeting impressions of reality or mood. The artists used bright colours and sketchy brushwork.

Installation: Exhibit often containing movable parts which are important to its meaning. Came into vogue in the 1970s.

J

Jawa demam: Form of kris hilt meaning 'fevered Javanese'; also known as *keris semenanjung.*

Jawi: Malay writing based on Arabic script.

Jerunai: Burial pole of the Melanau of Sarawak. Also called *kelidang.*

K

Kacip: Areca nut cutter which forms part of a *sirih* set.

Kadazandusun: The largest indigenous ethnic group in Sabah, comprising both the Kadazan and Dusun peoples.

Kain: Cloth or textile.

Kain dastar: Handwoven headcloth worn by men in Sabah.

Kaki kain: Bottom edge of a traditional sarong.

Kasut manik: Beaded slippers worn by Nonya women.

Kayan/Kenyah: Sarawak indigenous ethnic groups settled in the northeastern highlands.

Kebat: Iban term for ikat.

Kebaya: Malay woman's blouse, traditionally worn with a sarong.

Kelabit: Sarawak indigenous group centred in the Bario Highlands.

Kelarai: Panels made of interwoven bamboo or *bertam* strips.

Kendi: Spouted water vessel.

Kepala kain: Decorative middle panel of a traditional sarong.

Keris: Dagger with a curved or straight iron blade with a damascened surface.

Keris pekaka: Literally 'kingfisher', a type of kris hilt from the east coast of Peninsular Malaysia.

Keris tajong: Type of east coast kris hilt with long extended beak or nose, used previously by warriors and royalty.

Kerongsang: Set of three brooches, usually silver or gold, joined by an ornamental chain.

Khat: Calligraphy.

Kijang: Barking deer; also a Kelantanese coin bearing an image of this animal.

Kilirieng: Pole used for storing burial jars by the Kayan.

Kolam: Decorative floor patterns created using rice flour (*rangoli* in Hindustani).

Kompang: Shallow frame drum.

Kong teik: Chinese funerary ceremony at which paper effigies are burnt.

Kongsi: Chinese clan house.

Kris: see *Keris*.

Kumang: One of the two Iban goddesses of weaving.

Kupang: Early Malay Islamic coin equal to 10 grains of gold.

L

Labu: Gourd-shaped container.

Labu Sayong: Pottery made in Sayong, Perak according to a traditional method.

Lapohan: Sabah pottery stove.

Limar: Single ikat ceremonial and prestige Malay textile, based on the double ikat silk *patola* textile from Gujarat in India.

Linangkit: Needle-worked panel used to join and decorate the seams of many Sabah costumes.

Lulong: One of the two Iban goddesses of weaving.

Lun Bawang: Sarawak indigenous ethnic group centred in the northeastern highlands.

M

Mak Yong: Ancient Malay dance theatre of Kelantan and Patani.

Maloh: Borneo ethnic group from West Kalimantan, Indonesia, who were itinerant metalsmiths.

Mandapun: Ornamental collar worn by Lotud, Bajau and Iranun women in Sabah.

Melanau: Sarawak coastal indigenous ethnic group.

Mengkuang: Plant of the genus *Pandanus* (screwpine); leaves used to make mats, baskets and bags.

Mimbar: Pulpit in a mosque.

Modern art: Art produced in the second half of the 19th century typified by a new individualized approach to art.

Modernism: A 20th-century divergence in the arts from previous traditions; the support of modern concepts and tendencies.

Mogah: Black cotton textile patterned with striped bands of red and orange woven by the Iranun and Bajau in Sabah.

Murut: Sabah ethnic group centred in the southwest hilly regions.

N

Nashki: One of the earliest cursive Arab scripts.

Naturalism: 19th-century approach to art in which objects are represented as they are seen rather than in a stylized manner.

Nielloware: A form of enamelled silver.

Nobat: Royal orchestra.

O

Orang Asli: Indigenous peoples of Peninsular Malaysia.

Orang Ulu: Minority indigenous groups mainly centred in the northern interior of Sarawak.

P

Painterly lines: Sensitive 'living' lines as opposed to harsh lines.

Pamur: Damasked dark and light effect characteristic of Malay kris blades.

Pandan: Plant of the genus *Pandanus* (screwpine); leaves are used to make mats, baskets and bags.

Parang ilang: Ornate knife previously used in Borneo as a fighting weapon for headhunting.

Penan: Hunter-gatherer indigenous group of Sarawak.

Pending: Belt buckle often made of silver or gold.

Perahu: Boat.

Peranakan: Local-born person or a person of mixed local and foreign parentage. *See* Straits Chinese.

Periuk: Cooking pot.

Periuk tanah: Traditional earthen-ware Sarawak cooking pot.

Petala indera: Bird-shaped figure-head of a royal boat or carriage.

Pewter: Alloy of tin and other metals, usually antimony and copper.

Post-Impressionism: French art movement usually associated with Cézanne, van Gogh, Gauguin and Toulouse-Lautrec who showed a greater concern for expression, structure and form than the Impressionist artists.

Post-modernism: Late 20th-century style and school of thought where art, architecture and literature reacted against the earlier principles of modernism by reintroducing traditional or classical elements of style. Social issues and discourse became more important than form.

Pua kumbu: Iban ritual blanket.

Pucuk rebung: bamboo shoots (a common Malay design motif).

Pusaka: Heirlooms.

R

Rattan: Plant used for mat-making and basketry.

Rawai: Iban women's rattan corset.

Realism: Painting and sculpture style that seeks to represent the familiar or typical in real life, rather than the idealized or romantic interpretation of it.

Repoussé: Form of decorating gold or silver objects by embossing a relief pattern on a metal sheet.

S

Sapeh: A lute of the Orang Ulu communities of Sarawak.

Sarimpak: Boat-shaped ornamental headdress worn by Bajau and Iranun women in Sabah.

School of Paris: Early 20th-century Paris artists who created in the styles of Cubism, Fauvism and Post-Impressionism.

Selendang: Shawl.

Semangat: Soul, spirit, or universal vital energy.

Sheath: Case or covering for the blade of a knife, dagger or sword.

Sirih set: container for betel leaf and areca nut quid.

Songket: Gold thread cloth.

Staining: Colouring gold jewellery.

Straits Chinese: Localized Chinese in Penang, Melaka and Singapore. Also known as Baba-Nonya and Peranakan.

Sugu tinggi: Iban women's silver ceremonial headdress.

Sungkit: Iban woven textile.

T

Tantagas: Lotud ritual specialists.

Tekat: Malay raised embroidery technique using gold thread.

Telepuk: Malay cloth printed motifs created with gold dust.

Teluk berantai: Chain of bays motif.

Tengkolok: Customary headwear worn by Malay men.

Tepi: Decorated border edges of a traditional sarong.

Touchmark: Maker's mark stamped on pewter objects.

Tradition or traditional: handing down from generation to generation of customs, beliefs etc., especially by word of mouth.

Tudung saji: Food cover.

U

Ukiran tebok: Carving with pierced and cut-out work.

Ukiran timbul: Bas-relief carving.

W

Wau: Kite.

Wayang Kulit: Shadow play; puppet theatre using hide figures.

Earthscape 2 (1992) by Yeoh Jin Leng, an artwork of raku fired pottery with copper glaze.

Bibliography

Abdul Halim Nasir and Wan Hashim Wan Teh (1996), *The Traditional Malay House*, Petaling Jaya: Penerbit Fajar Bakti.

Alman, E. and Alman, J. (1963), *Handicrafts in Sabah*, Kuching: Borneo Literature Bureau.

Appell, George N. and Appell, Laura W. R. (1993), 'To Converse with the Gods: Rungus Spirit Mediums', in Winzeler, Robert L. (ed.), *The Seen and the Unseen: Shamanism, Mediumship and Possession in Borneo*, Borneo Research Council.

Arney, Sarah (1987), *Malaysian Batik: Creating New Traditions*, Kuala Lumpur: Malaysian Handicraft Development Corporation.

Azah Aziz (2006), *Rupa & Gaya Busana Melayu*, Bangi: Penerbit Universiti Kebangsaan Malaysia.

Benggon-Charuruks, Irene and Padasian, Janette (eds.) (1992), *Cultures, Customs and Traditions of Sabah, Malaysia, an Introduction*, Kota Kinabalu: Sabah Tourism Promotion Corporation.

Chang, Tommy (1996), *Sabah Malaysian Borneo: Peoples and Places*, Kota Kinabalu: Tommy Chang Image Productions.

Chen May Yee (2003), *Born and Bred in Pewter Dust: The Royal Selangor Story*, Kuala Lumpur: Archipelago Press.

Chin, Lucas (1980), *Cultural Heritage of Sarawak*, Kuching: Sarawak Museum.

—— **and Mashman, Valerie** (eds.) (1991), *Sarawak Cultural Legacy: A Living Tradition*, Kuching: Society Atelier Sarawak.

Endon Mahmood (2004), *The Nyonya Kebaya: A Century of Straits Chinese Costume*, 2nd edn, Singapore: Periplus Editions.

Farish A. Noor and Khoo, Eddin (2003), *Spirit of Wood: The Art of Malay Woodcarving*, Singapore: Periplus Editions.

Gavin, Traude (1996), *The Women's Warpath: Iban Ritual Fabrics from Borneo*, Los Angeles: UCLA Fowler Museum of Cultural History.

—— (2004), *Iban Ritual Textiles*, Singapore: Singapore University Press.

Ghulam-Sarwar Yousof (1986), *Ceremonial and Decorative Crafts of Penang*, Penang.

Harris, Mark and Zainuddin Zainal (1990), *History & Culture of Malaysia*, Kuala Lumpur: The Pepin Press.

Harrisson, Barbara (1967), 'A Classification of Stone Age Burials from Niah Great Cave', *Sarawak Museum Journal* XV (30-31): 126–199.

Hill, A. H. and others (1998), *The Keris and other Malay Weapons*, Kuala Lumpur: MBRAS.

Hose, Charles and McDougall, William (1966), *Pagan Tribes of Borneo*, New York: Barnes and Noble.

Khoo Joo Ee (1996), *The Straits Chinese: A Cultural History*, Amsterdam and Kuala Lumpur: The Pepin Press.

Killmann, Wulf, Sickinger, Tom and Hong Lay Thong (1994), *Restoring & Reconstructing the Malay House*, Kuala Lumpur: Forest Research Institute Malaysia.

King, Victor T. (1993), *The Peoples of Borneo*, Oxford: Blackwell.

Kraftangan Malaysia (1999), *A Malaysian Touch: Textiles for the New Millenium*, Kuala Lumpur: Perbadanan Kemajuan Kraftangan Malaysia.

Lasimbang, Rita and Moo-Tan, Stella (1997), *An Introduction to the Traditional Costumes of Sabah*, Kota Kinabalu: National History Publications (Borneo) and Department of Sabah Museum.

Leigh, Barbara (2000), *The Changing Face of Malaysian Crafts: Identity, Industry, and Ingenuity*, Kuala Lumpur: Oxford University Press.

Low, Hugh (1848), *Sarawak, Its Inhabitants and Productions*, London: Richard Bentley.

Melaka State Government (2004), *The Guide to Melaka*, Melaka: Melaka State Government and Leisure Guide Publishing.

Maxwell, Robyn (1990), *Textiles of Southeast Asia: Tradition, Trade and Transformation*, Melbourne: Oxford University Press.

Muliyadi Mahamood (2004), *The History of Malay Editorial Cartoons (1930s–1993)*, Kuala Lumpur: Utusan Publications.

Munan, Heidi (1989), *Sarawak Crafts: Methods, Materials and Motifs*, Kuala Lumpur: Oxford University Press.

—— (2005), *Beads of Borneo*, Singapore: Archipelago Press.

Ong, Edric (1992), *Pua, Iban Weavings of Sarawak*, 3rd edn, Kuching: Society Atelier Sarawak.

Othman Mohd. Yatim (1995), *Islamic Arts*, Kuala Lumpur: Dewan Bahasa dan Pustaka.

Payne, Junaidi, Cubitt, Gerald and Lau, Dennis (1994), *This is Borneo*, London: New Holland.

Piyadasa, Redza (2001), *Rupa Malaysia: Meninjau Seni Lukis Moden Malaysia*, Kuala Lumpur: National Art Gallery.

—— (2002), *Masterpieces from the National Art Gallery of Malaysia*, Kuala Lumpur: National Art Gallery.

Raja Fuziah Tun Uda and Ong, Edric (2003), *Herencia Textil de Malasia exhibition catalogue*, Kuala Lumpur: National Art Gallery.

Roojen, Pepin van (1993), *Batik Design*, Singapore: The Pepin Press.

Roth, Henry Ling (1993), *Oriental Silverwork, Malay and Chinese*, Kuala Lumpur: Oxford University Press.

Sabapathy, T. K. (ed.) (1994) *Vision and Idea: ReLooking Modern Malaysian Art*, Kuala Lumpur: National Art Gallery Malaysia.

—— **and Redza Piyadasa** (1983), *Modern Artists of Malaysia*, Kuala Lumpur: Dewan Bahasa dan Pustaka.

Shahrum bin Yub and Mohd. Kassim bin Haji Ali (1998), *Gold Jewelry and Ornaments of Malaysia*, Kuala Lumpur: Muzium Negara.

Shaw, William (1970), *Tin and Pewter Ware*, Kuala Lumpur: National Museum.

Sheppard, Mubin (1972), *Taman Indera: Malay Decorative Arts and Pastimes*, Kuala Lumpur: Oxford University Press.

Siti Zainon Ismail (1997), *Malay Woven Textiles; The Beauty of a Classical Art Form*, Kuala Lumpur: Dewan Bahasa dan Pustaka.

Sulaiman Othman and others (1997), *The Crafts of Malaysia*, Singapore: Archipelago Press.

Syed Ahmad Jamal (1994), *Form & Soul*, Kuala Lumpur: Dewan Bahasa dan Pustaka.

Tettoni, Luca Invernizzi and Ong, Edric (1996), *Sarawak Style*, Singapore: Times Editions.

Turner, Jane (ed.) (1996), *The Dictionary of Art*, New York: Oxford University Press.

Werner, Roland (1997), *Mah-Meri of Malaysia Art and Culture*, Kuala Lumpur: University of Malaya Press.

Williams-Hunt, P. D. R. (1952), *Malayan Aborigines*, Kuala Lumpur: Government Press.

Woolley, G. E. (1929), 'Some Notes on Murut Basket Work and Patterns', *Journal of the Malaysian Branch of the Royal Asiatic Society*, VI(II): 291–314.

Zakaria Ali (1994), *Islamic Art in Southeast Asia: 830 A.D.–1570 A.D.*, Kuala Lumpur: Dewan Bahasa dan Pustaka.

Index

Picture Credits

A. Kasim Abas, p. 5, fish trap, baskets; p. 8, Iban baskets; p. 26, Malay village; p. 35, *bangau*; Kayan boat; pp. 38–39, tattooing implements, *congkak*. **Abdul Halim Mohd Noor**, p. 12, prayer mat; p. 61, *tekat* steps 2 and 3 (collection of Siti Zainon Ismail), prayer mat; p. 89, goldsmith. **Abdul Halim Mohd Noor/ Terengganu Museum Collection**, p. 8, *sirih* set; p. 19, *periuk* pot; p. 83, incense burner; p. 92, kettle, *sirih* set; p. 143, hilt. **Abdul Multhalib Musa**, p. 115, *Faltered Wings*. **Adam Ariel**, p. 76, *sugu tinggi*. **Agence France Presse**, p. 7, craft day; p. 134, photography exhibit. **alt.TYPE/ REUTERS**, p. 71, models wearing black *baju kebaya*, red caftan and blue short *baju*, children in shop. **Amman, Heribert**, p. 55, Saribas *pua*. **Anuar Talib**, p. 29, Bukit Gantang house, *sulur kacang*, carved wall and window. **Arkib Negara Malaysia**, p. 30, Dato Dagang's house; p. 34, houseboat; p. 48, Prime Minister; p. 59, RIDA shop; p. 60, woman with *tekat* frame; p. 71, woman and child; p. 101, Chinese musicians; p. 122, noblewomen. **Art Asia Pacific Publishing**, p. 131, UNIMAS. **Bank Negara Malaysia**, p. 84, coins; p. 86, animal and Melaka coins, *tampang*, money trees; p. 88, coins; p. 125, logo; p. 135, exhibition and book cover. **Batik Guild**, p. 59, handicraft items. **Bernama**, p. 70, tailor; p. 103, making *thoranam*. **Bezzant, Dennis**, p. 68, *sungkit* cloth and details; p. 80, *parang ilang* blade and hilt. **Cadman, M.C.**, p. 26, Sabah carving. **Chai Kah Yune**, p. 10, Buddha; pp. 28–29, tools, bamboo shoot border; p. 31, hanging bees, *kepala cicak*; p. 42, *daun pandan*; p. 57, frame loom; p. 62, floral border; p. 69, backstrap loom. **Chang Yan Yi**, p. 72, bamboo and butterfly motifs. **Cheah, Michael**, p. 92, bridal couple. **Chin Kon Yit**, p. 11, Melaka house; pp. 14–15, *mimbar* Masjid Terengkera and details 7–11. **Chuah Chong Yong**, p. 116, *Pre War Building For Sale: Welcome to the era of the biggest, the highest and the longest…… Phase I*. **Colfer, Carol**, p. 77, Melanau bead bracelet. **Cowie, Kiri**, p. 73, sari details; p. 135, Central Market. **Cross, Martin**, p. 59, batik shirt; p. 103, temple with *thoranam*; pp. 14–15, *mimbar* details 1–5, 12 and 13. **Éditions Gallimard**, p. 77, Melanau button. **EDM archives**, p. 4, batik; pp. 8–9, doily, Neolithic pots; p. 12,

Tree of Life; p. 18, Nonya porcelain; p. 19, Nonya dish; p. 24, indigenous pots (top), old ceramics; pp. 28–29, Terengkera Masjid, Kelantan palace wall and inset; p. 47, Penan mat; p. 48, *tengkolok*; p. 51, Malay weaver; p. 52, ceremonial batik, Negeri Sembilan royalty; p. 56, *kain tenun*; p. 57, pattern 2; p. 58, stamped sarong; p. 59, details drawing and painting batik; p. 61, royal *tekat* gifts; p. 63, calendering, dish covers; p. 72, Straits Chinese family; p. 80, swivel gun; p. 82, bell; p. 84–85, *caping*, boy, jug; p. 93, silver belts; p. 124, *Undang-undang Pahang*, FMSR poster; p. 97, *pohon beringin*; p. 98, spinning *gasing*; p. 122, Melaka Square. **Falconer, John**, p. 40, Kadayan house (Charles Hose); pp. 42–43, rattan factory; *pandan* mat, dyeing leaves; pp. 46–47, *pandan* mat. **Fatimah Chik**, p. 120, *Keyakinan*. **Federal Information Department Malaysia**, p. 48, *songket* weaver, Prime Minister; p. 56, weaving *kain tenun*; p. 78, tea set; p. 83, making brassware, p. 85, engraving pattern, p. 96, puppet theatre; p. 101, *nobat*; p. 128, school art class. **Fong, P. K.**, p. 5, Iban carving; p. 6, Iban shield; p. 36, Hudok mask; pp. 38–39, baby carrier, *kilirieng*; p. 69, *pua* weaver; p. 82, gong; p. 91, ring and drop earrings; p. 138, stone carving. **Freeform Design Sdn Bhd**, p. 125, cards. **Galeri Petronas**, p. 7, *Gotong Royong*; p. 106, *Coconut Plantation-Dawn*; p. 123, *Kerana Mu Malaysia*; p. 135, Galeri Petronas book cover. **Gallery of Colour**, p. 6, weaving; p. 59, boiling batik, women painting batik; p. 94, temple statues; p. 132–133, Shah Alam Art Gallery, Islamic Arts Museum Malaysia, NAG (current); p. 135, Galeri Petronas. **Gavin, Traude**, pp. 54–55, Iban shrine, *Gawai piring*, weaver tying threads, effigy pole, girls in *kain kebat*; p. 68, preparing dye and mordanting. **Ghulam-Sarwar Yousof**, p. 96, CD cover, Dewan Bahasa and Purwa puppets; p. 98, *Mak Yong*. **Goh, Patrick/ Muzium Seni Asia Collection**, p. 29, Kelantan tile, ship panel; p. 52, *kain limar* with calligraphy; p. 56, *songket limar*; p. 63, *kain pelangi*. **HBL Network Photo Agency (M) Sdn Bhd**, p. 23, shipwreck Chinese pottery; p. 38, Orang Asli carving, tattooing; p. 65, poster; p. 89, granulation; p. 102, Tua Pek Kong temple, decorating lantern. **Héron-Huge, Domitille**, pp. 102–103, temple *gopuram*, Indian sculpture and artisan.

Höfer, Hans, p. 78, Nonya bride. **Hose, Charles (courtesy of the British Museum, UK)**, p. 77, Kayan chief's wife. **Ibrahim Hussein**, p. 104, *My Father and the Astronaut*. **Islamic Arts Museum Malaysia**, p. 15, chest, *sirih* set; p. 39, Qur'an box. **Ismail Hashim**, p. 123, *The Bathroom*. **Jabatan Muzium dan Antikuiti Malaysia**, pp. 10–11, cave painting, tombstone; *pending*; p. 28, Kelantan Qur'anic panel; p. 32, migrants; p. 35, fishing boat (b/w); p. 38, *Petala Indra*; p. 65, beaded shoes, shoe pattern; pp. 76–77, Kelabit earrings, Orang Ulu necklace; p. 81, wavy *pamur*; p. 86, touchmarks; pp. 88–89, gold discs, *bunga mas*, earring, *caping*; p. 98, making *gasing*; p. 100, Kelantan musical ensemble. **Jabatan Penerangan Malaysia**, p. 70, *tengkolok*; p. 88, Agong, *Keris Panjang Diraja*, *Pending Diraja*. **Jegadeva Anurendra**, p. 119, *Running Indians*. **Katong Antique House**, p. 65, wedding purses. **Kedit, Peter** p. 80, Sarawak blacksmith. **Khoo Joo Ee**, p. 64, Nonya women. **Kraftangan Malaysia**, p. 18, pottery motifs and forms; pp. 20–21, wooden paddles, making Sayong pot; *terenang* pot; p. 25, assorted touristware; p. 40, Kenyah hat; pp. 44–45, baby carrier, Orang Ulu hat; p. 49, ikat souvenirs; pp. 58–59, batik motifs, screen-printing, hot wax, covering table, dyeing cloth, *canting* stylus, alpha batik; pp. 60– 61, *tekat* items, *bersanding*; geometric *tekat*; p. 62, *telepuk* steps; p. 66, geometric *kain dastar*; p. 69, *pua kumbu* weaving; p. 79, *taming sari*; p. 83, brass pot; pp. 84–85, *kerongsang*, kite ornament; p. 97, making puppets; p. 100, making *sompoton*. **Lamb, A.**, p. 40, back carrier. **Lat**, p. 105, *Kampung Boy*. **Lau, Dennis**, p. 31, Kenyah and Iban doors; p. 40, Penan baskets; p. 42, Penan women; p. 45, Penan headman; p. 68, *Gawai* procession; p. 78, Rungus woman; p. 84, Iban women; p. 91, Orang Ulu woman; p. 122, Penan group; p. 143, hilt. **Lee, Reggie**, p. 126, Malaysian caricatures. **Leigh, Barbara**, p. 137, pottery sculpture. **Leigh, Barbara/ Nena Rieb**, p. 22, potter Ramadas Chettiar, drying pots. **Leisure Guide Publishing Sdn Bhd**, p. 32, furniture maker; p. 65, making slippers; p. 72, shoemaker. **Lim, Bernice**, p. 48, people with batik. **Lim Joo**, p. 34, boat building; p. 43, making *rombong*; p. 57, *songket* steps; p. 73, tying sari; pp. 74–75, Sabah

costumes; pp. 76–77, Sarawak costumes; p. 83, brassware steps; p. 93, Nonya woman; pp. 98–99, *gasing*, kite shapes. **Lim, Lawrence/Sarawak Museum Collection**, p. 40, Penan mat; p. 82, Sarawak kettle. **Limkokwing University College of Creative Technology**, p. 131, building. **Malaysian Institute of Art**, p. 130, building. **Malaysian Timber Council**, p. 28, *cengal*, *nangka* and *kemuning* trees. **Malaysian Watercolour Organization**, p. 98, Ismail Bukhary painting *Gasing (Tiga Dalam Satu)*. **Maybank**, p. 135, Maybank exhibition, cover of art book. **Moh, Alex**, p. 122, Nonya woman, portrait postcard. **Mohd Farid Mohd Zainuddin**, p. 132, Ibrahim Hussein Museum and Cultural Foundation. **Md Yusoff Othman**, p. 123, surrealistic photo. **Muliyadi Mahamood**, pp. 126–127, black and white cartoons, magazine covers, animated cartoons. **Munan, Heidi**, p. 18, clay seat; p. 23, potter making tall vase; p. 25, Gerald Goh; p. 43, *jangka*; p. 45, Bukan-Sadong, Murut and Kadazandusun hats; p. 68, bark jacket; p. 77, various healing and protective beads, Melanau woman tying beads, Melanau healing beads; p. 91, *kokoro'on* necklace. **Muzium Seni Asia**, p. 14, *sura*; p. 125, brochure; p. 132, building. **Nadaraju, Vani**, p. 19, Indian pots; pp. 70–71, tying *samping* and *tudung*; p. 73. Indian couple; p. 100, Indian musicians; p. 103, deity, making flower garlands. **Nanyang Academy of Fine Art, Singapore**, p. 108, logo and campus; p. 110, 1957 class. **National Art Gallery Malaysia**, p. 104, *Portrait of My Wife in Her Wedding Dress, Woman Pounding Paddy, Forest, Pago-Pago, Sirih Pinang, Bujang Berani*; pp. 106–107, *Rock Forms, Penang, Pepper Farm*; pp. 108–109, *Tropical Life, Roadside Stalls, Still Life With Wine Jugs, The Dayak Longhouse*; pp. 110–111, *Yati*, Wednesday Art Group, *Spirit of Earth, Water and Air*, APS painting class, Mohamad Hoessein Enas, New Scene catalogue, *My Love … Have You Ever Suffered?*; pp. 112–113, *Wayang Kulit Kelantan, Hanuman Visits Sita, Sri Jingga Indera Kayangan, Collection, SEA Thru-flow 3, 49 Squares, DOT: The De-Tribalisation of Tam Binti Che Lat, Malaysian Story No. 2, The Great Supper, Al-Kesah, Kdek, Kdek, Ong!*; pp. 114–115, *The Link, Spirit of Fire, Gerak Tempur, Globes, Freedom Monument, Rebab*

Player I, Peristiwa Tanjung Antu, Coaches; pp. 116–117, *Immunity I, Man and His World, Situational Piece No. 5 for T.K.S., Who Am I?, Insect Diskette II*; pp. 118–119, Sulaiman Esa and Redza Piyadasa, *Towards a Mystical Reality* exhibit and manifesto, *Vietnam, She Was Married at 14 and She Had 14 Children*; pp. 120–121, *Tulisan, Tombstone, Surah Ar-Rahman, Verse 12, Khat Diwani; Nurani, Alif Ba Ta 71, Murakabah, The Greatness of God*; p. 125, *Penyanyi Pujaan*; pp. 128–129, Salon Malaysia, foyer National Art Gallery, book cover; p. 130, Tay Hooi Keat, *Plantscape*; pp. 132–133, Board of Trustees, logo, National Art Gallery at Jalan Ampang, *Self Portrait* of Mohd Hoessein Enas, painting Howard Barron, *Soloman Performing, Penang Waterfront*, book cover; pp. 134–135, Burlington House, Nanyang Gallery of Art. **National Heritage Board, Singapore**, p. 44, Sultan Idris College. **National Museum of Singapore/National Heritage Board, Singapore**, p. 64, bridal handkerchief; p. 84, anklets; p. 93, Straits Chinese children. **New Straits Times Press (Malaysia) Berhad**, p. 8, festival; p. 16, Indian potter; p. 20, modern pottery; p. 26, Peranakan bed; p. 36, Orang Asli carver; pp. 40–41, Malay weavers; p. 52, haircutting; p. 57, designing on computer, model; p. 58, models; p. 61, bridal couple; p. 71, traditional *baju kurung*; p. 78, making brassware; p. 81, kris carver; p. 89, buying jewellery; p. 94, *kompang*; pp. 102–103, making lantern and joss sticks; *kolam* competition; pp. 118–119, Ibrahim Hussein and *May 13, 1969*, Nirmala Dutt Shunmughalingam. **Ong, Edric**, p. 8, *pua sungkit*; p. 49, mordant ceremony; p. 56, indigo plant; p. 69, *pua* motifs. **Ong, Ramsay**, p. 38, *Gawai Kenyalang*. **Penang State Museum and Art Gallery**, p. 32, carving chest; p. 102, lantern procession, burning *kong teik*; p. 107, Suffolk House, *Sampan*; p. 110, *Keeping Nets*; p. 132, Gallery. **Peris, Eric**, p. 123, temple. **PETRONAS**, p. 125, logo, advertisment. **Picture Library Sdn Bhd**, p. 8, kite maker, woodcarver; p. 18, carving motif; p. 23, stack of pots; p. 26, Orang Asli carver; p. 44, Malay weaver; p. 59, drying batik; p. 72, silk shoes; p. 94, kite maker, Chinese lanterns; pp. 96–97, puppeteer, painting puppets; p. 99, cutting pattern (image 1); p. 100, *rebana* drums; p. 102, giant joss sticks. **Piyadasa, Redza**, p. 104, *The Barber Shop*; p. 118, installation *May 13, 1969*; p. 124, Qur'an. **POS Malaysia**, p. 49, stamps; pp. 124–125, stamps, logo. **PROTON**, p. 125, logo. **Radin Mohd**

Noh Saleh, p. 6, Iban hatmaker; p. 19, votive tablet; p. 21, carving pot detail; p. 26, rice and tackle boxes; p. 39, palace gate, bamboo containers, Sarawak bowl, cake moulds; p. 53, circumcision ceremony; p. 54, *kain pis*; p. 57, Tengku Ismail *songket*; threading *lidi*; p. 67, Rungus man; p. 70, *songket* cloths; p. 78, goldsmith. **Raja Airina Raja Dato' Ahmad Badiozaman**, p. 107, *Counter Hall*. **Raja Fuziah Tun Uda**, pp. 58–59, making metal block, Kenyah batik, duck batik, bamboo shoot and crackle details; p. 48, *songket* textile. **Raja Mohd Zainol Ihsan Shah**, p. 122, *Perahu Biduk*. **Regis, Patricia**, p. 16, Lotud potter; p. 67, jacket, *linangkit* pictures. **Rashid Esa**, p. 36, mask dancers; p. 101, *tongkungon*. **Ritchie, James**, p. 23, Chinese pottery factory; p. 25, large decorated vase. **Royal Selangor International Sdn Bhd**, p. 79, advertisement; pp. 86–87, logos, moulds, tools, steps making object, funnel, teaset bowl, clock. **Sabah Museum**, p. 18, *tugtugan*; p. 35, *lepa* decoration; p. 55, Lotud priestesses; pp. 66–67, folded *kain dastar, kain pis*; p. 74, Lotud priestesses. **Salinger, Rudin**, p. 37, bird cage (Thai style). **Sarawak Museum**, p. 13, *pua kumbu*, metalsmith; pp. 18–19, clay burial urn, Chinese flowerpots; p. 26, Kenyah carving; p. 31, longhouse; p. 37, hornbill effigy; *jerunai*; p. 39, carving longboat; p. 43, hunter; p. 45, building rattan wall; p. 60, embroidering shawl; p. 71, *selayah keringkam*; pp. 76–77, Kelabit family, Bidayuh necklace; p. 88, foil figures; p. 90, Bidayuh necklace, *rawai*; p. 136, Iban chest. **Sarawak Tourism Board**, p. 69, heirlooms; p. 90, Iban women; p. 125, logo. **Sather, Clifford**, p. 18, *lapohan*. **S.C. Shekar**, p. 97, puppets. **Shell Malaysia**, p. 80, workshop. **Singh, Gurmeete**, p. 12, Istana Kenangan. **Singapore Art Museum/National Heritage Board, Singapore**, p. 108, *Lim Hak Tai, East Coast Vendor*. **Siti Zainon Ismail**, p. 62, *telepuk* headcloth, stamps and motifs. **Smith, Ravi John**, p. 1, handicrafts; pp. 12–13, pottery, *kris*, kettle, purses; p. 16, decorating Malay pot, *buyung*; p. 19, *belanga* (top), *labu panai* and detail, *belanga* (below) and detail, *bunga pecah empat* and detail; p. 20, woman making pot; p. 22, various Indian pots; p. 24, indigenous pots (all except top), heirloom jars; p. 29, bird hilt; p. 30, Bank Bumiputra staircase, Rumah Penghulu Abu Seman; p. 37, bird cages and traps, except first cage (Noor Azlina Yunus collection); p. 39, coconut grater; p. 40, fish trap, fish basket; p. 43, *rombong* basket; pp. 44–45, *kuih* cover, Penan basket, fans, Sabah foodcovers, Melanau hat; p. 46,

food carriers, Sabah carry basket; p. 48, *kain dastar*; p. 57, patterns 1 and 3, *cuban* needle; p. 61, woman embroidering *tekat*; p. 66, horse *kain dastar*; woman weaving; p. 69, human figures detail; p. 76, jacket and skirt, orang ulu beadwork; p. 85, bag, brooches; p. 96, *Gedek* puppets; p. 99, making kite (images 2–4), competition; p. 103, *thoranam* detail. **Star Publications (Malaysia) Berhad**, p. 52, Sultan's coronation; p. 66, Rungus dancers; pp. 70–71, Malay family, fancy *baju kurung*; pp. 72–73, Chinese family, sewing cheongsam, Indian family, buying saris; p. 96, joss sticks; p. 102, cave temple; p. 106, Abdullah Ariff; p. 125, exhibition; p. 126, Lat; p. 130, boy painting. **Sui Chen Choi**, p. 42, rattan, *mengkuang*. **Syed Ahmad Jamal**, p. 3, *keris sepukal*; p. 10, megaliths; p. 20, *labu* (items 1–4); p. 29, *awan larat*, cut-out Terengganu panel; p. 38, kris and sheath; p. 48, *tika sila*; p. 53, *songket* peacock, Perak *tengkolok*; pp. 80–81, *tumbuk lada*, large kris blade, striped *pamur*, 7- and 9-curved kris, kris *jawa demam*; p. 85, *pending*; p. 89, *dokoh*; p. 111, GRUP, Artists' Association of Malaysia; p. 112, *The Bait*; p. 118, *One Fine Day*; p. 121, calligraphy exhibition; p. 128, paint-in, banner; p. 130, Selangor Art Society, teaching art class; p. 133, NAG at Jalan Sultan Hishamuddin, Paris exhibition. **Tan Chee Khuan**, p. 7, Wayang Kulit painting; p. 106, Yong Mun Sen; p. 119, Wong Hoy Cheong; p. 134, *200 Malaysian Artists* cover. **Tan Hong Yew**, p. 82, celts, turtle; p. 91, Bajau woman; p. 99, kite-flying. **Tara Sosrowardoyo**, p. 22, making lamps, workers checking fired pots; p. 102, Chinese altar. **Tara Sosrowardoyo/Muzium Negara Collection**, p. 82, bell; p. 83, selection of brass items; p. 89, scent bottle. **Tara Sosrowardoyo/Perak Museum Collection**, p. 6, *labu* pots; p. 19, *kendi* vessels; p. 20, *labu* pots (item 5). **Tay, Terence/Permanent Collection of Henry Bong of the Pucuk Rebung Royal Gallery-Museum**, p. 6–7, gift to U.N.; p. 12, *lepa-lepa*; p. 15, *kerongsang, tekat* panel; p. 27, fish charm; p. 32–33, Peranakan home; *fu* dog, door, day bed, sideboard, wedding mirror, Melaka lintel; p. 35, Kenyah mast head; p. 36–37, Seru carving, sun god and Iban masks; p. 39, Peranakan lantern, grave *kacapuri*; pp. 50–51, 16th century map, Ottoman jacket, *patola* cloth, Indonesian *batik, limar* cloths, *songket*, Iban weaver (contributor's aunt), *pua kumbu, kain dastar, kain kebat*; p. 52, *tekat* fans; p. 53, *songket* motif; p. 54–55, *sirat* loincloth, Iban spinning wheel, backstrap, spool and beater, *kelambi* jacket, Baleh *pua kumbu*; p. 56,

patola cloth; p. 61, octagonal *tekat*; panel with bedwork; p. 64–65, embroidered panel, *Nonya kebaya* and details (owned by Mrs Nellie Bong, contributor's mother), embroidered slippers, beaded mattress trim; p. 66, Bajau sash and pouches; p. 68, *kain kerab*; p. 72, phoenix and peony motifs; p. 81, *keris tajong* hilt; p. 88, hairpin, p. 90, *sugu tinggi*; p. 93, *pending, kerongsang* (owned by Mrs Nellie Bong, contributor's mother), hairpins, diamond earrings, ring, anklets, slippers; p. 95, *rebab*; p. 139, phoenix carving. **Teh Siew Lan**, p. 109, *Serene Village*. **Tenaga Nasional Bhd**, p. 125, logo. **Tenmoku Pottery**, p. 23, tea set. **Teo, Albert**, p. 91, Lotud priestess. **Terengganu State Museum**, p. 58, wooden stamp. **Tettoni, Luca Invernizzi**, p. 18, jars; p. 24–25, Iban pottery and beaters, dragon kiln; p. 36, Orang Ulu hairpin; pp. 38–39, wooden beaters, hornbill earrings and bracelet; p. 46, rattan mats, Melanau box; p. 60, *selayah keringkam*; p. 69, *pua kumbu* pattern details (items 1–4); p. 78, Sarawak woman; p. 82, cannons; p. 91, dragon-dog earrings; p. 101, *sapeh*. **The One Academy of Communication Design**, p. 131, building. **The Pepin Press**, p. 58, screen-printed batik, metal block; p. 80, *lading, badik, lembing, kerambit*; p. 84, *sirih* set; p. 89, tobacco box. **Tommy Chang Image Productions**, p. 9, *sundatang*; p. 18, *bobohizan*; p. 23, Sabah ritual jars; p. 47, Dusun hat weaving patterns, Murut weaver; pp. 74–75, *supu*, Kadazandusun priestess; p. 91, Bajau jewellery, tobacco pouches, belts; pp. 100–101, *korubu, sompoton, gabang*. **Tourism Malaysia**, p. 31, Istana Lama palace; p. 35, Terengganu fishermen; p. 56, men in sarongs; p. 69, Iban heirlooms; p. 124, website. **Ultra Dimension**, p. 72, Chinese boy; p. 124, fort. **Universiti Pendidikan Sultan Idris**, p. 131, building. **Universiti Sains Malaysia**, pp. 80–81, *keris sundang, keris semenanjung* and sheath, p. 128, gallery; p. 130, building. **Universiti Teknologi MARA**, p. 128, art class; p. 130, building. **Valentine Willie Fine Art**, p. 117, *Re:Looking, 1965: Rebuilding its Monuments*; p. 135, exhibition at gallery. **Wan Yahya, Amin and Delia**, p. 78, Malay couple. **Wong, K.F.**, p. 122, *Morning Prayers*. **Yahya, Seth**, pp. 72–73, Indian girl, woman in sari, pp. 92–93, crown, pillow end, curtain hooks, bead belt, purse, key ring, pearl earrings; p. 94, wedding. **Yayasan Kesenian Perak**, p. 134, Ipoh Arts Festival. **Yeoh Jin Leng**, p. 112, *Human Rot*. **Yunus Sauman**, p. 37, Sabah log coffin. **Zakaria Ali**, p. 14, *mimbar* detail 6; p. 116, *Curse*.